Praise/Endorsements

"I have been looking for this book for forty years. Most books that focus on betrayal recovery start with the betrayal. But not Todd and Amy's! Instead, in a back-and-forth, down-to-earth dialogue, they highlight how trauma, coupled with 'common smaller hurts' collected over the years, can influence patterns, responses, and choices.

"You will relate. Remember, marriages are more alike than they are different, and that turns the sidebar discussions into horizontal relationship gold.

"But best yet, the practice of loving and letting go reminds you of your inability to fix your spouse. So learning to love while not controlling and letting go without distancing is an art, designed in heaven and modeled by Jesus on earth. When you don't agree with the choices your spouse is making, loving them (like Jesus loves you) becomes the hardest practice of the human condition. *Letting Go* will be your guide."

Dave Carder
Author of *Torn Asunder* and *Anatomy of an Affair*

"This book is a vulnerable and insightful account of a couple's journey through recovery. Rooted in faith, it offers Christ-centered hope and guidance for healing and restoration in marriage. Beautifully written and deeply encouraging—an excellent read."

Abbe Barclay, MSW, LMFT, CSAT, CPTT

"As the leader of a support group for separated husbands, I've had the privilege of walking alongside countless husbands struggling to find hope when everything seems lost. Yet few journeys have moved me as deeply as Todd's. I witnessed a man broken by separation become a man restored by surrender—proof of what only God can do when we give Him full control. Through humility, perseverance, and faith, I watched the Lord rebuild not only his marriage but his heart. This story is a living testimony that with God, all things are possible. If you've ever doubted whether true reconciliation can happen, this book will remind you: Nothing is beyond the reach of God's grace."

Randy Pryor
Leader, *Hope for Separated Husbands*

"This engaging story unfolds as both partners, through honest reflection, share the life experiences that led to challenges in their marriage. Rooted in Christian values, it becomes a powerful account of forgiveness and redemption. With self-examination, understanding, empathy, and faith, they trace a path toward restoration. This book is an inspiring resource for couples seeking to cultivate lasting wholeness in their relationship."

Mary Beth Griffis, MA, LMHC, CSAT

"As Todd and Amy's pastor, I've had the privilege of watching their lives up close—their humility in brokenness and their courage in healing. What they share in *Letting Go* isn't theory; it's the fruit of deep personal transformation, hard won through tears, prayer, and surrender. Their story carries the kind of authority that only comes from walking through pain with God and coming out the other side whole. Todd and Amy don't just teach about restoration—they embody it. This book is evidence that there's nothing life can tear down that grace can't rebuild."

J. J. Vasquez
Lead Pastor, Journey Church, Orlando, Florida

"A deeply vulnerable and relatable account of how personal trauma shapes our development and relationships. Through Todd and Amy's story, we witness that even in the midst of devastation, lasting change, true healing, and genuine transformation are possible through Christ and a courageous commitment to the healing journey. This book is highly recommended for anyone walking through infidelity or longing for authentic connection. You are not alone—hope and healing are possible."

Julie Petersen, MC, LPC, LIAC

Letting Go

The Key to Holding On to Your Marriage

TODD & AMY UNDERWOOD

Letting Go

HigherLife Development Services, Inc.
2342 Westminster Terrace, Oviedo, FL 32765
(407) 563-4806, HigherLifePublishing.com

Published 2026
©2025 by Todd and Amy Underwood

Scripture quotations marked AMP are taken from the *Amplified® Bible (AMP)*, Copyright © 2015 by The Lockman Foundation. Used by permission. lockman.org.

Scripture quotations marked CSB have been taken from the *Christian Standard Bible®*, Copyright © 2017 by Holman Bible Publishers. Used by permission. Christian Standard Bible® and CSB® are federally registered trademarks of Holman Bible Publishers.

Scripture quotations marked GNT are from the *Good News Translation®* (Today's English Version, Second Edition). Copyright © 1992 American Bible Society. Used by permission. All rights reserved.

Scripture quotations marked ESV are from *The ESV® Bible (The Holy Bible, English Standard Version®)*, © 2001 by Crossway, a publishing ministry of Good News Publishers. Used by permission. All rights reserved.

Scripture quotations marked MEV are taken from the *Modern English Version*. Copyright © 2024, 2017, 2014 by United Bible Association. Used by permission. All rights reserved.

Scripture quotations marked NCV are taken from the *New Century Version®*. Copyright © 2005 by Thomas Nelson. Used by permission. All rights reserved.

Scripture quotations marked NLT are taken from the *Holy Bible, New Living Translation*, copyright ©1996, 2004, 2015 by Tyndale House Foundation. Used by permission of Tyndale House Publishers, Carol Stream, Illinois 60188. All rights reserved.

Cover Design by Todd & Amy Underwood and Staci Alexander
Book Layout by Cristian Kadu and Faithe Stephens

Printed in the United States of America

30 29 28 27 26   1 2 3 4 5

ISBN: 978-1-964081-78-6 (paperback)
ISBN: 978-1-964081-79-3 (ebook)
LCCN: 1-15069437031

Dedication

THIS BOOK IS DEDICATED TO our three boys: Gavin, Griffin, and Garrett.

You have lived through things no parent ever wishes their child to go through. You have witnessed our imperfections, our prayers, our perseverance, and our journey in going vertical with God. Every prayer, every tear, every chapter of our story was written so that one day, you'll know that our love is not perfect, but it is powerful when surrendered to God.

May you grow as men who love deeply, forgive freely, and trust that even in the hardest seasons, God is still writing something good. Never give up, even in the valleys. We love each of you more than words can ever say.

Epigraph

Letting go isn't failing or giving up—it's faith.

Contents

A Guide for the Journey: How to Read This Book xv

Foreword.. xvii

Prologue.. xxi

PART 1 : BEFORE WE KNEW BETTER 1

    Chapter 1: Stories We Told Ourselves.................................... 3

    Chapter 2: The Vows Before the Vows 25

    Chapter 3: Warning Signs and Wedding Bells 45

    Chapter 4: Cracks in the Foundation 61

    Chapter 5: The Curious Irony of "Iron Sharpens Iron" 85

    Chapter 6: Circles, Silence, and the Illusion of Coasting..... 105

    Chapter 7: Continental Drift.. 125

    Chapter 8: The Mirage of Power and Pastures 139

    Chapter 9: Eighteen Months and a Thousand Miracles 169

    Chapter 10: The Addict in All of Us..................................... 185

    Chapter 11: One More Try 199

    Chapter 12: Death and Resurrection 219

PART 2 : BRING IT ON 229

    Chapter 13: Going Vertical 231

    Chapter 14: Unmasking the Past 253

    Chapter 15: The Offense of Forgiveness............................... 277

    Chapter 16: What We'd Do Differently 295

    Chapter 17: Grief... 309

    Chapter 18: The Heart's Compass.. 335

    Chapter 19: The Sacred Order 359

    Chapter 20: Tidbits and Truths.. 377

What's Next.. 399

Resources: Books and Other Resources We Recommend 401

Acknowledgments 407

About the Authors 411

A Guide for the Journey

How to Read This Book

WE'RE SO GLAD YOU'RE HERE. Picking up a book on marriage takes courage. It means you care. It means you're willing to take an honest look at where things are and where they could be. Just by opening to these pages, you've already taken a big step.

The chapters ahead are designed to walk *with* you, not just talk *at* you. Sometimes it'll feel like sitting across the table from us as we tell our story; other times, it may feel more like a workshop where you get to pause and take a small step or action.

Here's a quick guide to what you'll find inside:

Part 1 – Our Story

The first part is our story—raw, honest, and real. We invite you to read reflectively, watching for moments when our story touches yours. Along the way, you'll come across brief **reflections** set apart from the main conversation, each offering a thought or question to help you pause and consider what's coming up for you. Do them as they appear or circle back later when you have more time to focus.

Part 2 – The Workshop

The second part is more interactive with questions, insights, and space for you to reflect on your own journey as we share how we walked through ours.

Accelerators

Scattered throughout, you'll find what we're calling **Accelerators**—short, stand-alone entries that offer a little extra food for thought paired with a simple action step, prayer, or reflection to help accelerate your growth in real time.

Resources

Near the end, you'll find several lists of our favorite books, workshops, and intensives that encouraged and challenged us. If you reach the end of our story and you're hungering for more, these resources can help you keep going.

As we set out together, we encourage you to engage with this book. Write in the margins. Highlight what stands out. Keep a journal close and be ready to write what comes. Most of all, keep your heart open to what God is saying or directing you to do.

Finally, take a deep breath. Settle in. You've already started the journey—and you're not walking it alone.

Foreword

―――――――――

IF YOUR MARRIAGE FEELS MORE exhausting than life giving, you're not alone. Couples never plan to end up distant or disconnected—it just happens slowly. One busy season turns into another. Conversations shrink. Hearts close.

I've spent over thirty years walking with hundreds of couples through that slow fade, and I've seen it all—pain, betrayal, resentment, silence. But I've also seen God do what no book, counselor, or human effort alone can do: restore what seemed beyond repair. That's why this book matters.

I've read countless marriage books and used many tools to help couples rebuild, but this one stands out. The book you're holding is one of my top referrals for couples in crisis. And trust me—if you think your marriage is bad, wait until you read Todd and Amy's story. Their honesty will shock you, their humility will move you, and their hope will inspire you.

Too many couples believe the lie that this is normal—that distance is inevitable, that once the spark dies it's gone forever, that cold love is just what marriage becomes. I've heard it in their voices—hopelessness masquerading as acceptance. But Todd and Amy Underwood want you to know something different: Your marriage doesn't have to die. Not today. Not ever. Not if you're willing to fight for it.

Todd and Amy didn't just survive a hard season. For over two decades, they walked through fire—the kind that tests your faith, shakes your trust, and forces you to decide whether you really believe God can restore what's broken. And here's the miracle: They let God turn their ashes into beauty. Their scars aren't signs of failure— they're proof of His power. Every page of this book carries their story, their hope, and their deep belief that God still brings dead things back to life.

This isn't another "how-to" marriage book written from theory. It's real. It's raw. It's a lifeline for couples who are drowning and a road map for those ready to rebuild. It's hope for every husband and wife who've quietly wondered whether their story is over.

As I read, I found myself nodding through the whole book— because Todd and Amy offer insights that challenge us to confront truths we often overlook. They name the excuses we make, the ways we pull away, and the habits that slowly turn love into distance. But they write with grace. They don't shame you into change—they invite you into healing. That's what makes this book powerful: truth and grace walking hand in hand.

And they don't stop there. Part 2 becomes a workshop for your heart—helping you reflect, rebuild, and rediscover what's worth fighting for. That treasure isn't a perfect marriage or a flawless spouse. It's the real person beside you—the one you promised to love. It's the life God intended when He designed marriage to reveal His love to the world.

So here's my challenge: Don't read this casually. Don't skim it or half listen while scrolling your phone. Read it like your marriage depends on it—because for some of you, it might. Read it with honesty and hope. Read it with your spouse if you can, letting these pages spark the conversations you've avoided. Or read it alone and let God stir something in your heart again—something that remembers why you said yes in the first place.

I believe with all my heart that what Todd and Amy share can spark the miracle you've been praying for—not because they have all the answers but because they've lived this. They've seen God restore what seemed impossible. He still breathes life into broken marriages. He still turns ashes into beauty.

Your marriage is ready. It won't be easy. It will take humility, honesty, and courage. But it's possible. Restoration is possible. Reconciliation is possible. And a marriage that's truly alive—not just surviving but thriving—can be yours.

Now turn the page and start fighting for your marriage.

—**Roger Gibson**
Marriage pastor, author, and speaker

Prologue

Todd Underwood

I T WAS A DARK AND stormy night . . .

I have always wanted to start a book like Snoopy did. I wonder how his stories would've turned out. How did Snoopy get to that dark and stormy night? We never learned his story because all we ever saw was him perched on top of his doghouse at the end of the story, living to tell the tale.

The doghouse part I can relate to just fine.

For me, though, it wasn't just one night. It was a whole, long season—a dark and stormy twenty-plus years of my life.

One dark and stormy night, I found myself alone in a cabin up in the northern Arizona mountains. At a time when you're "supposed to" be established—done with the chaos of start-ups and raising kids—somehow I'd managed to break my life. The world was shutting down from the COVID-19 pandemic. Work had stopped, and work had been my anesthesia. Our kids were nearly grown. We were entering the era of empty nesting. And my wife of twenty-seven years had just left me.

Everything I'd worked for, everything I trusted, everything I thought was solid—unraveled. It was dizzying.

What is happening?

My world spiraling out of control was a cold, hard shock. I was the guy who was always in control. I fixed. I built. I worked hard and got whatever I set my sights on. I didn't lose. I didn't break.

My world spiraling out of control was a cold, hard shock.

But there I was—broken. I was suddenly on the brink of divorce, alone in a dark room, staring into the loss of everything I held precious, my heart aching and no remedy.

Except it wasn't sudden at all. Blindness just made it feel that way.

How is this happening?

I didn't know how yet. But I know now that moment marked the end. And at the same time, the beginning.

For many years, I clung to the beliefs and behaviors I had learned in childhood. It wasn't until my life unraveled that I finally saw the truth: I didn't need to *hold on*; I needed to *let go*.

Today, as I write this, the sun has come out. I have recovered more than I started with. I'm a better man with a better life. Like King David at Ziklag, I can look back and say, "By God's grace, I recovered all" (see 1 Samuel 30).

So, that's good.

But before we move into the story of how God's amazing grace showed up and saved me from the pit I had dug for myself, we need to go back—

I have recovered more than I started with. I'm a better man with a better life.

back to the story where all the lessons are hidden in plain sight. And that leads me to my next point.

Why bother to hear our story?

Because it could unmask yours. Because it might shed light on the unraveling you feel but don't yet understand. What broke us is what breaks most—and what healed us didn't start with trying harder or walking away. It started with *process.*

We're not skipping to "the end," because process matters—a lot. It's not just about drawing conclusions—though you will. It's about getting into the trenches together, where real change happens.

It's about getting into the trenches together, where real change happens.

As you walk through the mess with us, you'll see the blind spots (long before we did):

- **The vows** we made to ourselves that wrecked the ones we made to each other
- **The beliefs** that paralyzed us
- **The self-protective measures** that sabotaged our trust

It's not just our story.

Having worked now with hundreds of men and women going through crises, healing their marriages, it's glaringly obvious that couples' situations can be different, but the underlying currents, misjudgments, and drivers are consistently the same.

You can drop the person aggravating you, but you're stuck with you. And without process, you'll take all those unlearned lessons to whatever's next.

God is inviting you to a process that ends the dark and stormy night—and that's not an overpromise. Even if the world around you changes not one iota, you'll get much stronger. It's the difference between the disciples panicking in the boat and Jesus sleeping like a baby. When He woke and saw the storm—the mess of our lives—He stopped it with three words: "Peace! Be still!" (Mark 4:39 NIV). That's power. And on the other side of this process, that power is yours too. You can have the sunny day.

You can drop the person aggravating you, but you're stuck with you.

So don't just see the mess. See God. See the process of grace at work in our story and you'll begin to see Him in yours. If He can meet us in our storm, He can meet you in yours. And once you've seen Him there, the dark night will break into day, and you will already be on your way home.

1

Part

Before We
Knew Better

Chapter 1

Stories We Told Ourselves

FATHERLESSNESS HAS BECOME RAMPANT IN our culture—even in two-parent households. It wasn't always this way. For most of history, children were raised side by side with their families, learning life by doing life together. Sons followed their fathers into their field or a trade. Daughters worked alongside mothers and grandmothers, tending children and the home. Work and family were woven into one fabric.

But somewhere along the way, the fabric tore. Work moved out of the home. School replaced shared life. Parents and children began to move on separate tracks, living parallel lives with fewer points of connection. The result has been generations growing up with less presence, less guidance, and fewer models of wholeness.

And the absence doesn't stay in childhood. In those earliest years, when our brains are wiring themselves around experience, we're already deciding what's safe, what's dangerous, what gets us love, and what doesn't. We learn quickly.

If hitting gets us what we want, we hit. If lying helps us avoid trouble, we lie. If hard work is rewarded, we labor harder. If being seen but not heard keeps us out of harm's way, we learn to stay quiet.

Like clay set too soon, the impressions of childhood become the cement of adulthood.

We do whatever seems to work. And beneath those behaviors, beliefs are taking shape. With every passing year, we become less malleable. Like clay set too soon, the impressions of childhood become the cement of adulthood. What once was instinct for survival becomes a lifelong strategy—sometimes destructive, often limiting, always powerful.

The stories we told ourselves in childhood start to feel like facts. The solutions we came up with, we get stuck with, whether we like it or not—not because they were right but because they were early. Unless something breaks the cycle, the story written in childhood keeps playing long after the credits should've rolled.

Amy — No Evil

Throughout the book, Amy's comments will be in this light font.

As a child, I thought secrecy was love.

If I kept things quiet, no one would be burdened. If I stayed low maintenance, I wouldn't add to the stress already in the room.

In hindsight, I can see that what it really came down to was this: Love meant protecting people from my needs.

The only girl of the family, I was the middle child sandwiched between two brothers, all of us born within eighteen months of each other. My parents had struggled with infertility, so they first adopted my older brother, and then—surprise—I came along. Shortly after that, my mom got pregnant with my younger brother, and then we were a zoo.

But we were a tight zoo. I never once thought of Ryan as adopted. He was just my big brother . . . who seemed to attract a lot of attention. He had some struggles in school and didn't always make things easy on Mom and Dad. So I did what I thought was helpful: I stayed out of the way. I became the pleaser, the one who made things easy. I figured if I could just keep everyone else okay, then I'd be okay.

Love meant protecting people from my needs.

My family were Christians, and I grew up going to church, but it wasn't something we did every week. I spent summers at Vacation Bible School, sang all the Sunday school songs, and was taught Christian values at home. However, once my dad started traveling for work, we drifted away from regular attendance.

I *lived* for Fridays, because that was when I got to see my dad again.

He traveled for work every week—out on Monday mornings, back on Friday nights. The second I heard the key in the door, I'd bolt across the house and leap into his arms. When Daddy came home, I felt like the sun had come back. He was fun and warm. My mom was affectionate too—we were a huggy family. Hugs meant, "I see you." They meant, "You did good." They were our love language.

But during the week, Mom had to carry everything—three kids, a full house, and no partner to help with the day-to-day. Now I see her strength so clearly. Back then, I saw her exhaustion—and I wanted to make it better. I wanted to be the reason she smiled, not cried. So I learned to scan her moods, respond to how she felt, and avoid anything that might upset the apple cart.

I didn't realize I was stuffing parts of me that weren't meant to be stuffed. I just thought I was being good.

So Mondays were sad days. As I got older and more involved in sports, I'd find myself thinking about what events Dad would miss that week. A recital. A game. Something small that felt big to me.

I didn't realize I was stuffing parts of me that weren't meant to be stuffed.

Looking back, that feeling never really left. Years later, when Todd missed things, I think it triggered that same ache. That quiet little voice that said, *I wish you were here to see this.*

During the week, life at home as a kid felt like living in a single-parent household. My mom was running in three directions at once, managing the house, the schedules, the homework, the moods. I saw how much she carried—and I loved her so much, I didn't want to add weight.

So I tried to stay light. Quiet. Good.

What I thought was maturity was really just suppression—but I didn't realize it then. I didn't know that my needs were normal—that they weren't selfish or burdensome.

I found joy in making my mom happy. If she smiled, I had done my job. If she was upset, I took it personally. I absorbed whatever she was feeling. That's how I felt connected. That's how I knew I mattered.

And that pattern—of wrapping my happiness around someone else's—would go on to shape every major relationship of my life.

What I thought was maturity was really just suppression—but I didn't realize it then.

Fatherless

Todd

My conservative parents met as high schoolers around age fifteen. Neither of them grew up in religious homes, but sometime during those impressionable teenage years, they walked into a Pentecostal church—and walked out Christians. Pentecostals were (and still are) loud. Emotional. A little wild. But even though the dramatic displays of Pentecostalism unnerved them, something gripped their hearts. They believed.

Nevertheless, being non-demonstrative as they were, they eventually ran the other way as fast as they could from the wild emotionality of Pentecostalism—straight into ultraconservative, legalistic churches that dictated everything from their moral conduct to the length of their hair.

These churches also had strong views on music.

One of my parents' favorite teachers in that stream taught that a "proper" Christian song should be composed of precise percentages of rhythm, harmony, and melody. Anything that deviated was sinful and satanic.

Throughout the book, Todd's comments will be in this heavier font.

There was no room inside that legalistic box. I hated it. I balked at the idea of someone else controlling me, especially when it came wrapped in religion.

And that's the danger with legalism: It doesn't just box you in—it trains you to run from the whole thing. Manipulative, oppressive, and fake, we throw the baby out with the bathwater so that we don't just reject control—we reject Christ.

I balked at the idea of someone else controlling me, especially when it came wrapped in religion.

That's what happened to me.

I grew up saturated in church: Christian school by day, services every Sunday—no exceptions. Sick? Dying? Didn't matter. We were going.

I knew the verses. I knew the doctrine. I could quote it all on cue.

But I didn't know Him. Not personally.

My mom did. She journaled and prayed and truly loved Jesus. She was soft and sort of private—totally unlike my dad.

Dad was a machine. He worked twelve-hour shifts six days a week. Sundays were for church and football naps. That was it. Dad didn't have hobbies or friends. Dad had goals. He had that boomer mentality of climbing the ladder as high and as fast as possible. I'm pretty sure it was fear that drove him—just like me, years later.

But he was a success. Dad actually *made* it. He was a senior VP once featured on the cover of *PHOENIX* magazine with the CEO. And when he got to the top, he found nothing there. Just burnout. Silence. Still working six days a week. The man who took us to church every Sunday had no room left for us. No joy. No peace. No rest. Just a life running on fumes.

He also had a temper.

Yelling was his fix-all—and if yelling didn't work, he just wasn't yelling loudly enough. One second—calm. The next? *Kaboom!*

We always knew it was coming; we just didn't know when.

When you grow up in that kind of volatility, you don't learn to communicate; you learn to calculate.

When you grow up in that kind of volatility, you don't learn to communicate; you learn to calculate. You learn how to keep the peace. Or how to win. Or how to disappear.

You don't learn how to feel safe or create safety. You learn how to survive.

And in my house, survival meant putting your nose down, doing your work, and avoiding those pesky, distracting feelings. In fact, avoid them at all costs, because to indulge them and, worse, express them might get you ignored at best. At worst, it could bring out the kaboom.

A Beach Boy in a Box

I was a true beach boy.

Born in Southern California, my earliest memories are sun soaked and salty—barefoot on hot sand, the ocean always in reach. Those waves did something for me. They felt like

What was your relationship with your dad like? Was he there for you, not just physically but emotionally? When you bring him to mind, what feelings rise up first—safety, distance, or something else?

home, like being loved. The waves were fun. The ocean was friendly—gentle, even. Like a friend who filled a gap I didn't know was there.

But from the very beginning, something was missing. The man I longed to know was rarely around.

For the first six to eight years of my life, I hardly saw my dad. He worked all day and studied nights at Cal State Northridge until he earned his degree. Our family was in aerospace. My grandfather was with the Howard Hughes companies for fifty years. My dad eventually became the contract administrator for the engines on the Rockwell B-1 bomber. However, after President Jimmy Carter killed the program, the aerospace industry collapsed, and jobs in California dried up.

So we moved to Arizona.

And I felt shoved into a box—hot, dry, and empty.

To my ten-year-old beach-loving soul, Arizona was a nightmare. An ugly, beachless desert. Blistering heat, cacti, cowboys, and no ocean. We had no family there.

Without the waves, without the water—and without a dad— maybe the childhood angst just had nowhere to go. The ocean, the beauty, and the comforting lushness of California was gone, and I had to come up with some way of surviving.

Also, right before the move, my baby sister was born. It was a triple whammy. All at once, I'd lost my home, my family, and Mom's attention. And the beach . . . did I mention the beach?

Too Big, Too Soon

The first time I remember feeling afraid around a man, I was in the fourth grade. I was tall for my age—already five foot seven—and that confused people. I looked older, and unfortunately, some adults responded to me like I was older. A friend invited me to a youth event at her church. The youth leader—probably in his late twenties or early thirties—started paying attention to me. Too much attention.

We started in a group setting, doing some kind of activity, and then as everyone else began to leave, he tried to keep me behind. He never physically held me there but asked silly questions and made frivolous chatter so I wouldn't go.

And then I realized: I was the last one left.

That's when I felt it.

I remember feeling an aversion. Disgust. A need for avoidance. I was hesitant to be near him. My whole body wanted out. I didn't have the words "boundary violation" in my vocabulary—but I did have instincts. And they were screaming.

When just the two of us were in a room, he would touch my back or my leg, stroke my arm . . . It made my skin crawl. I hated being alone with him. So I learned to avoid it. I made sure I left the room when the other kids did. I watched the exits. I stayed alert.

I had good instincts and acted on them.

At the time, my dad hadn't been traveling long. I still felt connected. Still felt protected. I knew I was loved, which helped me stay grounded. It wasn't until years later, after more and more

> Sometimes our bodies know something is wrong before we have the words for it. A "feelings wheel," a tool often used in professional counseling and therapy, can help give language to what you're experiencing.

I didn't have the words "boundary violation" in my vocabulary—but I did have instincts.

distance and absence, that I began to feel the growing void where a father's affection, attention, and sense of safety were supposed to be.

The second memorable experience feeling uncomfortable around the opposite sex wasn't so easy to escape. By the sixth grade, I was already boy crazy. Maybe some women can relate. It was definitely not uncommon.

I was at the softball field, waiting to be picked up after practice. My mom was doing what she always did—getting one brother to practice, picking the other one and me up, managing everything all at once. I was used to waiting. I never blamed her. She was juggling so much.

The details of that evening are blurry, but I remember this: I was alone for a little while. Then I wasn't.

A group of four or five boys approached me. I don't remember all their faces. I had been talking to one of them earlier, giggling with my girlfriends, feeling that early buzz of middle school attention. I thought he was cute. I thought we were just playing. When I saw them coming close, I didn't think anything of it.

They had pinned me down—laughing, holding my arms and legs.

Until suddenly, I was on the ground. They had pinned me down—laughing, holding my arms and legs.

I remember feeling scared, frozen, wondering if this was a joke—or if something was really wrong. I think they touched me. I don't remember how far it went. That part is hazy. But I do remember the fear and the pressure I felt—not from them but from *myself.*

They treated it like we were just playing. And I felt like I had to play along.

I knew something was wrong, but I blamed myself. Maybe I had asked for it. Maybe I invited it by smiling too much. Maybe I had crossed some invisible line by liking the attention in the first place.

That's the part I didn't understand yet—that the attention I needed wasn't romantic or sexual.

I needed to be seen as a child—not pursued as a woman. I needed to feel loved—not lusted after. But I was already starting to confuse the two.

*I needed to feel loved—
not lusted after.*

And here's the truth: I *did* want to be seen. I wanted attention. Part of me loved being tall enough in the sixth grade to look older and get noticed. I loved looking more mature. I loved when people saw me and didn't think, *She's just a kid.* It made me feel special.

But that "love" had a shadow.

When the Lines Blurred

Still, I had a love-hate relationship with being tall.

One minute, I hated being teased and called "Too Tall Call" (Call was my last name) or made to feel like a freak. The next minute, I loved the advantages it gave me. I loved when it got me into places I didn't belong. I loved the attention . . . even though I didn't yet understand the kind of attention I was getting.

And I didn't know there was a difference. I didn't know that being looked at wasn't the same as being loved. I didn't recognize that even though it lit me up for a moment, it still left me lonely on the inside. I didn't yet know that certain kinds of attention want something *from* me, while real love wants something *for* me. I didn't realize that what I truly needed was *connection*—parental, fatherly, motherly, even brotherly.

> As children, we don't have the maturity to know any better. Even though we blame ourselves, many things that happened to us in childhood were not our fault.

What I was reaching for wasn't sexual at all. But I was clueless.

So when those boys pinned me down—laughing like it was nothing—I didn't tell a soul. Not my mom. Not my dad. Not my friends. Deep down, I thought I had asked for it. And if I had asked for it, who would protect me?

If the boys had crossed a line, *I* must have sent the wrong signals. If I felt uncomfortable, *I* must have misread the situation. If I got hurt, *I* must have brought it on myself.

I didn't yet know that certain kinds of attention want something from *me, while real love wants something* for *me.*

After it was over, I convinced myself it wasn't "that bad." And besides—I thought—*I'll get in trouble*. My parents had made it clear: no dating until I turned sixteen.

That's when something shifted in me.

I stopped believing I could fully trust my instincts. I stopped believing I had a right to say no. And I started holding myself accountable for other people's wrong behavior.

I stopped believing I could fully trust my instincts.

Yes, I felt scared—like something wasn't right—but I didn't know what. I didn't have the words. So I assumed it was me. I was just "being dumb." Was it funny? Was it assault?

That word *assault* wasn't even in my world yet.

What I did know was this: I didn't like it. I didn't feel safe. I didn't think it was right. And whatever it was, I believed it was better kept secret.

Spock

Our idea of travel was visiting grandparents back in California. We didn't take vacations. When I later married, and Amy considered regular travel and vacations to be normal, we didn't stand a chance. What was normal for my family was to work year-round and never take breaks.

Our family's idea of a break was church—nonnegotiable— even if one of us was sick. That was the height of my social activity outside school. I was too shy for dances or parties. Social situations terrified me, though I couldn't have told you why.

At one point, around eleven years old, I decided I wanted to be Spock from *Star Trek*. Spock was a logical, half human–half Vulcan and had to suppress his emotions so he would not be "clouded" by feelings. I tried it for a couple of weeks. I practiced being entirely logical and flat—at school, at home—and even did the hand sign: "Live long and prosper."

It didn't go well. I still had feelings. I just had nowhere to put them.

How did your family handle emotions? Were they welcomed or dismissed? Encouraged or controlled? Did you feel free to express what you felt, or did someone else decide what was acceptable? Did your spouse have a similar or very different experience?

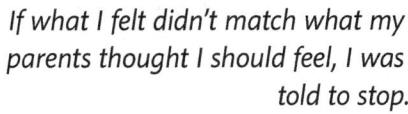

If what I felt didn't match what my parents thought I should feel, I was told to stop.

> Our bodies give signals, but they aren't meant to be the guide. Let them inform you, not rule you.

But as a kid in our house, emotions had to either be approved or were considered unacceptable. If what I felt didn't match what my parents thought I should feel, I was told to stop. "Stop crying, or I'll give you something to cry about." Nice.

As far as I was concerned, there were only four emotions: happy, sad, angry, and tired. I never developed emotional maturity—emotional quotient or "EQ"—because emotional maturity had nothing to do with survival in my house.

So I tried to stop. Tried to stuff it. Tried to out-logic my own humanity. But it never worked—and I was too young to name what I needed. What I needed was permission to feel. What I got was what a lot of kids with busy, successful, religious parents got: silence, shutdown, and shame.

When It's Safer to Give In

Later that summer, I found myself in a different situation—one that would reshape me for many years to come.

There was this boy. Older. Tall. Cute. And most importantly, he paid attention to me.

We had met at the baseball fields. I was only twelve—just about to start seventh grade—but I let him think I was in high school. I liked the way he looked at me. I liked how I felt when he did.

One lazy afternoon, my girlfriend and I rode our bikes to his house. She left early. Maybe she sensed something I didn't. I stayed—not because I was confident but because I was *wanted*.

Something inside me started to feel nervous, but I didn't know how to leave.

Something inside me started to feel nervous, but I didn't

know how to leave. Not without seeming rude. Not without ruining the moment.

And honestly—I don't know **what** I thought was going to happen. I had never even kissed a boy before. But it's not like we were going to break out the board game Sorry. When it was over, I would be left feeling . . . really sorry.

It started with hugging. Then, my first kiss. It escalated quickly. Too quickly.

I tried to pull back. I started to feel afraid. I wanted to stop. I was in *way* over my head.

Oh my gosh, I thought. *How do I get out of this?*

I shouted "*Stop!*" over and over and over while fighting to get away from him.

But he didn't stop.

He pinned me down—his knees on my arms. My arms were hurting. I put up a fight, but he said, "No one's going to hear you."

Still, I resisted a little while longer. But when I realized he wasn't going to stop, I stopped fighting. I gave in. I laid still—hoping it would be over soon.

I rehearsed my facial expression of nonchalance: Everything's fine.

And then I was raped.

I rode my bike home, crying the whole way, my arms aching from where he'd pinned me. I was bleeding and in pain in my private part. I also had pain in my heart, knowing I had just been violated.

I was angry at him. Angry at myself. Angry at my friend for leaving me. But I knew I could've left too. So it wasn't her fault.

As I got closer to home, something in me hardened. I wiped my tears away. I rehearsed my facial expression of nonchalance: *Everything's fine.* I figured out how I was going to get inside the house without anyone seeing the truth.

Okay, I told myself. *You're done. Dry your tears. Figure it out. Go inside and play the part.*

I did what I had learned to do best: I blamed myself.

I walked into the house like nothing had happened. No one knew. No one asked. No one could see that I was bleeding on the inside.

In the days that followed, I did what I had learned to do best: I blamed myself.

Yeah. It's your fault. You shouldn't have been there. You shouldn't have lied about your age. This is what you get for pretending to be older.

I told myself that over and over.

It's amazing how a perfectly good character trait can get twisted into something destructive. I wanted to be honest. I wanted to take responsibility for my actions. But in trying to be mature and self-aware, I became convinced of something that wasn't true.

It's amazing how a perfectly good character trait can get twisted into something destructive.

Yes, I had lied about my age. Yes, I had stayed when I should've left. But those were *immature choices*, not invitations. A twelve-year-old's mistake is never someone else's permission to violate them. But I didn't know that.

Not then.

And I didn't have the wisdom or understanding to tell someone more mature than me and let them teach me. So I carried the guilt.

And that story—the one where it was *all my fault*—became a script I couldn't stop running.

I never told my friend. I never told my parents. I never told a soul. I tried to cope the best way I knew how: Move on. Stay quiet. Keep going.

But my body held on. From every inappropriate touch to the trauma of being raped, my body was keeping score. I wouldn't find out how until later.

When Creative Outlets Are Medicine

By high school, music had become my outlet.

My parents fully supported it—bought me a guitar, paid for lessons. I didn't like the songs I had to learn, so I quit the lessons and taught myself.

I played in bands, wrote my own music, and practiced constantly. Music was the one activity that allowed me to feel what I didn't feel safe saying. The strings sang for me and gave me a voice that had no other outlet.

Music was the one activity that allowed me to feel what I didn't feel safe saying.

Without my knowing it, music would become more than a hobby. It became my own personal therapy. My worship. It may have saved my marriage. It may have saved my life.

I never turned to another woman or reached for alcohol or porn. God had already given me something. He gave me

What's your creative outlet that helps you process and release what you feel?

music. He put a guitar in my arms. With it, I could cry, scream, plead, praise—without ever opening my mouth.

Music made sense to me, and it still does.

One night when I was fifteen, my band landed its first real gig at a local venue.

Technically, it was a bar—but more of a music hall. Travis, my friend and the drummer, went. We were stoked that both our dads were there to support us. They sat front and center and seemed to hit it off great.

And then I saw it: Travis's dad ordered a beer. Instant panic.

In my house, alcohol wasn't just discouraged—it was forbidden. I'd never seen my dad drink. Never heard him talk about it. So I braced for impact. I spent the rest of the night convinced I'd lose everything—my music, my chance to play, my dad's respect.

I went home already mad.

"I'm running away!" I declared.

They just stared at me, stunned.

In my house, alcohol wasn't just discouraged —it was forbidden.

"What's wrong? Why are you acting like this?"

Huh?

It turned out that my parents didn't think anything was wrong. There was no punishment. No lecture. No explosion.

It wasn't till years later that I got more of the story. When my dad was drafted into the Marines, he was diagnosed with

Hodgkin's. At the time, he drank occasionally. But when cancer hit, he made his own deal with God: *If You heal me, I'll never drink again.*

God healed him, and my dad kept the vow. He never touched alcohol again. But he never told me that story. Not when I was young. Not when I panicked after the gig. Not when it could've helped me understand.

And maybe that's just the way it was. In our family, anything that touched the heart was mostly untouchable.

In our family, anything that touched the heart was mostly untouchable.

The "Yeah, But . . . " Syndrome I

Defense That Kills Connection

I was, and sometimes still am, the king of the "Yeah, but . . . " Nothing kills connection faster than defending yourself with a comeback. Most of us do it—maybe men more than women. The moment our wives bring something up that sounds like criticism, we jump in to prove it's not as bad as they make it sound:

"You forgot to take the trash out four times this week."

"Yeah, but I did take it out once."

"You're always late."

"Yeah, but it never starts on time anyway."

"You don't spend time with me anymore."

"Yeah, but we just went out last night."

I had a "Yeah, but . . . " for everything. What I didn't see was how my comebacks made Amy feel—like I was telling her she was wrong for feeling the way she felt. Every "Yeah, but . . . " chipped away at her spirit.

In my men's group, I started learning another way. Instead of defending myself, I could listen for the feelings behind her words. Instead of saying, "Yeah but . . . " I could say, "You're right. I'm sorry. That's something I need to work on."

Now, I know what you're thinking. You've got a "Yeah, but . . . " for me right now. *Yeah, but what if she's exaggerating? Yeah, but what if it isn't totally true? Don't I need to set the record straight?*

Here's what I realized: When Jesus stood before Pilate, He didn't defend Himself. So, why do I feel the need to? When I try to "win" by proving Amy wrong, I'm actually shooting myself in the foot. We're one flesh (see Mark 10:8). In marriage, if one loses, we both lose.

We can be right and still be wrong if we miss the hurt our spouse is trying to convey. So what if I drop my defenses and validate the pain behind her words—even when the details aren't exactly right? "I can see why you'd feel that way. I'm sorry. I'll work on it." That doesn't make me weak; it makes me more like Jesus.

This is still one of the hardest things for me. I look to Jesus's example and pray for His strength to drop my "Yeah, buts." When I do, I make room for healing instead of hurt—and that changes everything.

Accelerator

For one day, pay attention to how often you say, "Yeah, but . . . " Each time you catch yourself, stop mid-sentence and try one validating response: "You're right . . . I hear you . . . I'm sorry . . . I'll work on that."

Bonus: At the end of the day, journal about one conversation that felt different because you dropped the "Yeah, but . . . "

Chapter 2

The Vows Before the Vows

FROM OUR EARLIEST YEARS, LIFE wounds us. Sometimes it's big—loss, neglect, violation. Sometimes it seems small but still manages to knock the ground out from under our feet. Either way, we scramble to protect ourselves. We make promises that feel like safety in the moment.

Children carry many attributes we adults would do well to preserve—imagination, wonder, hope, excitement. But the one thing children don't have yet is *perspective*. They don't know the long-reaching effects when a wrong belief is cemented or a vow is made. Over time, our hidden promises begin to harden into patterns.

Over time, our hidden promises begin to harden into patterns.

A vow to stay thin and never gain weight can turn fruitcake at Christmas or chocolates on Valentine's Day into threats instead of kind gestures. A vow to never be slowed down or held back can twist even the miracle of pregnancy into a death sentence.

What once felt like salvation and protection begins to sabotage us. Fear distorts our perceptions of reality, and old vows quietly dictate new reactions. Sometimes, simply recognizing those vows is enough to start untangling the web. But when they remain hidden, operating from the shadows of the mind, we forget they're even there.

And then love sweeps in and changes the scenery.

The emotional highs of being chosen, pursued, and wanted feel like a fresh start—as if the old story is over and a new one has begun. On the mountaintop of romance, fear retreats into the shadows. The vows slip into the closet. For a time, they stay hidden in the glow of affection and dreams.

Yet even there, something else is at work. Alongside the weight of old fears are the sparks of real love—moments of laughter, desire, connection, and joy. Those seeds are worth planting. Like the wheat and the tares, they may grow side by side. Some may try to choke the others. But mountaintop moments *can* bear fruit strong enough to carry you through the famine—when things feel barren, when everything else seems to pull you apart. Those moments may not erase all the old vows, but their fruit *can* hold up love long enough for grace to do its deeper work.

Mountaintop moments can bear fruit strong enough to carry you through the famine.

Carrying More Than I Could Bear

Everybody knows *that girl*.

The one whispered about in the school hallway. The one who "made her bed" and now has to lie in it. The one people judge without knowing her story.

Most of the time, she can't even see her story. That "scarlet letter" isn't proof of some fatal flaw she was born with—it's the symptom seeping through the bandage of an unhealed wound. The boundaries she was never taught got crossed, and she was left to gather the pieces with the mind and maturity of a child.

I made it my job to keep everyone else comfortable—meet everyone's needs—until I was starved and chasing anything that promised a rush.

I took on the shame of what was done to me. I made it my job to keep everyone else comfortable—meet everyone's needs—until I was starved and chasing anything that promised a rush. The quick sugar hit, the candy high. The guy who seemed hard to get, who gave a little and expected a lot.

I became easy prey.

That's the thing about sexual trauma—and most trauma: It rewires everyone differently.

I was still just a child, but something cracked inside me. I didn't have the maturity to process rape. And, like so many, I didn't ask for help because I was afraid.

So instead, I carried it with me—into my choices, my patterns, my search for love.

By seventh grade, the stage was set: I always had a boyfriend. By eighth, I'd become promiscuous—not because I didn't value myself but because I thought this was the way to get what I needed.

I wanted safety. I craved affection. I longed to be chosen. I wanted anything that could make me feel alive instead of numb—to be treated like a person instead of just a body.

I believed that if I gave sex away, I'd be loved and wanted. That boys would value me and want to keep me. So I gave myself freely. I offered my body liberally. And when I was fifteen, I got pregnant.

I wanted safety. I craved affection. I longed to be chosen.

I remember the strange rush of it—the fear, the disbelief, the secret thrill of *Maybe I'm really going to be a mom.* But the excitement was fleeting.

Fear took over.

Where I came from, pregnant girls didn't stay in the same school with the "normal" kids. There was a school right next door for "those" girls. They were sent to an alternative campus, like outcasts. We looked at them the way the Old Testament looked at lepers. Every day I saw them and thought, *Those poor girls. . . . Their lives are ruined.*

They were seen as statistics who brought shame on their families, and I didn't want to be one of them.

So I went to the crisis pregnancy center. I told my boyfriend, but I felt alone in every possible way.

At that time, my faith was also starting to stir—I knew that having an abortion was wrong, and I was convicted about it. I hadn't sorted out all my beliefs, but I believed in God, and I believed this mattered.

Yet . . . I didn't want to disappoint my family. I didn't want to be found out. I didn't want to be "that girl."

So I vowed that no one would ever find out—that I'd protect my image at all costs. I decided to pay the highest cost imaginable—and terminate the pregnancy. Death was the fruit of my silent promise.

I told myself I had to do it because appearances were more important than truth. More important than God. I thought the only way to preserve the illusion of having it all together was to "erase" my mistake. But nothing is ever truly erased. The body keeps score. It always does.

So one day, I ditched school. My boyfriend took me to the clinic and paid, and it was done. No parental consent required. No questions asked. I recovered at his house.

By evening, I was home. Pretending. Again.

My dad was out of town. My mom was doing what she always did—caring for us, managing the house, running herself ragged. She had no idea what I had just been through—not because she didn't love me; she did. But I got so good at suppressing my needs, my pain, my presence that she didn't even know what to look for. And I didn't give her the chance.

When I *did* go to my parents with issues, they never shut me down. But I learned to choose carefully what I shared. I just didn't like exposure. I didn't like how it changed their countenance, and

> Have you ever made a silent vow—"I'll never . . . I'll always . . . "—that still shapes the way you live or love today?

I thought the only way to preserve the illusion of having it all together was to "erase" my mistake.

I was terrified they would look down on me. The little things, I might share. But the big things—the ones that mattered, the ones I had no business going through alone? No way. Those stayed hidden.

I didn't want to hurt my mom. I didn't want her to feel pain, shame, or disappointment. She had a picture in her head of how we looked on the outside—and I didn't want to ruin it.

And it wasn't just me. In our family, we didn't deal with hard things. We kept things light. We stayed on the surface. We smiled. We swept things under the rug.

In our family, we didn't deal with hard things. Because, really . . . what would people think? What if they knew I'd been sexually active? What if they knew I'd gotten pregnant? What if they knew I'd been raped?

I refused to be the girl who brought shame to the family. So I smiled and stayed silent. Again.

Rules and Rebellion

Thank God my parents didn't hold me to ultraconservative Christianity, with the belief that playing rock music meant I was going to hell—but they did send me to small, conservative Christian schools my entire childhood. It was never a perfect fit.

Naturally independent and always an entrepreneur at heart, I couldn't take the box of religion, from the very start—especially after we moved. In my mind, I lost everything—I hated being controlled. I may not have been allowed to feel much, but I felt the oppression of control keenly. Maybe that's why, later, I turned into a professional control freak. I vowed to never let someone take away everything I held dear.

Like many kids, I experienced trauma in ways I couldn't name at the time.

My life felt dictated. I couldn't choose what I ate, where we went, or what we did. The weight of rules was everywhere. No shorts in 120-degree weather. Hair above the collar. Severe punishment for breaking school rules—including corporal discipline for being sent to the principal's office.

So I rebelled.

Where do you find yourself needing to be in control—circumstances, people, or both? Would you say it's healthy or out of balance? Can you trace when that started?

If I couldn't grow my hair long, I spiked it punk style. I leaned into the "rebellious" label just to claim a sliver of identity. To be fair, being rebellious in that environment was nothing. I mostly got straight As—but straight As were never good enough. Not for my parents. Not for my teachers. At conferences, they'd say, "He's doing great, but he has so much more potential."

The weight of rules was everywhere.

Potential may be one of the cruelest words in the English language. They wanted *more*? Than *straight As*?

I was never the kid to get into serious trouble, but in a world of strict rules, with severe punishments, it didn't take much to be branded a rebel. I still remember the blows from the "holy" paddle smashing against my rear end, or sometimes across my knuckles for a more lasting sting.

What "god" do you trust when life feels out of control— success, image, money, relationships?

The paddle hit. The message also hit: Whatever I did was never enough. I could work my fingers to the bone, outdo everyone around me, and they still wouldn't be satisfied. So I learned not to care whether they were satisfied. I just aced everything so they'd at least be appeased, and I could mind my own business.

Perfection became top priority. I turned ruthlessly efficient— get it done fast, get it done right, leave no room for complaint, and still finish, with time left for what I actually wanted to do.

Whatever I did was never enough.

That sliver of power, that ounce of choice—that's what I called "freedom." But it wasn't the kind that comes from God. It was counterfeit. It was a so-called freedom that I could control and a god I could "trust"—because it was up to me.

And who bought me this freedom? Where'd I get it from? Not from prayer. Not from love. *From work.*

Hiding Bruises

The pattern continued: relationship to relationship. Trying to patch the leak with more love—or what I mistook for love.

Eventually, I added another layer to my cover-up: hiding bruises.

The boy I was dating became increasingly abusive. He left finger marks on my arms and neck. He hit me—hard. To this day, the ringing in my ears is a souvenir, a reminder of being struck in the head. Blows I never should have taken.

He was careful not to put marks on my face—only on my arms, my sides, my neck. The parts I could cover. So I did. Even in the middle of the Arizona summer, I wore turtlenecks and long sleeves. And somehow, no one asked. I don't blame them. I was just too good at whatever I set my mind to. I'd promised myself no one would see whatever messes I'd made or the mess I might've been inside, and I made it my job to *ensure* that no one ever questioned the real story. If someone looked at me funny, I flashed them my best "It's fine, I'm fine" smile, and people believed me.

The boy I was dating became increasingly abusive.

Eventually, I got out of that relationship—but never slowed down long enough to ask why I kept finding myself in the same kind of story. At that time, being "equally yoked"—finding someone with Christian values—wasn't on my checklist. I didn't know what I didn't know. I just traded relationships, always hoping the next guy would be different. That someone would finally see me, love me, protect me. That a knight in shining armor would show up and rewrite the ending.

Spoiler: No one came galloping in on horseback.

Not until chemistry class.

The Father-Son Bond

Because I excelled in many fields and topics, and because I was always pushing myself, I was often successful. Working was never my challenge. Knowing when to stop—that wasn't even on my radar. Simply put: I never stopped.

Eventually, my dad went back to the university to get his MBA. By then, I had a master's degree too and was teaching chemistry at a local community college. He tried to follow suit but couldn't land even a part-time gig teaching.

After two years of nothing, he decided to buy a business—a family venture. The idea was that the family would run it with him. He found a retail music store, and I wasn't opposed; I was a musician. But I didn't want to *own* a music store. So he paid me minimum wage and expected a lot. We clashed constantly.

I was a hardheaded twenty-something. My dad was a burned-out executive trying to build something new.

I was a hardheaded twenty-something. My dad was a burned-out executive trying to build something new. There were lots of arguments, but there were good times too. I thought maybe we were inching toward better days, vaguely holding on to the Disney-like hope of a "best" that was yet to come.

The best never came.

A Good Catch

He had long, blond hair, sun-kissed skin, and looked like Fabio, the 1990s pop culture icon who appeared on the covers of about thirteen hundred romance novels. He looked like he'd stepped straight off a California beach.

Yup, you guessed it: I eventually married "Fabio," my college chemistry professor. We met while I was taking prereqs for nursing school. At the time, I was dating someone else—but there was something about "Fabio."

For starters, he wasn't just "a guy." He was a man. A little older, established, confident, and—most dangerous of all—hard to get. He didn't chase. He didn't even flirt. He was my teacher. And with that little girl's vow still running in the background—not to be seen as *that* girl, with the scarlet letter, but *that* girl, who caught the good guy with the clean look and the responsible savings account—Todd seemed perfect.

A good man. A safe man. The kind of man you would want to bring home to Mom. And his natural sense of boundaries, stability, and propriety only made him more attractive.

He wasn't just "a guy." He was a man. A little older, established, confident, and—most dangerous of all—hard to get.

I wondered if I could get him to notice me.

So I asked a lot of questions in class—though I was far more interested in the teacher than the teaching. I tossed my hair. Smiled that girlish smile. Did everything I knew to draw his attention, even while pretending to ask for help in chemistry.

He was always kind, always smiling—but never gave me the answers. He'd just say, "Go back to your desk and read the directions."

Eventually, I stopped hinting and just came out with it: "Would you ever date a student?"

I completely caught him off guard.

Todd's shy. I think I probably scared him a little—but I saw the flicker in his eyes. He noticed me.

Not Your Mama's Chem Teacher

After Amy's first class with me, I secretly hoped I'd see her again—especially since I knew she still had one more chemistry class to take. I may have "helped" her decision by mentioning how awful all the other teachers were and how little homework I gave.

Sure enough, next semester, there she was, sitting in my lab again. One evening after class, Amy and I were walking out together when she spotted a little tag still dangling from the zipper on my jacket.

My heart raced just talking to Amy.

"You ski?" she asked.

"Nope. Snowboard," I said.

She laughed. "Oh, you're one of those. The ones who sit down in the middle of the run and mess it up for everybody else."

I grinned. "Only when we're waiting for the skiers to catch up."

We went back and forth like that for a few minutes—her teasing about snowboarders, me firing back about skiers—until I invited her to hit the slopes with me sometime.

My heart raced just talking to Amy. She was beautiful, with a contagious smile, and just fun to be around—even if she didn't like to read directions. She was coy, a little quiet. A little like my mom. And the more time I spent around her, the more I wanted to. I didn't want to wait for a ski trip, so I came up with something sooner.

Our first actual date wasn't on the slopes—it was at one of my band's concerts. She came, and I remember noticing how at ease she was there—comfortable with the music, with the crowd, and with me. That was the start. And for the record, she earned both of those As the proper way.

Mountaintop Moments

More and more, I found myself saying yes—to a man who loved Jesus, who loved me, and who offered safety, stability, and security. Being with Todd started to feel like a new chance at life.

He was the first Christian man I'd ever dated, and he inspired me. Made me want to change. Made me feel like I *could* change. A new name. A new identity. A fresh start.

Maybe I was committing myself more to an idea than to a person. I dreamed about the life I wanted to step into, the things I wanted for myself. I wasn't thinking about the relationship in terms of serving him but in terms of how he made me feel, or how he might make my life better.

I dreamed about the life I wanted to step into, the things I wanted for myself.

It wasn't all black and white, but one thing I did know was this: I was truly falling in love with Todd. He was fun. Spontaneous. Attractive. All the things I love most about him today were already there, even if I didn't see it yet.

We had been dating for ten months when I experienced one of the most unforgettable days of my life.

It started with breakfast—just the two of us. Such a treat! Slow. Sweet. Romantic. Then church. And I thought that was it. Standing outside after church, Todd handed me an envelope and then vanished. Inside was a puzzle.

Unexpected, I thought. *He's up to something.*

Before I could finish putting the puzzle together, his sister, Julie, suddenly pulled up.

"Your ride awaits," she said with a grin. "Let's go."

We had been dating for ten months when I experienced one of the most unforgettable days of my life.

I jumped in the car, and what followed was a full-day scavenger hunt, hand designed by Todd and Julie.

As she drove me through his extravagant, meticulously planned course, each stop offered a clue, a new puzzle piece, or a memory hidden for me to find like treasure.

Todd had thought of everything—inside jokes, favorite places, sweet notes inside hidden envelopes. By then he had his pilot license and co-owned a plane, so naturally he programmed a short flight into our day. When we reached his hangar, the clues had already pulled me through the mall, little cafés, even the stores we'd wandered through when we'd first started dating. Each one built on the last, like a living timeline of our story.

He didn't miss a single detail.

There he stood, waiting on the wing of the airplane. He opened the plane, and then we buckled up and took off. The desert dropped away beneath us, brown giving way to blue before we landed for lunch and lifted back into the sky.

After we touched down, Todd was still being mysterious.

"Wait here," he said, escorting me out of the plane onto the tarmac. "I'll be right back."

And just like that, he took off again!

I stood in the hum of the runway, shielding my eyes against the sun as I watched the little plane lift into a cloudless blue. My heart raced, my mind flipping through possibilities I couldn't quite piece together.

What are some ways you and your spouse connect without words?

Suddenly, Julie appeared again. "Time to go."

The afternoon was filled with more clues, more stops, more gifts. One stop held a surprise I didn't understand until later—a helmet.

I *heard* Todd before I saw him—his dirt bike rumbling across the horizon. He pulled up, grinning, helmet off, eyes soft. I climbed on behind him, and we rode—fast, breathless, alive—Todd in front, my arms wrapped around his waist, the wind in my face. I'd always loved the way Todd felt in those moments. Our rides were like freedom. I could feel his strength in his back as we glided through open roads and desert turns.

The roughness of the dirt bike made the experience feel wild, while Todd's control over it made me feel even more feminine—and safe.

The roughness of the dirt bike made the experience feel wild, while Todd's control over it made me feel even more feminine—and safe.

These were exhilarating moments. In the years ahead, dirt bike rides would become one of the few ways we could still connect— even when everything else felt like it was coming apart.

By sunset, the last clue had led me to an open stretch of desert. We wound our way to a hidden spot no car could reach, tucked into a mountaintop clearing where the air felt thin and the horizon stretched in every direction.

A table was already set.

His parents had been there earlier to prepare it and then quietly disappeared. The whole family was in on it!

Candles flickered. Dishes reflected the last of the daylight. Everything glowed. I stood there, captivated by the beauty of the moment and the sense that I was stepping into a new kind of promise.

Todd got down on one knee and asked if I would marry him.

I said yes.

> Immature love asks, "How do you make me feel?" Mature love asks, "How can I serve?" Where do you see yourself in that shift?

Mountaintop Clues

I had always been a planner. So when it came time to propose to Amy, I went big. I wanted it to be epic—something she'd never forget.

The day had taken me weeks to plan—and it was worth every minute. From the handmade puzzle I gave her that morning to the last clue at sunset, every stop was designed to say, "I see you." I wanted her to *feel* how much I knew her—and loved her.

The day had taken me weeks to plan—and it was worth every minute.

By sunset, I was waiting in a hidden spot in the mountains, my dirt bike ready. We rode fast down desert roads—in a flurry of wind, dust, and adrenaline—before ending at a table set for just the two of us.

I asked her to marry me.

She said yes.

We were on top of the world.

It's staggering how quickly a man can abandon the very things he once pursued so passionately.

The "Yeah, But . . ." Syndrome II

Hearing Emotions Beneath the Words

In heated arguments, emotions can take over. Our spouses may start using words like "always" and "never." Sometimes they exaggerate, even say things that aren't completely true.

Our instinct is to defend ourselves. We zero in on the details—*Yeah, but that's not accurate . . . Yeah, but it didn't happen that way . . . Yeah, but you're forgetting what I did last week.* Before long, we're building our case instead of building connection.

But what if instead of reacting to the words we listened for the emotion behind them? *"You're never home!"* might really mean *"I feel lonely."* And *"You don't want to be with me anymore!"* might mean *"I don't feel wanted."*

It's not easy, but it changes everything when we step back and ask questions like these:

- "Can you help me understand what's really bothering you right now?"

- "Is there something I've done—or not done—that made you feel unseen or unheard?"

- "I can tell you're hurting. What do you need from me right now?"

Sometimes the issue isn't even us—it's stress from work or something they can't name yet. But showing we care about the feelings beneath the words creates safety instead of shutdown.

When we let go of the "Yeah, but . . . " and tune into emotion, we stop making our spouse the enemy. We become allies again.

Accelerator

Try one of these three approaches this week:

Option A: Practice + Visualization

- Pick one question: "Can you help me understand what's really bothering you?" or "What do you need from me right now?"

- Practice saying it out loud.

- Visualize yourself asking it in the middle of a tense moment instead of reacting.

- Ask God to help those words come naturally the next time emotions rise.

Option B: Reframe the Reflex

- Recall the last time you felt defensive. Write down the exact words you wanted to say—your "Yeah, but . . . "

- Visualize those words being placed into a box and carried away.

- Now reframe your "Yeah, but . . . " into a question that would draw your spouse closer instead of pushing them away.

- Pray: "Lord, retrain my reflexes. Help me trade 'Yeah, but . . . ' for curiosity and compassion."

Chapter 3

Warning Signs and Wedding Bells

H UMAN BEINGS CRAVE INTIMACY. WE'RE all made to give and receive care, compassion, and affection—but not everyone grows up knowing how.

In some homes, if someone is hurting, you give them space. In others, you give more than space; you leave them alone until they get hold of themselves—by themselves. If something goes unsaid, *it stays that way.*

If you—or your spouse—grew up in a home where the deepest things stayed buried, where everyone avoided talking about what mattered instead of developing the skill to notice, you may have strengthened your ability to ignore vital signs when something is off. If that's all you've even known, chances are good that's what you'll build.

In a house that lacks closeness and communication, you either learn to guess or you stop asking altogether. Your

In a house that lacks closeness and communication, you either learn to guess or you stop asking altogether.

Growing up, how did your household communicate emotional needs? How does your communication style differ from your spouse's?

brain stops picking up signs or warnings, and your attention to those red flags grows dull. Even if things start going off the rails, what you have learned is to just keep moving. You stay quiet and push through. You figure out how to get on without the "distraction" of relational needs.

In other households, maybe you fight. You bicker. You start throwing arrows and darts until you forget what you were mad about in the first place and, little by little, find that you like each other less and less.

Where there's too much drama, with too many land mines between you, disinterest becomes defense. Some of us were taught to confront, battle, and push others away. Others learned to plow through and disconnect quietly. Sooner or later, the gap shows up, and you use explanations like "We grew apart."

But is that true? Did you "grow" apart because you both actually grew? Or did something unhealthy make its way into your marriage that went unchecked until it *tore* you apart?

Maybe you carried unspoken grief into your relationship . . . and called it normal. Maybe you were taught to "just keep going." Maybe you pushed through red flags and flashing warning signs because no one ever told you it was okay to pause.

One way or another, whether today or tomorrow, in this relationship or the next, whatever's inside that's left untouched, unprocessed, unresolved, or

Maybe you pushed through red flags and flashing warning signs because no one ever told you it was okay to pause.

unhealed will keep working from behind the scenes—quietly, relentlessly—until it's brought into the light.

A High, a Crash, Silence . . . and Then Numbness

"Call your mom."

Three little words that changed everything.

I had convinced my dad to go with me to a big annual music convention in California called NAMM (the National Association of Music Merchants). It's the largest global nonprofit music trade organization.

It was my idea of a perfect trip: just the two of us—father and son—flying there together in a plane I would pilot. I saw it as a chance to connect, maybe build something new into our relationship, and hopefully not argue. I was excited. He was nervous—about flying, especially with me at the controls. But he agreed.

That morning, I got to the airport early to prep the plane. While waiting for Dad to arrive, I cleaned it from top to bottom till it sparkled.

It was my idea of a perfect trip: just the two of us—father and son—flying there together in a plane I would pilot.

Then Amy showed up at the hangar.

"Call your mom" was all she said.

I found a pay phone.

"Mom?"

"He's gone, Todd. Your father's gone."

I froze, unable to process what I was hearing.

"Huh?"

"On the bathroom floor of the music store," she choked out. "Massive heart attack."

Clunk.

That was the sound of my heart and everything in me hanging up—not the phone, not the conversation, but me. The ironclad grip and control I thought I had on life slipped right through my fingers.

My dad was gone. Gone with no goodbye. And there was nothing I could do about it.

My dad was gone. Gone with no goodbye.

I threw the phone violently and collapsed on the tarmac, emitting a scream before I could stop it. We never made it to NAMM—never got to the bonding . . . or the building.

He was forty-nine.

Into the Deep End

After the engagement, everything should've been joyful. And for a few brief moments, it was.

We got engaged on a Sunday. By Thursday, my soon-to-be father-in-law was gone. Just like that. A massive heart attack left him on the bathroom floor of the music store. No warning. No hugs or long talks or prayers together or goodbyes.

Todd went quiet . . . and I didn't know what to do. I still had my parents and grandparents. I'd never lost someone that close. Because Todd wasn't outwardly expressive, I assumed space was what he needed. I thought that giving him room was loving him. I missed him, but because one of my personal vows was not to burden anyone, I sucked it up and carried my own grief alone.

I didn't see the pattern that was beginning to form: If I reached toward him, he stepped back.

I was used to being needed—I thrived on it even. And Todd didn't seem to need me. Looking back, I don't think he took the time to grieve about the loss of his father at all. He didn't fall apart. Life didn't stop. The week after the funeral, we were back in the shop—pricing guitar picks and restringing instruments like nothing had happened.

Todd carried the grief like he carried his responsibilities. Make the funeral arrangements. Run the store. Keep your head down and plow through the work. I tried to help—packaging guitar strings, organizing shelves—but he didn't ask for much, and I didn't know how to offer more.

We were newly engaged, still young enough to think love could power through anything. And I still believed it could!

But Todd was in shock. The center of his life had suddenly and brutally shifted, and I didn't have a blueprint for how to be there. He let himself cry once or twice. Mostly, he worked. I wanted to comfort him, but nothing seemed to help. So I assumed giving him space was helping and serving him—and in that sense, my need to be needed was being fulfilled.

When your spouse is hurting, how do you respond? Do you feel afraid to approach—unsure how to comfort and easily pushed away? Or do you draw closer?

Because Todd wasn't outwardly expressive, I assumed space was what he needed.

But it's clear to me now: We never talked about how his dad's death was affecting him. We never paused. Never processed. We just kept going. And somewhere in that forward motion, I started falling behind.

Todd felt like he had to be everything to everybody, including me, which meant there wasn't much left of him for any one of us. He wasn't looking for comfort. He was looking for stability—something that wouldn't suddenly change and break his heart. If I was there and not dead, it was probably enough.

Todd felt like he had to be everything to everybody, including me, which meant there wasn't much left of him for any one of us.

So he worked. And I planned a wedding.

Could we have paused? Should we have taken the time to grieve, heal, and notice the warning signs?

Absolutely.

Did we? No.

The Cost of Carrying It All

When you're in your twenties, you think you have time. Everything lasts. The people you love will always be there.

The death of my dad shattered that illusion. I didn't know something like that could even happen. Having to pick up the pieces in the days and years that followed—without tools, counsel, pastors, or support—set the course for the next quarter century of my life.

My mom was devastated. She was just kind of a zombie—always sad, blank, not wanting to make decisions. My sister, Julie, was only sixteen—more than seven years younger than me. I felt like I had to be a parent for her.

So I stepped in—not because I had a plan but because someone had to. I hadn't gone to business school. I had zero interest in running the music store. In fact, after watching how miserable my dad had been in corporate life, I'd sworn never to follow that path.

But there I was—trying to run a business I didn't understand, dealing with customers six days a week, and struggling to make payroll, all while stuffing away my grief.

What about my new fiancée and future wife?

Amy was the light in the darkness for me during this time. She was outside all the hurt and chaos of Dad's sudden passing, and her constant presence helped me get through each day. The only problem was . . . I didn't tell her that.

There I was—trying to run a business I didn't understand.

I was "there" for my mom and sister. Amy was trying to be "there" for me while I went through life with tunnel vision. I could see her warmth and her care for me. I wasn't *trying* to push her away. I just couldn't respond. Couldn't seem to reciprocate. And I didn't know how to bring her in.

So everything else that had been moving forward—every other part of my life—froze. My music. My dreams. Our engagement. The future with Amy—everything.

The real problem, though, wasn't that I *needed* the pause, or even that I did pause, but that I stood still while Amy kept moving forward. I stepped out while Amy jumped in with both feet.

The signs of our sudden disconnect were there all along. I just didn't act on them, think about them, or even so much as look at them. And that's the thing about warning signs: They're helpful only if you stop and face what they're telling you—to slow down, take a pause. But I believed the way to succeed at carrying all the responsibilities was to put my head down and burrow into the work. I had no skills and no clue about how to love someone else in the middle of that.

And here's the crazy part: One of the most foundational truths about marriage is almost never said out loud. It's not first about *being* loved but about being *a lover* in the truest sense—whole enough, healthy enough, and present enough to carry someone else's heart in the balance of your own life. If only I had known *that* at the time. . . .

That's the thing about warning signs: They're helpful only if you stop and face what they're telling you—to slow down, take a pause.

Red Flags

Premarital counseling reminds me of a defensive-driving course. Everyone says it's smart. It's the wise and responsible thing to do—so you do it. You might sleep through half of it and forget everything five minutes after you walk out, but in the end, you get your insurance discount.

At the end of premarital counseling, you get your box checked off. Let's be honest: Most couples walk in thinking, *We're already getting married. I've already sent the invitations. I've bought the dress and paid the deposits.* So we nod along. We take every quiz. We answer questions about conflict and communication and whether we prefer showers or baths, and then we continue to plan our wedding—to say nothing of planning the marriage.

But while it's arguable that we probably should, most couples don't go into premarital counseling looking for reasons *not* to get married.

When it was our turn, sure enough, red flags arose.

For example, I would still go out with my girlfriends—my *single* girlfriends. And sometimes we'd end up at a bar. We weren't hunting for guys—it was just our thing. Something familiar, fun . . . free.

Most couples don't go into premarital counseling looking for reasons not to get married.

But to Todd? It wasn't harmless. And it wasn't the right kind of "free."

He still carried the weight of something that had happened earlier in our relationship—when he found out I was still spending time with an ex. We had "moved past it" (or so we told ourselves), but some part of that wound was still raw.

We were sitting in counseling when it blew up.

"This is what single girls do," Todd said. "They go to bars to meet guys. Why would you want to do that if you're marrying me?"

I explained that I didn't want to meet other guys at the bar. I just wanted to be with my friends. I also didn't want to be controlled.

If you're seeing warning signs in your relationship, don't rush past them or ignore them. Premarital counseling and marriage counseling aren't a box to check—they're a chance to face truth.

"If that's what you want, then I don't want to get married," Todd said. And just like that—the wedding was almost called off.

I froze. I couldn't believe what I was hearing. This was supposed to help us prepare—not blow us apart. And suddenly, we were done?

I honestly don't remember how we got back on track. I know we didn't pause. Didn't process. Didn't really resolve anything. We just . . . kept going. *Again.*

At that time, I didn't know how to use my voice, but I'd recently discovered one solution that seemed to work when nothing else did: tears. Sometimes, crying got me what I wanted. It helped me "win" the fight. But in the long run, I was losing the war.

Warning lights were blinking everywhere. If we could go back now—if we could sit with our younger selves in that season—we would've told them, *It's okay to pause in order to work things out. Don't ignore. Don't rush in. Don't pretend everything is fine when it's not. It's okay to slow things down.*

The wedding was almost called off. . . . *Don't pretend everything is fine when it's not. It's okay to slow things down.*

Instead, we did what we'd been doing. We kept moving forward—again— right past the moment that should've made us stop and ask bigger questions, that should've been a wake-up call. But we did not slow down. So when the next signal came—louder, sharper, and right on the edge of "I do"—we did what we'd learned to do.

Once the initial emotions subsided, we pushed through. We kept going—patched it over and carried the bruises, the chaos . . . all the unspoken words with us.

Full Speed Past the Signs

Then came the counseling.

We'd chosen a pastor from my youth group years prior. He was a good man. But premarital counseling is only as helpful as what the participants are willing to confront.

Amy still liked going out with her—single—friends. Sometimes they went to bars. To her, it wasn't a big deal. To me, it *was* a big deal. Especially because earlier in our relationship, she was still keeping ties with an ex, which I didn't much appreciate. It still stung.

"This is what *single* girls do," I said. "They go to bars—to meet guys. You're not single anymore. Why would you want that?"

We argued. The pastor tried to mediate. But Amy didn't like to feel controlled—and I didn't want to feel disrespected.

Premarital counseling is only as helpful as what the participants are willing to confront.

Eventually, I'd had enough.

"Okay," I said. "I'm done. If that's what you want, then I don't want to get married."

I meant it. In that moment, I was ready to walk.

But I didn't.

Somehow, we moved past it. How? I don't know—we had no process. We had this all-or-nothing way of reacting to things, which was immature and totally ineffective. We didn't pause. We didn't think it through or go deeper. Most likely, once we "felt" better, once it all blew over, we did what we'd already learned to do: Put on our sunglasses, block out the glaring truth, and go full speed . . . right past the warning signs.

Throwing the Keys Away

The night before our wedding, everything exploded.

Looking back, it wasn't new—it was the same pattern we'd already seen in counseling. If I wanted something Todd didn't want, he would just shut me down—no warning, no discussion, no room to explain where I was coming from. Just a flat *no* and nothing else.

We had this all-or-nothing way of reacting to things, which was immature and totally ineffective.

It had already been an impossible couple months. Todd's dad had just died. We were grieving and planning a wedding at the same time. I was juggling timelines, flowers, photography—trying to keep the plates spinning—while Todd tried to hold up the rest of the world.

Little did I know that our pattern was just a tiny glimpse, a mild start, of the next two decades.

By the time the rehearsal dinner rolled around, I thought we were past the hardest part. Everything was ready. Family was flying in. Dresses were steamed, tuxes pressed. I'd confirmed the photographer for the morning of the wedding—an early call time at the church so we could capture Todd and his groomsmen getting ready.

Our pattern was just a tiny glimpse, a mild start, of the next two decades.

So I told Todd to be there early.

Without even looking up, he said, "No. I'm not going that early."

I blinked. "What do you mean *you're not going*?"

"I'm not doing that," he said flatly. "That's too early."

I tried again. "Todd, the photographer is already booked. This is what we planned."

"Nope. Not happening."

I could feel the heat rise, the tears well up. This wasn't just manipulation; this was sheer frustration. There we were, standing in the music store, customers within earshot, arguing over wedding logistics like it was a contract dispute. Only I wasn't a client. I was his fiancée. And this was our wedding.

Feeling desperate—and fixated—I zeroed in on one thing: Todd getting to the church at the scheduled time.

The argument followed us into the car and all the way to his house. By the time we pulled up, my face was soaked with tears. I felt disheveled and a mess. I needed to get home and get ready for the rehearsal dinner, not be in a fight the night before our wedding.

I kicked him out of my car, wanting nothing more than to get away from him. But Todd insisted, "We need to talk."

The argument followed us into the car and all the way to his house.

"I need to go," I replied. "My parents are expecting me."

"No," he said, his voice firm. "Not until we work this out."

Refusing to let go, he blocked my door, reached in through the window, grabbed my keys, and threw them who-knows-where.

At first, I just sat there, blinking, stuck, my car parked cattywampus in the street, mascara smudged, emotions raging. I screamed, *"The wedding is off!"*

Then I stormed into his house and headed straight for the phone in his sister's room, screaming all the way through the living room for the whole house to hear.

The house that was now full of family: grandparents. Aunts. Uncles. Cousins. All there. Every one of them heard me.

I called my parents. Somehow I pulled myself together. Smiled for all the guests. How did we resolve it? I honestly couldn't tell you.

At some point, Todd agreed to show up for photos.

Whether it was because of the crying, the chaos, or the threat to call the whole thing off, I'll never know. But here's what I do know: The "how" matters. And however it came about, that night hardwired something in me. I realized that if I pushed—or cried—hard enough, I could get my way—not because we met in the middle or because we came to a mutual understanding but because one of us broke first.

I realized that if I pushed—or cried—hard enough, I could get my way.

And that's the kind of "win" that costs more than it gives—whether you're holding the keys or throwing them. And here was yet another sign. Another red flag warning us that we weren't ready and we needed to stop. Take a break. Let go.

Back then, it just felt like another fight we got past. Now, I know it was a flashing red light we blew right through.

But we threw the keys away instead of inviting God into the process. And we wouldn't lay eyes on those "keys" again for twenty-five years—not until the world stopped, life collapsed, and we were forced to start over.

Can you relate to Todd's "kaboom"? What's beneath the surface of the outbursts— whether yours or your spouse's?

Not About the Dish Towels

Amy tried. She and Julie helped in the store. My mom came in just to be near us. We were all there, orbiting grief, doing our best to make it work. Sometimes it was even nice just to be together.

But I didn't know how to talk about what I was carrying, so I exploded over stupid stuff. One day I saw the wedding registry list and just snapped. It was all plates, curtains, and kitchen stuff.

We threw the keys away instead of inviting God into the process.

"Why is there nothing for a guy?" I blurted out. "At some point, don't you think we're going to need a drill? A hammer?"

Looking back, Amy had been trying to include me the whole time; I just wasn't present. Throughout our engagement, I wasn't engaged. And when I couldn't articulate what was wrong, I lashed out about dish towels.

As the wedding rehearsal rolled around, the pressure built to a breaking point. Amy had scheduled early morning pre-wedding photos. To me, it felt excessive. The day was already going to be long. Why add three hours just for pictures?

I resisted. Doubled down. Refused to go.

I didn't know how to talk about what I was carrying, so I exploded over stupid stuff.

In hindsight, it wasn't about the time. It was about control. And stress. And all the grief I hadn't faced.

I'd been living in fear for months—fear of losing more people, fear of failing the business, fear of not being enough, fear of leaving Amy, like my dad had left my mom. I was terrified we wouldn't make ends meet, that I'd let everyone down.

In hindsight, it wasn't about the time. It was about control.

I wouldn't have said I was afraid—because I didn't know I was. But fear was driving me.

My dad had always operated with the philosophy, "If it is to be, it's up to me." In my family, if something needed to be done, you did it yourself. You climbed. You pushed. You finished it.

So I took it all on, even though I wasn't built to carry it alone. My God was big enough—but my faith wasn't big enough to let Him take the wheel. I didn't trust that He was in control, even when I couldn't be.

My God was big enough—but my faith wasn't big enough to let Him take the wheel.

And *that*—if I'd been paying attention—was the biggest warning sign of all.

Chapter 4

Cracks in the Foundation

*M*OST MARRIAGES DON'T COLLAPSE IN a single moment. They fracture slowly—under the weight of a thousand small hurts, unspoken needs, and misunderstandings that pile up over time. The fight isn't really about dishes or dollars or sex. Underneath, something deeper is smoldering.

The fight is really about expectations never voiced. Insecurities triggered and never resolved. Fears that rise to the surface—or worse, are confirmed—like catching your spouse in an affair or being married to someone who suddenly changes their mind about having kids. Each one leaves its mark. And the longer those wounds go unnamed, the deeper they sink. If it isn't seen, recognized, and named—how can it be healed?

These are the hidden fractures—the places where couples miss each other without even realizing it. The silence. The offhand joke. The tiny decisions that seem harmless but leave emptiness behind. Left unspoken, they spread

What advice might you give Todd or Amy? Where does their struggle mirror your own—or what insight or question about your own marriage is surfacing?

into cracks big enough for the foundation to shift—and eventually, the house can come down.

We ask ourselves whether it was ever "meant to be," but part of God's purpose in marriage is not just happiness—it's transformation. It's to become more like Christ, which is to be perfected in love. Modern culture treats marital union like more consumer entertainment: A husband *should* provide this, and a wife *should* do that. A "real" man this and a "real" woman that—standards shouted louder than Scripture. Caught up in our worlds and our personal concerns, we miss not only the point but the source of true satisfaction.

Jesus said, "It is more blessed [and brings greater joy] to give than to receive" (Acts 20:35 AMP).

If your marriage is suffering a joy deficit, the problem may not be whether *you're* getting enough of what you need and want—but whether *your spouse* is.

The Other Woman

A man shall leave his father and his mother, and shall cleave to his wife; and they shall become one flesh.
—Genesis 2:24 NASB

After Todd and I got married—surprise, surprise—we had no idea what we were doing.

We'd said our vows, but like most newlyweds, we didn't know what they meant.

We'd said our vows, but like most newlyweds, we didn't know what they meant. Not really. "One flesh" sounded great. I didn't realize it meant leaving behind the very people who had shaped my entire life.

Scripture says that when we marry, we should stop clinging to our parents and "cleave" to our spouse. Well, I had no idea what that meant—or how to do it. In biblical times, there was real preparation—not just for the wedding but for the marriage. Daughters were *raised* to serve a husband and run a household. The first year of marriage was dedicated entirely to the new household.

Today, we add a whole person into the most intimate parts of our lives like we'd just brought home a hamster: We know it needs a good cage and a couple daily meals. Give it a wheel and stop by whenever you want some entertainment.

So when I got married, nothing much changed. I still lived ten minutes from my parents. I talked to my mom every single day—sometimes multiple times a day—for hours. I loved my parents. I was close with my mom. I trusted my dad. Staying connected felt natural and normal.

I'd failed one of the most important parts of marriage: leaving my childhood home, Mom and Dad, and all they provided.

What I didn't see was that I'd failed one of the most important parts of marriage: leaving my childhood home, Mom and Dad, and all they provided—not just physically but emotionally. I hadn't separated from them enough to truly become one with Todd.

And he could feel it.

There's nothing wrong with having a good relationship with your mother as a married woman—but I was openly venting my frustrations about Todd to her. Whatever I didn't like—what he was or wasn't doing—I shared with her.

What
tiny hurts
might be piling
up inside?
Name one—
and name
what you
need.

My mother was "the other woman" in my relationship with my husband.

And she always responded with full support—for *me*. Whatever I wanted, she was on my side. She'd offer suggestions for what I might say or do to persuade Todd or improve the situation. It felt helpful in the moment. It felt validating. I didn't realize I was creating an atmosphere that made Todd feel invalidated—like an outsider in his own home.

And after a while, it ticked him off.

He wasn't rude about it. He didn't bad-mouth her. He just asked, "Why are you sharing so many intimate personal details of our marriage with your mom?"

He just asked, "Why are you sharing so many intimate personal details of our marriage with your mom?"

Cringe.

Knowing what I know now, I would never do that. He and my mom already had a rocky relationship. Telling her my complaints probably didn't make the situation better for either of them. But clueless as I was, when he started making comments and showing disapproval, I just felt torn between them. I didn't know I was *supposed to* choose. I didn't want to choose.

And it wasn't just my mom. There was also someone else.

Vacations

Are you kidding me?!

That was my reaction when Amy suggested we go on vacation with her parents for two weeks. To me, it was wrong on so many counts. We had just gotten married. It was supposed to be the two of us—leaving and cleaving, building our own life.

Besides, how was I supposed to get away? I was teaching, running the music store, managing employees. The shop was open six days a week. And, oh—we had no money.

It didn't help that our honeymoon had been a disaster. I had gotten severe food poisoning from something at the reception and spent four days bedridden. Amy was stuck in the hotel room, bored out of her mind, until she finally escaped to the pool. But she forgot sunscreen and came back red as a lobster, burned from head to toe.

By the time I could get out of bed, I hadn't eaten in four days. When I tried to walk, I took about five steps and—slam—hit the deck. In a whole week, we had maybe two days of actual honeymoon vacation.

I wasn't much for vacations anyway. Before that trip, vacations weren't even a thing for me. In my entire childhood and young adult life, I went on

We couldn't have been more different.

exactly one vacation with my parents—ever. That was it. In my mind, vacations were rare, extravagant, maybe even wasteful. You earned them; you didn't expect them.

Amy was used to going on vacation with her family several times a year. So when her parents offered, she heard "fun and familiar." I heard "not us, not now."

We couldn't have been more different.

The Other Guy

How can you affirm your spouse this week, no matter the result?

I honestly had more confidence in my dad than in Todd. Todd was a new husband with his first house and a lot on his shoulders. Dad was the "handyman" who could do a little bit of everything, from hanging a picture or ceiling fan to fixing appliances. If Dad could do it, I let him—oblivious to how much I was hurting my husband.

Case in point: After our trip to Hawaii, Todd had this dream of turning a corner of our yard into a little Hawaiian oasis. I should've encouraged him and cheered him on. It was something he wanted to do just for us, by himself, a gift from his heart. But I didn't trust that his version would look nice or be done "right."

I compared Todd to my dad, who in my eyes could do everything perfectly.

Today, I know the outcome matters less than the process—that he needed to enjoy it, and I needed to appreciate him. Even if it turned out awful, we would've learned what *not* to do and had a good laugh!

Instead, I doubted. I compared Todd to my dad, who in my eyes could do everything perfectly. My dad was, in essence, "the other guy" in my relationship with my husband.

I probably thought I was being practical, but what Todd saw was my lack of confidence in him. Without meaning to, I was withholding what Todd needed most: my approval and my belief in him. I just didn't know. I didn't see. And no one else thought to show me.

Without meaning to, I was withholding what Todd needed most: my approval and my belief in him.

I wanted closeness with Todd. I really did. But I felt more connected to my parents than to my husband. Now I think it's normal that it takes a little time to transition from being a daughter to becoming a wife. At the time, though, I wasn't expecting such a rude interruption to everything I'd known and valued.

So when Todd started refusing all the things I wanted us to do together—when he declined again and again—I didn't adjust or fight for it. I just took the path of least resistance. I went to the familiar. To the people I knew *would* engage, listen to, support, and understand me.

Especially in the beginning, that meant my parents. The emotional current of my life kept flowing toward the home I'd come from rather than the one I was trying to build.

We'd said our vows, but I was still bound by other vows—silent ones I'd made to myself. A vow to avoid being a burden. A vow to hide my needs and meet them secretly so

Those personal vows we make as children . . . keep running in the background, affecting everything we do.

no one could tell me no. A vow to protect my image of holding everything up. *I'm fine. It's fine. Everything's fine.*

Those personal vows we make as children, under pressure and without wisdom, don't just evaporate. They keep running in the background, affecting everything we do. Even if they go quiet for a while, sooner or later, every vow will catch up with us.

Not Enough

I often wanted to ask Amy, "Is this a marriage with you, me, and your mom? Or is it just us?"

After a while, Amy was talking on the phone with her mom constantly, whether I was out working or home waiting for her. It left me feeling disrespected, like I wasn't enough for her. In reality, I probably wasn't being enough because I was hardly present. Things were rough for me. I was working three jobs, I'd lost my dad, and my mom wasn't doing well. We were still waiting for that newlywed glow that everyone talks about.

Amy compared me to her dad a lot—not exactly confidence boosting. But ex-boyfriends were also in the picture.

Why would she feel like she had to go back to one? To me, that only meant one thing: I wasn't enough. Six months into our marriage, I came home while she was talking to an ex—the one she'd dated the longest.

Six months into our marriage, I came home while she was talking to an ex—the one she'd dated the longest.

I started yelling: "What are you *doing*?!"

Clearly, I hadn't yelled enough the last time, before we got married. I hadn't made a big enough impression that this wasn't okay. So this time, I raised my voice—brought in the "kaboom" like I'd learned from my dad. Loud meant serious. Loud meant *You'd better get it this time.*

But honestly? I still didn't understand what was going on between us. I've heard so many guys talk about this at marriage conferences, in books, in private conversations. We don't understand what our wives are actually asking for.

Amy would come home stressed and wanting to talk all about her day, while I'd be thinking, *Why do you want to relive this again?*

Most men make assumptions, thinking, *She needs me to solve something.*

So I gear up. Get my pen and paper. Start looking for the problem. Start building the fix. But she doesn't *want* me to fix it. She wants me to *feel it* with her. She wants me to connect. But I never had to connect before. In my house, I wasn't allowed to feel. Feeling angry was fine. Being tired from working hard was good. But feeling and venting frustrations was unacceptable.

So I had zero experience listening to anyone's emotional problems. When Amy brought her stress to me, for whatever reason, I internalized it as failure. *She thinks I'm not there for her. I never do enough. I've fallen short. I let it go this far. I can't save her, fix it, or make it better.* And out of that narrative—which existed entirely in my head—I felt disrespected.

When your spouse is stressed, do you take it personally and push back, or do you pause to pray and bring comfort?

When Amy brought her stress to me, for whatever reason, I internalized it as failure.

And that disrespect then hit at my self-worth, which made me defensive.

So I was either in problem-solving mode, or I would shut down because I felt inadequate and, therefore, attacked. Underneath it all was one and the same fear: *I'm not enough.*

While it wasn't true that I, as a man, was not enough, it was undoubtedly true that I wasn't doing enough to hold on to my marriage. I wasn't maturing, healing, or becoming a husband to Amy. I was holding on to my ways, my hurts, my boxes—while letting *Amy* go by neglecting her needs.

In fact, I was actively pushing her away. I didn't want to hear about her day. I didn't want to know how she was feeling.

And because those were her primary ways of connecting, what it all added up to was this: I didn't want Amy.

Money or Me?

"You can't write off trinkets."

Words to *cringe by*—if you're me. Words to *live by* if you're Todd.

At twenty-one years old, I came into marriage with no savings. Right or wrong, I still think that's pretty typical. I wasn't lazy or irresponsible; I just wasn't quite . . . Todd.

I'd been working since I was sixteen—I had worked hard and paid my own car note and insurance, and I liked stopping for a sixty-nine-cent Thirst Buster or swinging through the drive-through for a cheeseburger.

I wasn't used to someone telling me I couldn't spend less than a dollar on lunch.

Todd was a saver.

Once, after a long twelve-hour shift, I wanted to grab a burger on the way home. Todd said no.

"*Really?!*"

"We don't need to be spending money on eating out."

It was sixty-nine cents.

"Are you kidding me?"

I wasn't used to someone telling me I couldn't spend less than a dollar on lunch. He watched over everything I did with our money.

Meanwhile, I had landed my first real job—as a nurse on the night shift in the neonatal ICU. I'd always wanted to work with babies. It was intense. Beautiful. Stressful. And I loved it.

Todd didn't get it.

That alone would've been okay—but he didn't ask about it either. When I'd talk about my day, there was a lot of nodding and . . . silence. He didn't ask questions. He didn't respond emotionally. He showed no curiosity nor any signs that my passion for this new nursing career meant much of anything to him.

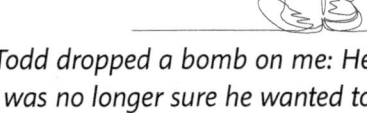

Todd dropped a bomb on me: He was no longer sure he wanted to have children.

I felt ignored. Silly. And abandoned.

To make matters practically dismal for me, around that same time, Todd dropped a bomb on me: He was no longer sure he wanted to have children.

I. Totally. Panicked.

Oh my gosh! I'm in this for the long haul—with no kids?!

"Todd—all I ever wanted was to be a wife, a mom, and a nurse!"

Most days, my face was soaked in tears, and my heart felt like it was being pushed through a meat grinder. *What is this marriage I'm in?*

Todd's way of abandonment—and what felt like trampling all my dreams—bled into everything. I loved decorating our first house. I would go to craft shows with my mom and pick out small touches, imagining how they would feel inside our home.

"You can't write off trinkets" was his response to my treasures.

Money can divide—or it can be surrendered. What place does it hold in your marriage?

Talk about raining on someone's parade.

Thunk. That was the sound of my heart sinking yet again. I was just trying to make a house a home.

"Why is my stuff not valuable?"

"Because you can't write it off, Amy—it's not tax deductible. And it can't be sold."

He'd grab something like a computer or a piece of equipment. "See this? I can sell this. Can you sell that pillow on the couch? That picture frame on the wall?"

"No, but it looks nice."

I'd dismissed his landscaping dream the way he dismissed my pillows.

"And as soon as you've touched it, what value it had is already lost."

The irony is, I had done the same thing to him. I'd dismissed his landscaping dream the way he dismissed my pillows. It looked and sounded different, but it was the same lack of care . . . and it caused the same sort of wound. I just had no idea.

I knew he was smart with money. That was part of why I loved him. He had savings, security, direction. He was responsible. So when he said no, I was bummed . . . and I assumed he was right.

"We have to save," he would say. "Put that money away for a rainy day."

What mattered to me didn't matter to him. And slowly, I started to believe maybe I didn't matter either.

Looking back, maybe that *was* the rainy day, because all those little no's started chipping away at me. What mattered to me didn't matter to him. And slowly, I started to believe *maybe I didn't matter* either.

Your Heart Needs a Pressure Valve

My mom hadn't been feeling well. The doctor said it was a bad flu, but earlier that week, I had noticed a massive blood clot on her leg. She'd had clots before, but this was concerning.

On Friday, I stopped by her house after work and noticed that the clot was gone. *Gone* gone. So where did it go?

On Sunday, my sister called.

"She's having trouble breathing," she said. Then, as an afterthought, "Did you notice the blood clot is gone?"

"Yup," I said.

"That's not good," Julie replied.

I agreed. "If it gets worse, she needs to go to the hospital."

"She doesn't want to go."

"Well, she doesn't have a choice. She's going."

Julie took her. It took forever for someone to see her. As it happened, Amy was working at the same hospital and was able to check on her while we waited. Amazing. God is always in the details if you look for Him.

Eventually, they admitted Mom into the ICU. They said it was

God is always in the details if you look for Him.

sepsis and pumped her full of antibiotics. Then I got the call: "You need to come down."

I happen to have a photographic memory. As soon as I walked into Mom's hospital room, I took one look at the machines and the vital signs and flashed straight back to my days helping Amy study for nursing school.

"This is textbook pulmonary embolism," I heard myself say.

Silence.

"Amy, didn't we just read about this?" I asked. "O2 saturation's down, and pH is down. The clot we saw is gone."

I flagged the doctor. He was a third-year resident—still in training—and there was no attending physician on duty to oversee or step in. This was supposed to be world-class medical care?

"She's *septic*," he insisted.

"I'm not a doctor," I told him, "but this is classic PE."

"You don't know what you're talking about."

Who says that!

"What would it hurt to give her blood thinners?"

"I did X-rays. She's septic," the doctor said, dismissing me.

When we subpoenaed Mom's medical records, they all were magically "lost."

I debated finding someone higher up. Someone with authority. Someone who'd listen. But I didn't. Instead,

I stood there and rubbed my mom's feet—like she used to do for me when I was little.

"If you need to go," I whispered, "we'll be okay."

Ten seconds later, the crash cart barreled down the hallway as hospital staff forced us out. I don't think I made it to the end of the hallway before she was gone.

The autopsy confirmed it: pulmonary embolism. PE. Like I said.

She had a known history with clotting. I'd told the doctor what we saw. He ignored it. We called it malpractice. When we subpoenaed Mom's medical records, they all were magically "lost."

Right then and there, I lost all trust in medicine. A bitter root went deeper. And to make things worse, this was the hospital where my wife worked. Trust—in general—may have gone almost completely out the window at this point.

My dad had died suddenly at forty-nine. Now my mom at fifty-one. I started asking myself, *Do I even want to bring kids into this world?*

Before that, I figured we'd have kids when the time was right. But now? Everything felt wrecked.

In the span of just a few years, I'd lost my dad, then my mom had died an untimely and preventable death. The music store got dumped on me. I was carrying business responsibilities I never asked for while trying to pursue my own dreams. If I was feeling sorry for myself, I didn't let myself know it. Instead, the shock, the injustice, the

Work might get hard, but never as hard as facing the mess inside.

burdens—it all was too much. I went numb. Checked out while doing the tasks that seemed required of me. In fact, I threw myself into the tasks primarily. Work might get hard, but never as hard as facing the mess inside.

Doing Life Together—Apart

I'm sure you've heard the saying that opposites attract? Well, Todd and I were opposites. Like, truly.

I am a morning person; Todd is a night owl. I love noise, people, energy. Todd likes peace, silence, and solitude. I like to dress up. He doesn't even own a tie.

Once, my hospital threw a black-tie gala. I was excited. I already had the perfect gown. I knew Todd didn't love getting dressed up, but it was just one night—at least that's what I tried telling him. Our conversation went poorly. I begged. I even cried. He still refused to go.

He didn't stop *me* from going. He just didn't care to join me. So I took my brother as my date.

"Why are you here with your brother?" people kept asking. "Where's your husband?"

Is this going to be my life?

"Are you sure your husband's real?" That was another one I got a lot, in some form or another. "Or do you just Photoshop him in family pictures—because we *never* see him."

It happened a lot. At work parties. Family picnics. Trips. Out loud, I'd laugh it off.

Inside, I wondered, Is this my new normal—doing all the things I love . . . alone?

Inside, I wondered, *Is this my new normal—doing all the things I love . . . alone?*

I went salmon fishing in Alaska, took a New England bus trip, drove my dad's rebuilt '57 Chevy up the Pacific Coast Highway, did all these beautiful things—with my parents. Todd was always invited. Always welcome. He always had reasons why he "couldn't"—but really, he just didn't want to. Whatever he was holding on to, it clearly wasn't me.

During this time, I wasn't having any affairs. I was trying to let go of that old coping lifestyle, so I could hang on to this new life. But I was also trying to create some semblance of a lifestyle I could tolerate with Todd. No trinkets. No drive-through cheeseburgers. No conversations about things that mattered to me. And now add to the list no going on trips together. I tried and tried, but nothing I said or did could get Todd to budge.

"Somebody's gotta work to pay for all that," he'd say.

I understood. But it still felt like he didn't care about what mattered to me. He didn't love—or even appreciate—anything I loved. And that's a big downer. It certainly didn't make me feel like we were close or connected. I'm sure it played on my insecurities. Todd was the smart one. My desires weren't smart; they were wrong. Maybe I shouldn't have wanted throw pillows and camping trips. Maybe I was just twisted inside, longing for things I *shouldn't* want. To me, it felt like he wanted me to play dead. Expect nothing fun and embrace only everything "safe" until retirement.

Whether I admitted it or not, deep down, I felt abandoned. Like I'd entered the single most important relationship with someone who . . . maybe wasn't for me.

Did I marry the right person? Is there a right person? Is there such a thing as a soul mate? No spouse can complete you. Only God can do that. Marriage is God's gift to help us become more like Him, not to fill the God-shaped hole in us.

Whether I admitted it or not, deep down, I felt abandoned.

Penny Wise and Pound Foolish

I have always been frugal—not just to save for saving's sake but so I could do "bigger and better" things. When I might do those things, I'm not sure I ever thought through. But I'd watch people blow money on Thirst Busters or candy at the movies and think, *Why? I would never do that. Not even a soda. Not even once in a while.*

So when Amy came along—full of joy, freedom, and spontaneity—I didn't know what to do with her. Her carefree spending hit something deep in me: fear. Fear we wouldn't make it. Fear I couldn't provide. Fear I was already failing.

I didn't see it that clearly at the time. All I knew was I got angry. Over hamburgers that cost less than a dollar.

Her carefree spending hit something deep in me: fear.

Years later, in counseling, I started to understand something about myself: One thing I hated more than anything was getting in trouble for something I didn't even know I'd done wrong—or something I had no power to prevent. Have you ever had that happen? That feeling of being blindsided—called out, punished for someone else's stupidity or mistake—was unbearable to me.

If I blew money we needed, okay. I could own that. But if someone else spent it and we all had to suffer for it? That felt like *I* was the one being chastised for another person's negligence. That made it an injustice. And that made me mad.

One day, Amy was on her lunch break. She bought a burger— two bucks, maybe less. I saw the charge and immediately started grilling her about it.

"What was this for?"

"I grabbed a hamburger . . . Todd, I was starving."

"We have food at home. We don't have money to spend two dollars on you eating out."

"It's just a burger. It's not a big deal."

But to me, it was a big deal. It was another leak in the dam. Another crack in the system. Another sign we weren't going to make it. I escalated. I treated her like a child. Called her out. Made finances a point of constant tension.

Eventually, she'd be crying. Only then would I start to soften—realizing maybe I'd pushed too hard. But I was still too clenched inside to really bend.

All I could think was *We're not going to make it. We have to scrimp. Every penny has to go to savings.*

Amy would crack down for a while. Cut back. But eventually, the cycle would repeat. And we tried everything: workshops, budgets, monthly spending limits. We even set up a "hamburger fund"—twenty dollars a month for her to spend on anything she wanted. She tried. We both tried.

But that old cycle always came back. Fear. Reaction. Retreat. Reset.

Every round left us a little more worn down, another fissure in the trust between us. And around we'd go—like hamsters on a wheel—trying and failing, striving and burning out.

We were striving for the wrong things. Always fixing symptoms, never the roots.

We were striving for the wrong things. Always fixing symptoms, never the roots.

When You Don't Know the One You Love

As a nurse, I care for others all day. I know my job. I think I'm pretty smart at my job. The people at my job were beginning to recognize that, and I was doing well.

But at home?

You might remember that Todd was my chemistry professor when we met. He's a science buff, and being a pilot, he's borderline obsessed with weather. So one day I asked, just being curious, "Why do they name hurricanes?"

Todd answered without missing a beat. "Because hurricanes circle the earth and come back the next year," he deadpanned. I bought it.

"Oh!" I said, surprised.

Totally bought it. I mean, if you're not into weather trivia, how would you know that's not a real answer? Well . . . it wasn't.

It was a joke. I didn't get the joke. So I asked a follow-up question: "Then why do they rename them the next year instead of keeping the same name?"

He didn't say anything then. But later, in front of a bunch of people, Todd decided to *run* with the story.

"Oh yeah," he said, laughing, "Amy thinks Hurricane Hugo from three years ago is still circling the globe!"

 Everyone cracked up. I laughed too. But inside I was mortified. *Is he seriously making fun of me—in front of all these people?!*

Todd had a habit of turning my confusion into a punch line.

I smiled. And I laughed. But I felt *so stupid.*

It wasn't the first time. Todd had a habit of turning my confusion into a punch line. He didn't intend to be mean. He just thought it was funny. The person who was supposed to be closest to me had no idea how insecure I was.

It's not all his fault.

I didn't speak up. I didn't say it hurt. I just kept laughing along, covering up the hurt and humiliation for as long as I could. But whenever this sort of thing happened, after the laughing faded, I'd go quiet. Sometimes I wouldn't say anything for days, but the whole time, I was repeating the moment in my mind. Then I'd reach a boiling point and finally explode.

"Why would you treat me like that?!"

To him, it was out of left field. But to me, it wasn't just about a hurricane joke—it was about being made to feel *small*. Repeatedly. Sometimes publicly.

He genuinely didn't get it—and I didn't think that was a free pass. Aren't we supposed to care, to know, to be aware of what hurts and what lifts up the person we supposedly love? Shouldn't we know what hurts them or makes them happy? I had raging insecurities, that's true. And my guy was clueless.

Truthfully, I was clueless too.

So we laughed with everyone else, and I got even better at hiding. I hid my hurts. Hid my feelings. *I hid what excited or bothered me because either way, Todd wasn't interested.* And the more I hid, the easier it became—until hiding felt more natural than connecting.

Are there times you might be expecting your spouse to be a mind reader? Do you have hurts or insecurities you feel they "should" be aware of but maybe aren't?

The more I hid, the easier it became—until hiding felt more natural than connecting.

Can't Fix What I Don't Know's Broken

Amy told you the hurricane story. Here's my side of it.

I'd go for the easy joke—not to be mean to my wife but because it got a laugh. And when you're in a room full of people and you can make them laugh—it's fun. It felt like connection to me. I didn't realize I was doing it at Amy's expense. In fact, I had no idea, because she always laughed along.

She didn't tell me how much it hurt. She didn't express her feelings to me, and I genuinely didn't know it bothered her. But it did. Deeply. And if I didn't know it, how could I know to stop?

One time, Amy was showing me a picture. She had this huge smile, beaming. Something came out of my mouth—I don't remember exactly what I said but it was something like "You've got a real horse smile there."

I wasn't saying she looked like a horse, that she was ugly, or that there was anything wrong with her smile. But that's what she heard.

And for years, she didn't want to smile. She would only half smile to hide her gums, especially in photos.

I was so numb to most of my own feelings that I didn't pick up on the cues.

Several years later, when she finally told me, I was devastated. I hadn't meant it that way at all. Words I thought were harmless had left wounds—and I had no idea.

Obviously, I was far from being in tune with my wife's feelings. Stuffing emotions away has a way of making you insensitive—numb. Maybe my low EQ was part of why I was so blind. Emotions aren't *just* feelings; they're part of human intelligence. They give us information. When you're in touch with your feelings, you're more able to do what Jesus said to do in Romans 12:15: "Be happy with those who are happy, and weep with those who weep" (NLT). But to do that, you have to actually notice.

I was so numb to most of my own feelings that I didn't pick up on the cues. Not by a long shot.

I hadn't seen how my words—my "jokes"—were cutting into her. I wasn't aware that the person closest to me already felt so unsure of herself. I needed her words. She needed my awareness. We had neither.

What we did have were childhood wounds and insecurities festering and playing in the background, coloring everything. I was poking straight at the places she hid, and she was poking at mine—by choosing her mom, her dad, and ex-boyfriends over me.

Instead of letting marriage inspire us to heal and grow, our lack of connection and communication was doing just the opposite. And it affected everything.

That same mindset showed up in my business too. For me, the *task* was everything. If you'd asked me back then what mattered more, people or the work, I'd say the work. Hands down.

Now? I'd say you can't run anything—marriage, business, life—without valuing the people first. But I didn't know that yet.

When a marriage leaves too much empty space out in the open, something—or someone—eventually sneaks in to fill it.

So I steamrolled people. I joked. I pushed. And I didn't see what I was breaking.

Those small, early cracks in our relationship were starting to spread. A chasm was forming between us. And when a marriage leaves too much empty space out in the open, something—or someone—eventually sneaks in to fill it.

Chapter 5

The Curious Irony of "Iron Sharpens Iron"

> *As iron sharpens iron, so one person sharpens another.*
> *—Proverbs 27:17 NASB*

*E*VERY MARRIAGE IS PERFECTLY DESIGNED to heal—or to destroy.

Why? Because marriage isn't built on compatibility; it's built on transformation. What if your spouse's strength is *meant* to meet your weakness? What if their perspective, their wiring, even their flaws were meant to sharpen and refine you—drawing you into something bigger than yourself as you learn to love? We often say that love conquers all. In marriage, that could mean love will cause us to change rather than attack the person showing us our need for change.

But here's the catch: Marriage works only if you're willing to lay down your old self—the

Marriage isn't built on compatibility; it's built on transformation.

"me" that existed before "us." Entering marriage means killing the version of you that insists on keeping life as it was. In marriage, you become "one"—unless you refuse to change. Hence, the key to holding on . . . is letting go.

Let go of control, secrecy, fear, and pride. Hold on to love, union, unselfishness, and fulfillment.

Otherwise, the same strengths and weaknesses designed to help us mature and refine turn into weapons. Instead of slowly peeling back the bandages and healing the childhood wounds, you grip the wound while pushing away the one who came to help heal you.

Marriage works only if you're willing to lay down your old self—the "me" that existed before "us."

Iron sharpens iron, Scripture says. Sparks fly, edges grind, and what was once dull is forged into strength. But that works only when two people are willing to be sharpened. When they're not? The friction just causes pain. What was perfectly designed to heal now becomes perfectly designed to destroy.

Our marriage had become the irony of iron: What was meant to sharpen had begun to slice. Sparks designed to ignite change were instead building a fire hot enough to burn it all down. Still, hope remained because we knew this: Enough rain—enough prayer, enough surrender to God—can quench even the most raging wildfires.

Sparks designed to ignite change were instead building a fire hot enough to burn it all down.

Anatomy of an Emotional Affair

When someone starving is suddenly presented with a beautiful feast, they probably don't stop to ask questions. They eat.

Affairs don't usually start with fireworks.

They start with small talk and the lure of satisfying a deep-seated hunger. And if you're hungry, you eat. Or if you're starved—for affection, attention, touch—well, you eat more. It may not be real sustenance. It may not even be that good. But the sweetness covers the bitterness of your loneliness, and all you know is . . . now you're craving it.

That was me. And I told myself it wasn't an issue at all: *You're fine. It's harmless. This is just friendship.*

Sure, I believed it. I *wanted* to believe it. I needed to think it was okay. He made me feel valued. Just seeing me cheered him up. At home, Todd wasn't usually happy to see me. Mostly, he *didn't* see me except when something needed to be done.

Maybe attention isn't the same as connection. And maybe flattery isn't love. But at least it was something I could feel. Something sweet that I could taste.

"Hey, I like your hair."

That alone just lit me up.

"Is that a new scrub top?"

I drank the Kool-Aid®, felt the sugar rush—and wanted more.

Nothing dramatic. Just some guy . . . noticing the little things. I was thirsty, and he offered me Kool-Aid. I drank the Kool-Aid, felt the sugar rush—and wanted more.

And I told myself another lie: *I'm strong enough not to cross the line.* I thought I could handle it. But little by little, I was stepping into a trap.

As time went on, he started asking about my patients, my assignments. The friendship progressed from superficial chatter and little pick-me-ups to feeling something deeper. We started getting to know each other. And what had started as scattered moments in the day began to feel like something else.

Not lust. It wasn't that. I didn't want to date him. I wasn't even interested in him romantically.

But I also didn't have a "feelings wheel"—a diagram of a circle with seventy-two emotions built around six core feelings. I'd never even heard the term "emotional literacy." I wasn't thinking consciously about what I felt or what I needed. I just knew it felt good.

Now I can see why. What felt so good had less to do with him and more to do with what I longed to have with Todd—what Todd refused to give: *connection.*

My friend at work was warm and attentive. At home, Todd was distant and quiet. When I tried to talk with him about work, he listened like it was a checklist: *Is there a problem? Something to fix? Something broken? No? Then why are we talking?*

What felt so good had less to do with him and more to do with what I longed to have with Todd—what Todd refused to give: connection.

He didn't care. He really didn't.

So I split myself in two.

There was Work Amy, and there was Home Amy. I could flip the switch between them. I'd come home, walk the dogs with Todd, do all the normal things—but never talk about what I really cared about or any of the day's events. Not the codes I'd been part of. Not the stress, the problems, or the weight I was carrying.

Marching orders for life: Keep everything easy for Todd. Starve at home. Get filled up at work.

Because I was already getting fed emotionally at work, I didn't need it from home. Todd was free from the burdens of my life. I got my sense of identity, validation, and worth from working in the NICU, from my coworkers, and from my new friend. It made me feel better. And it set me free to give Todd what he wanted: cooperation, smiles, "peace and quiet."

Wash. Rinse. Repeat.

Todd and I still had fun. We still rode his motorcycle through the neighborhood. Still had moments that reminded me of when we were dating. But the deep, soul-level connection I longed for—where we'd comfort each other, process life together? That was growing somewhere else.

It's not an "emotional affair," I told myself. And I believed myself—until the day we crossed a line.

Up to that point, the "friendship" had been out in the open. I wasn't hiding it from coworkers. I knew nothing was going on—at least not like that. I wasn't drawn to him "that way." I just soaked up the attention.

Then—a touch. A moment. A choice. A transaction.

It wasn't sex. But it was intimate. And it shattered me.

And suddenly—it wasn't just emotional anymore.

What is an "emotional affair"? How can you tell when a friendship has crossed the line?

I never imagined it would go this far. It wasn't sex. But it was intimate. And it shattered me.

In an instant, all my old patterns came rushing back, transporting me to that day on the field when the boys had held me down. To that summer afternoon when my friend had left, I had stayed, and I had ridden home on my bike bleeding, vowing to hide the attack.

The same voice that had spoken to me then was speaking to me now: *You always get yourself into these situations. How do you get out?*

I felt stuck. I didn't want this. But I was *doing* this. Why?

Because I "owed" him. That was the transaction.

He'd "paid" attention to me, right? And I'd taken it. I'd soaked it up. I'd built a double life around it. I had no idea the significance of what I was doing until he came to collect.

You know it's killing you, but it feels good, and you don't have anything to take its place.

I wanted it to stop—but I didn't want him to stop paying attention to me. Maybe it's how smokers feel. You know it's killing you, but it *feels* good, and you don't have anything to take its place. Add to the mess that he was a coworker, which made everything riskier. A blowup could cost me my job.

So I did what I'd always done: I people-pleased. Nodded. Smiled. Laughed. Looked fine on the outside . . . while screaming inside.

How do I get out of this?

One day, he invited me to his house. I knew it was wrong, but I went. And it quickly turned sexual. It didn't last long. Almost as quickly, I froze.

"I can't do this!" I shouted. Seconds later, I was dressed and out the door.

I'm grateful to say I never spoke to him again. Out of the blue, he ended up getting transferred out of the nursery, and I was suddenly set free. *Thank You, God.*

It felt like a get-out-of-jail-free card. No mess. No fallout. I didn't have to say anything. And neither did he. We just . . . stopped.

But inside? My heart was shattered.

Okay, I told myself. *It's over. Now what?*

I had no idea how to tell Todd. Infidelity meant that he had biblical grounds to leave me—and I fully expected him to. But I didn't want to lose our marriage.

> *Infidelity meant that he had biblical grounds to leave me—and I fully expected him to.*

So I made a decision: I wouldn't tell him. I'd live with it. I'd carry the guilt all the way to the grave.

Famous last words . . .

Addicted to the Mess

By adulthood, chaos felt normal to me. I had no real frame of reference for "easy" or "healthy." My earliest boyfriends had always cheated on me. I had cheated on them. I had one long-term relationship that was physically abusive, but truthfully, we

Is there something in your life you know needs to change, but the pain and effort required feel more daunting than staying where you are?

had abused each other in so many ways. There was always drama, betrayal, secrets, lies—flowing like water. Like second nature.

Instead of developing healthy skills, like cooking, running a household, or studying Scripture, I learned to master secrecy. Secrecy wasn't just survival anymore; it was something that fed me, made me feel in control. I didn't know how to function without it. When relationships got messy, I felt the stress—but stress felt like home. It was *peace* that felt foreign.

So if things went smoothly, I panicked. Dating someone who didn't make me compete with other girls or work hard for his attention—that's what freaked me out. There was even this one guy in high school who was super sweet, honest, and never did anything I can remember to hurt me. I sabotaged it—not quite consciously—but I was jittery and unstable. So I lost the good guy and just kept going.

When it happens, you scream, "Like I said! I knew it all along." But really, it was a self-fulfilling prophecy. You made the way for it. It's not *everyone's* pattern. It's yours. It was mine. And I lived with it on repeat.

It's like I needed the mess to *feel*. I guess it was easier to suffer and squirm than to change.

Stress felt like home.
It was peace *that felt foreign.*
Healthy felt foreign, and shame was familiar.

That pattern must've started with the rape. After that, something officially split inside me. There was the Amy everyone saw—put together, upbeat—and then there was the version no one saw, the one still bleeding from the day she'd stayed back when she should've left.

Healthy felt foreign, and shame was familiar. So later, even though I wasn't having a new affair, I still carried the old one inside. That was my chaos. I went about my day—going to work, folding laundry, laughing with Todd in the kitchen—while shame burned beneath the surface. I could stay busy enough to forget for a little while, but it never left.

Many Sundays at church, it hit me hard—my heart breaking under the weight of conviction and secrecy. Every sermon felt like it was aimed at me—God seeing straight through my facade. And screaming above it all was that voice: *You need to tell him!*

Monday . . . Tuesday—I'd be riddled with guilt for a few days. Then, just to function, I'd shove it back down. Get back into the swing of things. Smile. Fold laundry. Take good care of babies in the NICU. Try to be a good wife.

But one Sunday, Todd came straight out and asked, "Is there something you need to tell me? Anything I should know?"

I think the preacher's words, the message, and the screaming voice inside took over, because when he asked, I don't even remember hesitating.

"Yeah," I said. "There's something I need to tell you."

He lost it.

Looking back, I don't recommend this, but he wanted details—all the details—and I gave him what he asked for. In some ways, compliance can feel like the right thing, but every answer just made it worse. His anger snowballed. Words flew. And eventually, I found myself curled up on the

In some ways, compliance can feel like the right thing, but every answer just made it worse.

Based on what you know so far, what would it mean for Todd to "own his part"? Do you think he was partly responsible at this point?

floor, Todd kicking me. Not hard. Not to injure. Just enough to say, *Get out.*

He called my mom.

"Come get your daughter," he said as I sobbed.

And then he let it all out. He told her everything he could cram into just a few minutes—which was a lot. The affair. The rape. The abortion. My past. My shame. All of it.

My response to myself?

You did this. You deserve it. Take the berating. Take the shame. Put on your big-girl panties. Suck it up. He has every right to say whatever he wants. Every right to treat you like this.

And so I let him.

I packed a bag, and my mother picked me up. I went home with her and stayed for a while. For about a week, Todd refused to answer any of my calls. He wouldn't let me go to our house.

But I was desperate to talk. To explain. I wanted to make things right. But I also wanted to say, *It wasn't all me. You played a part too.* I believed that if I could just help him see it—own his part—maybe we could move forward.

I believed that if I could just help him see it—own his part—maybe we could move forward.

So I made a plan.

We didn't have kids yet—but we had dogs. And we loved our doggies. We even took them to Glamour Shots to have professional photos taken. *Hello, 1990s.* They were our world.

If I take the dogs, he'll have to talk to me.

So I waited until he wasn't home, grabbed the dogs, and drove around.

On cue, he called.

"Bring them back."

"They're my dogs," I said.

"No. They're *our* dogs. And they live here."

"Well . . . if you want them back, you'll have to talk to me."

And with that, the silence broke.

What do you think about Amy's tactic? Was it good or bad? Wise or just manipulative? What would you do?

Blindsided

Being cheated on wasn't just disgusting; it was enraging. All I wanted was to be able to do my work, provide for my wife, and trust that everyone was staying in their lane without me having to play cop.

As I mentioned, I didn't appreciate emotions, but this whole situation was making emotions unavoidable. I was tired of "suddenlies." Tired of getting hurt emotionally. Tired of finding out jaw-dropping revelations after the fact.

My dad had died. My mom had died. And now, something in me wanted to die.

The fact that I was tired is an understatement. Amy's confession felt like being blindsided by a freight train—and then, as I lay there bleeding, finding I was the only one around to sweep up the debris.

My dad had died. My mom had died. And now, something in me wanted to die.

I was the kid who wanted to be Spock, right? After Amy's confession, I wanted to go back to that—being logical, detached, and free from emotions and attachments. Taking control of the situation. It seemed other people just couldn't do the right thing.

Do I have to do everything?

I equated peace with not feeling.

I had tried living in a way that was godly. To me, being "blameless" meant don't steal, don't lie, don't cheat, and make an honest living. Wasn't I doing all those things? So why was I being punished?

The Bible says to seek peace. Psalm 34:14 (NASB) says, "Turn from evil and do good; seek peace and pursue it." I wanted that. I thought I was doing that. However, I equated peace with *not feeling*. Kind of a big difference. But I didn't know that.

Today, I know that Galatians 5:22 puts peace right alongside love, joy, patience, kindness—all feelings. Even gentleness assumes sensitivity: You can offer a gentle touch only if you can actually *feel* how much pressure you're applying.

What I was calling peace had no basis in reality. True peace doesn't leave you afraid of pain; it gives you strength in the face of pain.

What I reached for wasn't biblical peace. It was emptiness. Stoicism. Numbness.

I was "comfortably numb," like the Pink Floyd song says—edging ever more dangerously toward being dead inside. What I reached for wasn't biblical peace. It was emptiness. Stoicism. Numbness.

To achieve it, I had to get better at stuffing down the emotions that stirred up whenever I thought about Amy's affair. To keep those feelings from coming back, I had to stay within a tiny comfort zone where I was driving and where I cared deeply only about the things that I was in control of.

The comfort zone became my idol.

What I was really seeking was a way to steer clear of suffering. I'd stopped trying to be happy long before. Now I was just trying to survive.

As time went on, I told myself I was aiming to be just like Spock: logical, detached, untouchable by feelings. But what I was becoming wasn't Spock; it was closer to a Borg: part human, part machine, stripped of individuality, emotions dismissed as "futile."

Amy's confession was a sledgehammer to my chest.

I reeled. I exploded. I yelled. I screamed. I called her mom and exposed everything I could, like a dump truck unloading in one big heap.

Lashing out didn't make me feel better, but it did exhaust my emotional capacity so I could return to being numb.

Lashing out didn't make me feel better, but it did exhaust my emotional capacity so I could return to being numb. I didn't think about her mom, her dad, anyone else. I was too busy wanting to crawl into a hole and die.

Abide

"Just tell me what I need to do to save my marriage."

That's basically what I told my new Christian counselor during the separation that followed my first confession to Todd.

I didn't say this outright, but all my actions and responses showed it: I wasn't there to process or unpack or heal. I was in fix-it mode. *Tell me the steps. Give me the list. I'll do whatever it takes.*

The counselor gently tried to explore where some of my patterns came from—like how my dad's absence growing up might have shaped my need for affection and attention. I listened, but I didn't take it seriously. Not yet. I wasn't ready.

Still, it was in that season that, for the first time, I really started thinking about what it meant to have a personal relationship with God—beyond knowing *about* Him.

I'd always believed. I had no doubt that God was real. If you'd asked me back then, "Do you know God?" I would've said, "Absolutely!"

But the truth? I knew about God. I didn't *know* God.

I even remember saying to my counselor, "I know God's real, but I can't *feel* Him. I'm supposed to get my needs met by Him, but He's not here to hug me. I can't feel His arms around me."

I knew about God. I didn't know God.

Growing up, physical touch was my top love language. My parents were so affectionate—always giving warm hugs and kisses. We're a touchy-feely family. That had been my normal.

So the idea that God could meet my needs was hard for me to grasp because He was not physically present, like my family was.

My counselor challenged me to study every verse in the Bible that included the word *abide*. So I did, and I learned a lot. I read and even understood, at least on paper, what it meant to "abide in Christ." It means that I'm in Him and that He's in me. But it was too abstract. Not quick enough. Not something I could go *get*, grab onto, or control.

What does "abide in Christ" mean to you personally? Do you find this easy to understand and experience, or challenging?

The way I was thinking and operating, the best I could do was grasp it with my head—but my heart had a harder time catching up.

And at that time, I wasn't all that committed to figuring it out. I didn't think Christ was the issue—I thought *I* was. I thought, *I'm the one who can't say no. I'm the one who keeps lying. The one who can't be trusted. Who needs too much. Who can't seem to let her husband's love be enough.*

So instead of running to God, I kept trying to fix myself.

Todd started seeing the same counselor—sometimes alone, sometimes with me. We stayed in counseling for about a year. Slowly, we were spending more time together. I'd go back to the house to get some clothes. Sometimes he'd ask me to stay. Eventually, to sleep over.

We stayed in counseling for about a year.

We still loved and missed each other. And, eventually, he asked me to move back in.

Like all the times past, there was no big, formal reuniting moment. I came home. And while being back together felt good in many

What do you think of the word *deserve*? Do you find yourself using it often? How might your beliefs about what you deserve affect your actions?

ways, it also revealed how much pain Todd still carried. He was hypervigilant. Constantly checking on me. If I went to work, he wanted every detail. If I went to lunch, it was "Who were you with?" and "What did you talk about?" I'd wanted conversation—I got interrogation. Close enough?

I'm fine. It's fine.

Soon I took a new job at a different hospital, so I could be closer to home. That helped because we could see each other more. But still, Todd was relentless. His questions didn't stop. The constant reminders of what I'd done didn't stop.

He made sure I never forgot.

Biblical Grounds

Deserve is a heinous word.

I remember saying to my counselor, "I'm not the one who cheated. I don't deserve this."

He didn't argue. He just said, "Let's find out what you actually *do* deserve."

Then the counselor took me straight to Christ and described what He did for me—for all of us. What I really deserved without Him was eternity in hell. Separation from God. What I got instead—what we all got instead—was grace.

What I really deserved without Him was eternity in hell. Separation from God. What I got instead—what we all got instead—was grace.

Sin is sin. We're all guilty. Yet He forgave us—went to the cross for us—while we were murdering Him, slandering Him. We killed Jesus. That should've destroyed our own future.

But He didn't let that happen.

Jesus had "biblical grounds," but He didn't play that card. While we spat on Him and called for His murder and condemnation, He cried out—for us: *Forgive them, Father.* He had every right to slam the door in our faces, but that's not what He did. He never gave up on us . . . even though we've all gone back to our sin again and again.

This was the gospel I said I believed. The one I said I lived for. I let it sink in.

We talked about forgiveness—not just the kind that makes peace but the kind that literally bleeds for the very ones who cut Him. The kind of forgiveness Jesus gave me: undeserved.

My counselor affirmed that yes, I had "biblical grounds" for divorce. But he also asked me to consider modeling my next move after what Jesus had done for me. And what did Jesus say about divorce?

When the people of Israel asked, "Jesus replied, 'Moses permitted you to divorce your wives because your hearts were hard. But it was not this way from the beginning'" (Matt. 19:8 NIV).

And 1 Corinthians 7:12 says, "If a brother has an unbelieving wife and she is content to live with him, he should not divorce her" (TPT).

Amy wasn't an "unbeliever," but even in that case, the Scripture barely gave room for divorce.

If I could control all the variables, maybe I could protect myself from being betrayed again.

The truth was, Amy wasn't walking away. She wasn't done. She wanted to come back. And I had to ask myself, *How can I walk away from Amy, who is asking for my forgiveness, and still expect God to forgive me?*

And what's more—I still loved her.

So as we started talking and seeing each other again, we didn't fight. It's more like we drifted back toward each other. She'd come for dinner, sometimes stay the night. Eventually, she moved back in.

But even then, I couldn't let go of the fear.

People are just too weak, I reasoned. *I have to be the strong one.* I thought if I could control everything around me—my schedule, my home, my wife—I would finally feel okay. If I could control all the variables, maybe I could protect myself from being betrayed again.

So I nitpicked. I turned over every stone. I grilled Amy, coming and going. I absorbed myself in work, and when I came out of the cave—I inspected.

The idea that my wife needed love, affection, or healing? I'm not sure I thought even once about that.

While I was holding on to control as my savior, I was blind to what I was letting go of.

I didn't ask God what Amy needed. I asked if I was still doing something wrong—missing something He was trying to teach me—not how to love, but how to be better at preventing problems.

Yet while I was holding on to control as my savior, I was blind to what I was letting go of.

I was already juggling three jobs, but later, when my friend asked me to be an associate pastor, I said yes. *It's for God*, I told myself. And it was something that mattered. Maybe if I did something that mattered, I would earn enough brownie points that God would protect me from being blindsided again.

But even in the middle of serving others, I prioritized my own needs above everything else. If Amy wanted to do something and it cut into my rest time? Not happening. If Amy wanted to travel, socialize, see something beautiful, and it didn't seem necessary for my survival, it was an easy no.

I never told her she couldn't do something *herself*. I'd just say, "You go ahead—I need to rest" or "I have to work." If she wanted to go to a golf tournament with her parents? "Cool. I'll be here. Sleeping in."

It never occurred to me that stepping back like that might leave her vulnerable—tempted by other men who were willing to give her the closeness that I cut off.

I just figured you get married, you make a commitment, and you don't cheat. That's marriage, and that's the deal. Period. I didn't see that offering her zero connection and zero intimacy was failure on my part. I thought we'd succeeded. We weren't fighting all the time, so clearly, we had something most couples don't after a shock like that.

I didn't see that offering her zero connection and zero intimacy was failure on my part.

Fine. Great. We're not fighting. Let's move on. We can just coast for a while.

Turns out, coasting isn't really moving forward; it's moving backward. The road stretches out ahead of you—and you're not stretching with it.

Chapter 6

Circles, Silence, and the Illusion of Coasting

WHEN SOMEONE GETS CAUGHT IN a lie, in an affair, some marriages shatter—like a house already cracked and thus easily destroyed by an earthquake.

Other couples survive—but survival isn't the same as healing. What happens after the tragedy determines a lot about a couple's future. The initial shock of betrayal may fade, but without real repair, the damage doesn't heal. It either gets buried so deep no one can touch it or your house becomes a minefield—anywhere you step, a bomb could go off. Some slip into silence, mistaking the absence of conflict for peace. Others fight and make up in endless circles. At least if they're fighting, it feels like *something's* happening, right?

But whether it's silence or circles, both are really just forms of coasting.

The initial shock of betrayal may fade, but without real repair, the damage doesn't heal.

Coasting isn't the same as enjoying the fruits of your labor or taking a well-earned rest from conflict. Coasting is floating over a shipwreck you refuse to look at. It requires just enough avoidance to keep the peace, just enough detachment to keep the household running, just enough denial to maintain the status quo. You fight because you think that's accomplishing something, or you keep the peace on the surface because you mistake civility for progress.

It's like moving back into a house after the quake. The walls are still standing, you put the furniture back in place, and life goes on. But the foundation is cracked—and unless those hidden breaks are repaired, another tremor is all it takes to bring everything down.

Coasting is always moving backward.

That's how many couples survive after a confession, a crisis, or a season of pain. They don't heal. They just resume, returning to the rhythm of carpool lines, paychecks, dinners, and routines. It might feel like reconciling, but it's really just drifting. Coasting. And coasting is always moving backward.

Joy, Exhaustion, and the Early Years of Parenting

"It's time," he said.

"Time?" I asked, clueless. "Time for what?"

Todd and I had taken a walk down to the lake when, out of nowhere, he handed me a dozen red roses. They were beautiful . . . and so unexpected. At that point in our marriage, I didn't get flowers often, so I couldn't help but wonder, *What's the occasion?*

We sat in the grass, talking about where we were in counseling and what might be next. That's when he told me he'd had a dream—and felt like God had spoken to him.

"I think it's time for us to have kids," Todd declared.

Drop the mic. Stop the presses. This was music to my ears! Without thinking and overwhelmed with joy, I jumped into his arms.

I think it's time for us to have kids.

I was so elated, I didn't even notice
we had rolled into a patch of queen
palm trees, and one of the sharp fronds sliced my forehead open. I thought nothing of it until we got home and I passed a mirror. There I was: smiling, roses in my arms, with blood running down the side of my face.

Of course, we had to snap a picture. Roses. Big smile. Bloodied face. The moment that marked our decision to start a family. Perfect.

And it *was* perfect. Oh, how I loved being pregnant! I loved feeling the babies move. Our second son followed quickly after the first, just fourteen months apart—so close, they were nearly "Irish twins." Number three came three years after the first.

I didn't have much morning sickness, no major complications— and all three deliveries were fast. With my firstborn, there wasn't even time for an epidural. Just four hours after my water broke, I became a mom. All natural. Start to finish.

Three babies in three years. Yup. Three in diapers. Three in car seats. And one busy mom.

Those early days were everything I'd hoped for. I loved breast-feeding. Things got dicey when I was breastfeeding one, spoon-feeding another, and potty training the oldest—all at once. But I didn't care about the discomfort, the crying, the sleepless nights. *I was a mom!* Looking back, it's a blur, but a beautiful one. Sticky faces, messy hands, and sweet little grins filled our home.

Sticky faces, messy hands, and sweet little grins filled our home.

Todd, though, saw it all differently. To him, three meant we were outnumbered, and his focus shifted even more to providing. He was okay with rocking and cuddling—as long as they weren't crying or fussing. He tried to help, filling in as the fun playmate, but when they were sick, fussy, or really needed care, he bowed out.

For me, the chaos felt oddly familiar. I'd grown up in a trio—three kids within eighteen months of each other, thanks to Mom's unexpected pregnancy following my brother's adoption. But for Todd, this was foreign territory. So while I focused on surviving, he threw himself into providing.

Thank God for grandparents. My parents were amazing. Because Todd worked from home, he and my mom split the childcare. Some days, the boys stayed home with Todd, and other days, with my parents, just ten minutes down the road. We never needed day care—a huge blessing. To this day, the boys have a close bond with their grandparents.

We never needed day care—a huge blessing.

Because I loved motherhood so much, I longed to stay home full time. But that never felt like an option. I'd occasionally say, "I wish I could work less" or "I'd love to stay home," and Todd would say, "We can't afford that." That ended the conversation.

By then, Todd had left teaching to build his own business. I carried our health insurance. And I loved being a nurse. I loved caring for the NICU babies. Sometimes, honestly, the hospital even felt like a break. I'd cut back to two days a week, and in those shifts, there was quiet. I could breathe. I wonder sometimes if things might've been different had I been able to stay home. Work was another life—another place where I could easily build one.

What's more valuable to you: One parent being at home with the kids, or both parents working? Does your spouse agree?

Working from Home Yet Never "Home"

While Amy loved the newborn season, I went all in on provision. And this was one of the busiest, most demanding phases of my life. We'd just welcomed three kids into the world—one right after the other. We'd sold the music store—it wasn't a viable long-term solution to support a family. And I'd launched a computer hosting business, which provided more than enough money to support our family and allowed me to work from home.

On paper, it sounded great. In reality, the job never stopped.

It ran 24/7/365. There was always a computer down somewhere, even at three a.m. on a Sunday. So home became work. Work took the place of home. In that sense, I was always home—but never *home*.

My business partner was an early riser, so we split the day.

When work drains you that much, family gets pushed to the edges.

He worked from around four a.m. to eight p.m., and I took the late shift—eleven a.m. until around three a.m. That way, we overlapped during peak hours and kept the business covered twenty-three out of twenty-four hours, every day of the week.

Financially, it was a breakthrough—finally. But the schedule was soul sucking. And when work drains you that much, family gets pushed to the edges.

So while I never felt safe to shut off work for long, I could at least pop out of the office sometimes to swim with the kids, grab their lunch, check in. That was fine, as long as I could do it on my own terms. I left my work when I felt I could, not when someone needed me. A meltdown or a mess in the kitchen didn't matter if a client's server was down—work came first.

Even though I was physically in the house, I could not be counted on.

I realize now that many of these things that had seemed so urgent would still have been there an hour or two later. But my fear-over-faith mentality and immaturity prevailed.

It frustrated all of us: I was there but not really there. Eventually, we hit a breaking point, and I had to spell it out: Even though I was physically in the house, I could not be counted on.

Sleeping Giants . . . and Tiny Adults

Todd is a great father. But in those early years, with three baby boys all at once, he didn't have the patience—or maybe the capacity—to be fully present. He was a night owl then, often working until two or three in the morning, which meant he slept until eleven a.m. The vibe in the house was *Don't wake up Dad—unless you're bleeding . . . or dying.*

That left me on full duty by sunrise. I tiptoed through the house with three boys under five—juggling cereal bowls, diaper changes, toy negotiations, and grocery runs—like it was my full-time job. Because it was.

To be fair, this setup had its perks. Todd took the late-night bottle feeding, which let me sleep a little more through the night. I was always grateful for that. But keeping three little boys quiet in the morning—ages one, three, and four—was like trying to mute a thunderstorm.

Todd wasn't absent; he was on another planet. When the boys and I saw Dad, he was locked into work—his eyes on a screen, his mind on a million other things.

Keeping three little boys quiet in the morning—ages one, three, and four—was like trying to mute a thunderstorm.

"You can't count on me."

Did I just hear that right?

"You can't count on me," Todd informed me.

Yup. He's saying the quiet part out loud.

"Even though I'm here, *I'm not with them*. You have to treat it like I'm not home."

He wasn't wrong. But it hurt to hear.

I couldn't understand why the man I loved—the one with such strength, wit, and deep integrity—couldn't just watch his own kids while I ran to the store. I wasn't asking for miracles; I was just trying to make it through. To survive.

Judging from how things turned out, I guess I didn't. Eventually, I just stopped asking. And then, one morning, we caught fire—literally.

I was on shift at the hospital when the phone rang. I answered casually . . . until I heard the tiny voice.

"Mommy?"

I froze, trying to make sense of the fact that my little boy had memorized my work number—and was using it—*while his dad was home.*

"The cabinets are on fire."

You know those moments when you realize something is just crazy—like spending hours baking a cake with all your heart, only to drop it and watch it splatter across the floor on the way to the table? You just stand there, blank and paralyzed, emotions swelling inside you. Sometimes, it's so devastating that you almost decide not to react at all.

A fire rose from my chest. It was our eldest son. Five years old. Home with Dad, but on his own. Making breakfast for himself and for his brother—or trying. And our under-the-cabinet toaster oven—a supposed space saver—had caught fire.

I could barely breathe.

"*Where is your father?!*" I yelled. "Go get Daddy!"

Todd, groggy and disoriented, was already stumbling down the stairs, roused by the smoke alarm.

"I'm up! I'm up!" he shouted, hearing me yelling through the speakerphone.

Yes, he was up now. But not before our preschooler had the presence of mind to call my work number, put me on speaker, and calmly report a kitchen fire.

When people hear that story, they say, "Wait—your husband was asleep while the kids—babies—were just . . . *up*?"

Yup. They knew not to go outside. We had a pool fence. And they knew not to wake up Dad unless someone was dying or bleeding. And now we added house fires to that list. But that was the rule. That was the culture.

That was our life.

It makes us laugh now. But in the moment? I was fuming. Not just at the toaster. Not just at Todd. But at the whole setup. At how normal it had become for our son to call me instead of going to his father. At how casually we had trained our children to function like tiny adults in a world of sleeping giants.

Three Kids, Three Houses, Three Mortgages

Around that time, we decided to move—because of structural issues with the house, our eldest starting kindergarten, and rising crime in the neighborhood, including a double murder just a few doors down. To me, it felt like a window of time and opportunity—before all three kids were in school and before we got too entrenched.

Unfortunately, it was 2008—the height of the financial crisis. We chose a small mountain town an hour and a half

How do
you respond
when your
plans don't
work out?

north—away from friends and family but closer to Amy's dream: cooler weather, pine trees, occasional snow, and far less traffic. We both dreamed of something smaller. It felt like perfect timing.

We listed our house in Phoenix, certain it would sell fast.

It didn't.

The global financial crisis hit. The market crashed. And just like that, we were stuck. Two cities. Two houses and a cabin. Three mortgages.

Running on Empty

Gymboree, gymnastics, "Mommy and Me" at the library, plus passes to the zoo and science museum. I served on the board of Moms in Fellowship at church. During those early years, I kept the kids and myself busy—probably too busy. If I wasn't working, we were going—*somewhere*.

I told myself I wanted to give our boys all the good stuff—the memories, the movement, the experiences to shape their little bodies and brains. And that was true. But if I'm honest, I was also trying to keep the anxiety from catching up with me. If we kept moving, maybe the loneliness wouldn't catch me.

Todd wasn't there for most of it. That's not a dig—it's just the truth. He was always working.

If we kept moving, maybe the loneliness wouldn't catch me.

So I did it all myself, and at first I didn't mind. I loved being with them. I loved seeing their faces light up. When they started kickball, I cheered the loudest. Todd went to Saturday games but never to the weekday practices. That was okay, I thought. *I can do this.*

I didn't realize that was the beginning of something much bigger. The start of a thousand miles in the car. The start of every backpack, diaper bag, and car seat being mine to load. The start of me becoming the point person for everything—again and again.

But I wasn't just giving them memories; I was trying to give them strength. When I was younger, being on the field gave me confidence, energy, and a healthy sense of worth as a kid. I wanted my boys to have that too. To feel strong. To feel joy. To feel free.

Little did I know that I was operating partly on wisdom, partly on fear—the infamous FOMO: *fear of missing out.* And somewhere along the way, fear and striving turned joy into strain.

I was always moving. Always with the boys. Always surrounded by people. Yet I started feeling more alone than ever. Watching other families show up together, I was becoming silently and secretly embittered by Todd's absence.

I'm fine. It's fine. Everything's fine.

That was my mantra. But the truth? I was draining myself dry. Trying to fill everyone else up while I ran on empty.

A Marriage Stretched Thin

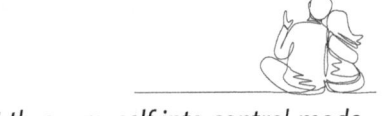

On top of working constantly just to keep up with three mort-gages, I had just lost more than $120,000 in a Ponzi scheme

I threw myself into control mode—cutting corners, watching numbers, trying to outrun the storm.

Is there an area of your life where you keep pushing harder, even though deep down you know it isn't helping? If God is asking you to let go, what would trusting Him there look like?

with a friend who wound up in jail for it. There went my inheritance.

It was a special kind of torture.

Not just because of the money, but because I saw how fragile everything I'd built really was. I thought I was being smart, even cautious. But all it took was one crash and one bad decision and suddenly I couldn't protect us. Instead of loosening my grip, I doubled down. I threw myself into control mode—cutting corners, watching numbers, trying to outrun the storm. It didn't matter that my striving wasn't working. I just did more of it.

This triggered something deep in me. I was already wired to save, plan, and avoid financial ruin at all costs—as if our safety and comfort could come only from money. Suddenly, we were hemorrhaging cash trying to keep three roofs over our heads. The pain was almost unbearable. I felt so out of control financially. I let fear, not faith, run my thoughts and actions.

I let fear, not faith, run my thoughts and actions.

Meanwhile, as I was clinging to fear—as if fear could somehow save me, keep me sharp, motivate me enough to outlast the financial blows—I was losing everything else. My presence at home. My connection with Amy. My peace with God. Fear became my driver. The more I let it steer, the more ground I lost where it mattered most.

Looking back, it's almost too obvious: We moved because of structural issues—not cosmetic ones. The house looked fine on the surface. But underneath, there were cracks we didn't want to face. So we packed up, moved to higher ground, and hoped for the best—leaving the house but dragging the household's cracks with us.

We thought we were building a dream. But the truth is, you don't leave problems behind by changing your address. They stay with you.

So we found ourselves living not only in two cities but in two separate realities.

From one perspective: Three homes. Two lives. Two rhythms. A marriage stretched thin.

The reality: Three homes. Three lives. Three rhythms . . . and Amy starting to split herself in two. There was the Amy I saw and the Amy who was everywhere else.

We were building something— just not what we thought. We were building on two different tracks, with two different blueprints.

You don't leave problems behind by changing your address. They stay with you.

Monday through Friday, Amy was in Prescott with the kids. I stayed behind to work and "watch the house." Amy didn't buy that the house needed watching, but that was what I wanted—so that became the plan. I kept prepping it for showings, with no results.

Fridays after school, Amy packed all three kids—plus the dog—and made the hour and a half drive back to Phoenix for her weekend hospital shifts.

Two adults. Three lives. Not much room for God.

Nature Abhors a Vacuum

I was carrying everything.

I would work all night, sleep all day, and then pack us back up Monday morning—just in time to get the kids to school and start the cycle again. It was exhausting and completely unsustainable. It eerily mirrored my childhood: a dad who was gone all week, a mom who made everything work. I was becoming the very thing I'd once watched with wide eyes—and never in a million years thought I'd repeat. *How did that even happen?*

Doing your best in two different directions eventually pulls you apart.

Yeah, we thought we were doing our best. But to serve what? And whom? Doing your best in two different directions eventually pulls you apart.

And getting a nursing job in Prescott? Nearly impossible. The town was small, and the hospital didn't need what I offered. I was a specialty nurse, and there just wasn't room for me there. So we stayed tethered to Phoenix.

Todd insisted he needed to be there for work—and maybe that was true. His business was there. Our house was there. Our family was there. But looking back, it was a poor decision for our marriage.

I was still trying to believe in our plan, but inside, I was growing sadder, more isolated, more resentful.

We'd put the boys in private school—another decision that added stress. No bus, no shortcuts. Just me and my car. Back and forth, day after day. Pre-K lasted only a few hours, so some days, I drove back and forth twice. Our youngest son started speech therapy too—three extra appointments a week.

"Somebody's got to pay for all this," Todd would say.

I nodded. I got it. But I was the one carrying the load at home while Todd carried the finances. And even when we were both in Phoenix, it wasn't really *us*.

Tag—you're it. That was our "togetherness."

Todd did his own thing with the kids—mostly at the house. They'd swim in the pool, go on little hikes, and have fun together. He was the weekend dad; I was the weekday mom. The one managing routines, school drop-offs, homework, and discipline. I carried the weight. He got the splash.

Tag—you're it. That was our "togetherness."

It felt unfair. But what made it worse was the disconnection.

Growing up, my dad was gone all week too. But my parents made a point to be together on weekends. They were intentional about their time, even if it was limited.

Todd and I? We weren't together during the week. And we weren't together on the weekends. We weren't building toward togetherness. We were just surviving apart. Coexisting. Functioning. Passing like ships. Like one employee clocking out while the other clocked in. Housemates.

We knew it wasn't ideal. But we convinced ourselves it was necessary. Eventually, we got used to it—just like driving on a leaky tire that's slowly deflating, always on the verge of a blowout.

It was during that time that I met someone.

As soon as it started, I felt that sick twisting in my gut: *Oh no. Not again. I don't want to go back there. I don't want to be that person again. I've been there. I've done that. I hated who I became.*

But something in me was starving. If you keep going on empty long enough, something or someone else will come and fill the void. That's the law of nature, right? If something is left empty, something comes along to fill it. Or it will at least try. It doesn't have to succeed. You can notice it and do something different.

Grab a hobby. Fill the emptiness with something healthy. But if you're not intentional, it might be something destructive.

Well, I wasn't—and it was.

I felt so alone. Over time, I found myself in another affair.

It began like the first one. Just conversation. Someone I could talk to, laugh with, connect with—someone who *saw* me.

Todd was almost never there, so it was easy to carry on without him suspecting anything. And honestly, I didn't talk to the other person much either—not at first. When I'd go down to Phoenix for work, I was busy with the kids, the hospital, the household shuffle. But in those rare moments I didn't have the kids, our paths would cross. We'd connect for a few minutes here and there. Nothing serious. It was just "friendly" for a long time. I felt good just being seen and heard and having someone to laugh with. I wasn't aware of longing for more. I told myself it was innocent—just meeting a need.

If you keep going on empty long enough, something or someone else will come and fill the void.

Until one day, he reached in for a hug. And I felt it. That twinge. That shift. The hug was nice. Too nice. I knew it shouldn't feel that good. That was my red flag. But I ignored it.

There was that voice in my head: *Don't do it. Don't go back there!* But I brushed it off. *It's just a hug,* I told myself.

I told myself it was innocent—just meeting a need. The other guy gave me something different: a sense of companionship.

It's fine. I'm fine. Everything's fine.

Usually, I was exhausted by the time I had my nightly phone call with Todd—and our calls were pretty basic. We'd run through the day—kids, school, groceries, bills. That was it. Just the ordinary business of life.

The other guy gave me something different: a sense of companionship. He sat with me. Asked me things. Shared pieces of himself. Even in those brief moments, it felt like I was more than just a role to fill.

Todd and I hadn't connected like that in a long time. I wished we had—but he was busy providing, and I was busy surviving. Plus, I didn't think the conversations were that big of a deal.

I was wrong.

The "Yeah, But . . . " Syndrome III

Curiosity over Criticism

There's another version of the "Yeah, but . . . " that hits just as damaging as defensiveness: The one that shuts down ideas before they ever get a chance to breathe. I used to joke about calling them "rebutts" (spelled with two *t*'s) because that's exactly what they felt like—every idea got its backside handed to it.

Here's how it usually went:

"There's a conference I'd love to attend. My boss said I can get the time off if I put in for it now."

"Yeah, but who's going to walk the dogs and pick the kids up from school while you're gone?"

"We were invited to dinner at the Johnsons' next week."

"Yeah, but I have work to do. Who's going to make the money if I'm out having dinner?"

"I'll bet we could turn that empty room into a little reading nook."

"Yeah, but do you even know how expensive shelves are right now?"

Maybe the objections were logical. But logic didn't matter in those moments. What I heard was *Your ideas are impractical. Your excitement doesn't matter. You're asking for too much.*

That's the hidden cost of the "Yeah, but . . ." reflex. It doesn't just block a plan—it blocks connection. Every rebuttal chipped away at my sense that I was heard, valued, and safe to dream out loud.

The shift for us came when we learned that curiosity is stronger than criticism. Instead of cutting an idea off with a "Yeah, but . . . ," Todd could say, "Tell me more. What would that look like?" or "How do you picture us making that work?" Even if we couldn't always follow through, those questions kept the door open.

Every "Yeah, but . . . " shrinks the world. Curiosity expands it. One closes the conversation. The other invites possibility—and connection.

Accelerator: Dream Session

- Set aside time with your spouse for a short "dream session."

- Share one or two dreams with each other—big or small. Write them down together.

- Pick one dream and brainstorm what would need to happen to bring it closer to reality (time, cost, practical arrangements).

- Pray about it together.

Chapter 7

Continental Drift

SHOUTING MATCHES. SLAMMED DOORS. ULTIMATUMS.

Some fractures in a marriage are loud and obvious. Others are quieter but just as dangerous. Whatever may have gotten you to that point, after a while, all the ups and downs are just too much. Instead of letting go of control and manipulation, of trying to win or making your point, you let go of each other. You drift. The determination to fight wears thin. You stop caring.

Couples can share an address, a last name, even a bed, and still live two completely separate lives. From the outside, it looks like stability. But inside, the cracks widen. The walls are still standing, but the foundation is split. Without repair, the fault lines keep spreading until one tremor is all it takes to bring the whole house down.

That's the tragedy of parallel lives: the quiet drift that turns spouses into strangers. We tell ourselves it's enough to keep the routines going— school runs, work schedules,

What really holds a marriage together isn't the roof above your heads; it's the shared life beneath it.

dinners on the table. But what really holds a marriage together isn't the roof above your heads; it's the shared life beneath it.

When a family is connected—truly united—it's powerful. You get to build a culture, create a legacy, and hand down values and traditions that shape generations. A united home multiplies strength. It becomes a garden that bears fruit for generations—a skyscraper, tall and unshakable, standing against every storm.

But when that unity shatters, the opposite happens. The foundation goes untended. The cracks widen. The structure begins to tilt. Cracks become currents that carry everything away. The drift feels small at first, but over time that distance widens until it becomes devastating— eventually turning into a full continental drift.

That's where we were: building two lives under one roof.

Wanted

I knew I had crossed the line. But life kept moving, and it was easy to tuck it away—compartmentalize, shut it off, go back to Phoenix, work, sleep, repeat. I told myself I could stop. I *should* stop. But I didn't.

My desire to be desired had taken root.

My desire to be desired had taken root.

It felt good to be wanted. The other guy noticed me. He wanted to talk. He made me feel pretty. He reminded me what it felt like to be more than "just Mom."

Everyone else in my life needed something from me—meals, errands, discipline, coordination, energy. But he wanted *me*. And there were no strings attached. Life would get busy. Days or weeks would pass, and he didn't push or pressure. He just stayed steady. Even after long silences, he'd still show up. That made it easier to keep it going. Easier to protect the fantasy. Eventually, it fizzled out.

The house finally sold, and Todd moved to Prescott.

Right away, he started back in with the clichés: "We can't have all our eggs in one basket" and "We'd better have a backup." Money was always on his mind.

One thing I'd always admired about my husband was that he was a jack-of-all-trades. Anything he touched turned to gold. He'd built the computer business from nothing. And that was great, except . . . he hated it. Fixing computers was making him miserable. It paid the bills, sent the boys to private Christian school, and

When he wasn't working, we got the version of Todd that work left behind—frustrated, angry, temperamental, always tired.

provided for the family. But then, when he wasn't working, we got the version of Todd that work left behind—frustrated, angry, temperamental, always tired.

Up, Up, and Away

When we were finally all under one roof again, the kids were old enough to be in everything—sports, clubs, practices, rehearsals. It was nonstop.

Amy and I had a huge disagreement.

By then, for the most part, we weren't even fighting anymore. We'd have one big blowup followed by silence. It can seem sometimes like no fighting after years of battles is progress—but silence can be just as deadly as fighting in circles.

Amy did what Amy wanted to do. And I thought the kids were overscheduled.

I was overwhelmed. Life had become all about the kids and work—but nothing about us. Looking back, that was one of our biggest mistakes. We poured everything into everyone else and did nothing for our marriage. Your marriage is either moving forward or drifting backward. There's no such thing as coasting.

Financially, we were feeling the pressure. Work was hard to find, and my computer business was barely staying afloat. I hated it anyway, but I kept at it because it paid the bills. Sometimes we're so deaf, dumb, and blind to God's goodness and direction, He has to pry our misery from our hands just to show us something better.

Your marriage is either moving forward or drifting backward. There's no such thing as coasting.

"Todd, get out of it," Amy told me one day. "You hate it. It's not worth your happiness, and you're a *bear* to live with here at home. Get out of it and find something else that you love. We'll figure it out. We'll do what we need to do."

As good as the computer business had been, the writing was on the wall: It wasn't going to last much longer. And then what?

Todd kept clinging to work out of fear. If the opposite of fear is faith, what should Todd have been doing during this season?

I had always loved flying. I had gotten my pilot's certificate when I was seventeen. I'd even woven flying into our first date and my proposal to Amy. And teaching came naturally to me.

So I decided to blend the two. I became a flight instructor, starting at the bottom, with no clientele. I picked up flight hours any way I could, spending long stretches away from home, building up hours and experience. Amy only encouraged me: "If this is what makes you happy, do it."

It should've been a moment for unity—Amy cheering me on, me chasing a dream. But instead, it became another wedge.

I dove headfirst into flying, and Amy went full speed into kids, sports, schedules, carpools, homework, church—everything.

And my part in it? Nothing.

"I have to work. I can't." That was always my answer.

I was exhausted, which didn't make me passive—it made me harsh. I didn't want to fight, so whenever there was drama, I'd shut down—a quieter kind of argument. In some ways, worse than words.

Amy was juggling carpools, rideshares, pickups, drop-offs—then still driving herself an hour and a half each way to and from Phoenix for work. It was a full-time job just coordinating all of it, and she was doing it completely alone.

I refused to help unless she begged—and even then, I'd do it, but not without giving her an earful about how she was disrupting my work and making life harder for me. We

> How do you feel—really? Not just in this moment, but throughout your day. Can you pause to name your feelings—in irritation over small things or joy over simple moments? Try to be specific.

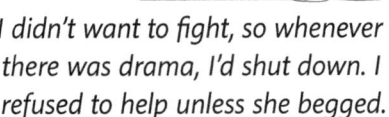

I didn't want to fight, so whenever there was drama, I'd shut down. I refused to help unless she begged.

weren't just in different cities—we were living separate lives, on different timelines, with different agendas, under the same roof. I had found something that made me feel alive again—up in the air, doing what I loved. Amy was on the ground, trying to hold a family together alone.

She wanted me there more. She talked about family trips and outings. I just wanted to rest. I started saying no to *everything*. No to the beach. No to camping. No to Disney. No to fun. Because *someone has to work to pay for all of this.*

Feelings—Nothing More Than Feelings

"This is too much," Todd told me. "You have them in way too many activities. If you can't do it, then we shouldn't be doing it—because you can't count on me. I have to work."

He'd said it before—back in the baby years. Now here it was again, resurfacing in a whole new season.

"You can't count on me."

Great. Thanks for the reminder.

That was always his answer.

Todd didn't go to games or practices. He missed school assemblies, spelling bees, and recitals.

Todd didn't go to games or practices. He missed school assemblies, spelling bees, and recitals. Maybe he showed up once or twice a year—Christmas, end of year. That was it.

And when spring break, summer break, fall break came around? He had no desire to travel with us. Didn't want to take time off.

That's when I would hear it again—the phrase that made my stomach turn: "Someone has to work to pay for all of this."

I was so tired of hearing that.

So, throughout the boys' middle school years, I traveled with my parents instead. Todd stayed behind "to work," of course. Still, I needed help with the boys. I wanted companionship. My parents wanted to spend time with us and their grandkids. But we had to go without him.

We went to the beach, Lake Arrowhead, camping almost every summer. We took multiple trips to Disneyland, stayed in a little beach condo. Todd never came.

Once or twice, he took a couple days off to join us camping, but never the whole week. Skipped fishing with the boys. Skipped walks on the beach. Grandpa did that. Grandpa let the kids bury him in the sand. Someone else was enjoying what God meant for Todd, and it broke my heart both for him and for the boys.

He said Disneyland was like Chinese water torture.

"How can you say that?" I asked him once. "It's the happiest place on earth!"

But Todd had grown up in California going to Disney. He hated the crowds. The germs.

That was one of the things I missed the most—recreational companionship. The joy of sharing adventures, memories, fun. I didn't just want a partner who paid for the memories; I wanted a partner who lived them with us.

That was one of the things I missed the most—recreational companionship.

What recreational activities help you feel connected as a couple? Are there new ones you'd like to explore?

There was one stretch, though, when he showed up. It was during the boys' soccer years. We finally told them they had to pick one sport—just one—because we couldn't keep running around every season, year-round.

No football. That was Todd's line in the sand. So they picked from the rest: baseball, basketball, or soccer. I was hoping for basketball. But they chose soccer—because that's what Todd had played. And I think, deep down, they were reaching for him.

Dad likes soccer? Then we'll do soccer.

And that's when Todd became their coach. For about three years, he showed up—not just as a provider, but in a real, consistent way. He was committed—obligated by responsibility to his promise—but I think he enjoyed it too. The boys loved it.

It was one of the only seasons when we all felt somewhat aligned.

Still, underneath it all, I was unraveling.

I still didn't know about the feelings wheel. And I definitely didn't know the power of naming my emotions. Looking back, I can see how many unspoken, unprocessed, toxic feelings I was carrying.

I tried not to care but, deep down, I was jealous and disappointed that our marriage was nothing like what I'd hoped for.

Over the years of distance and disconnect, I grew bitter. Angry at Todd for never being there. Frustrated that I had to manage it all by myself. Irritated and, honestly, embarrassed because I was always the mom showing up alone. I'd see all the couples at events—both parents coming to games or recitals—and I was the one sitting by myself.

I tried not to care but, deep down, I was jealous and disappointed that our marriage was nothing like what I'd hoped for. Todd didn't want to be there. I felt abandoned, ignored, depressed, and so, so lonely.

Was that all Todd's fault? No.

But I didn't yet know how to run to God. Not in the way that would've satisfied my longing and kept me anchored. Fulfillment wasn't impossible, but it would've taken faith. A kind of deep-rooted faith I just didn't yet have.

And ironically, Todd—despite all his flaws and emotional withdrawal—had that faith, at least more than I did.

He didn't go off the rails like I did. Because he had something I didn't. *Someone.* He had a closer relationship with God. I had kids. I had work. I had escape. But I didn't have the One who could actually restore me.

Todd—despite all his flaws and emotional withdrawal—had that faith, at least more than I did.

So I poured everything into my children. I gave them everything I had. And it *was* a beautiful time—for me and the kids. But for our marriage?

For years, I told myself it was just a season. Todd was focused on work, building our future. I figured once we were more established, he'd be around more. We'd reconnect.

But I was growing skeptical. And with that skepticism came indifference.

At least I have my kids, I told myself. *And a husband who provides. He can keep doing that part, and I'll just take care of the kids.*

In addition to being lonely, I was often completely overwhelmed. When I couldn't find a sitter or a ride for the boys while I had to work, I felt like a failure. Todd wasn't helpful. I felt inadequate as a mom.

Work didn't make me "whole," but it gave me an outlet. At least there, I felt recognized, wanted. I was affirmed by my contributions. One day, I was offered a management position. I said yes! But that came at a cost. It meant going back to work full time. More time away from home.

I eventually drifted and found myself in another affair with someone at work, slipping right back into the old pattern, flipping on and off who I was depending on where I was. I could be one person in Phoenix and then drive back up to Prescott and switch on "Mom mode." Circles.

Even when I was away in Phoenix, I still carried the mental load of home—organizing rides, coordinating everything—but I didn't worry about Todd anymore. I stopped trying to keep him happy. I thought, *You figure it out. Walk a day in my shoes.*

I eventually drifted and found myself in another affair with someone at work.

And the whole time, I felt guilty. Just not guilty enough to stop.

The need, the hurt, the feelings of abandonment and deprivation outweighed everything else.

I told myself, *This is the best I can do.*

I convinced myself I deserved this. That I had justification. This was my tiny slice of fulfillment. My little window of indulgence.

Even if it was a fantasy.

And that is exactly what it was—fantasy. Illusion. It was never real. I can see that now.

> Did you know that the biblical doctrine of "justification" has nothing to do with your actions, your behavior, your choices, or how "good" you are—and everything to do with Christ and how good He is?

But back then, I truly believed this was the only way I'd ever get my needs met. *Because I'm never going to get it from my husband,* I thought. *He just keeps not showing up.*

Are you trying to get needs met from your spouse that only God can meet?

"Call Me When They're Done with You"

After Amy got promoted to management, she was gone even more. More hours. More stress. More time away. And something shifted.

She wasn't just busy—she was different. Distant. Irritable. Something was off.

And then came the ankle.

We were heading out early one morning for our first family ski trip. As we pulled out of the driveway, Amy noticed the trash cans were still out. Not wanting another letter from the HOA, she jumped out of the Jeep—and suddenly, she was gone. A beat later, I heard a pounding on the tailgate, threw the Jeep in park, and there she was on the steep cement driveway, right behind the rear wheel. She'd slipped on the one patch of ice left there.

For a moment, I'm sure she was just relieved the Jeep hadn't rolled back.

The kids got out of the car and stared over her.

"Mommy?"

"Yes?" she strained to say.

"Does this mean we have to go back to school?"

Do you or your spouse have a "phobia" that puts a strain on your marriage? I learned much later in life that my fear of hospitals traced back to hidden trauma. As an infant, I had rolled off a table, hit the floor, and been left alone in a hospital incubator for hours. Sometimes an "irrational" fear isn't irrational at all—it's a wound from a real experience resurfacing.

She tried to get up, but her right ankle hurt—a lot. She managed to grab the back of the Jeep and pull herself up. I assumed she was taking herself to the hospital, and I was fine with that. I hate hospitals. Can't stand the smell, and at the time I was a full-blown germophobe.

Amy hobbled and hopped toward the house trying to manage alone, and I let her. I was backing out of the driveway to take the kids to school, when—*slam!*—down she went again, this time face-first as she tried to clear the threshold on one foot, now screaming in excruciating pain.

If it had been a sprain at first, it wasn't now.

I think I got scalded from the steam coming out of her ears. Amy was already furious that I would leave her alone while she was injured. Now she was livid *and* screaming in pain with a broken ankle. I was probably too numb for her anger to affect me much, but I completely deserved it.

So I did what I should've done the first time: I took her to urgent care.

But I didn't stay. I just dropped her off and said, "Call me when they're done with you."

Not my finest moment, I know. That's how far gone I was. I wasn't really there. Not then. And not in the many other moments that followed.

Then, one day, she brought it up—casually, like it was no big deal.

I signed us up for counseling at church again.

"I want to get my own place in Phoenix."

Huh?

"Less driving. Less hassle."

These were the things she said. What I heard was: *I want a separate life.*

I knew it wasn't good, but I was wiped out emotionally, spiritually, mentally. I worried about money more than marriage, more than Amy, more than my kids—or even my relationship with God.

It caught my attention.

I signed us up for counseling at church again. And get this: The counselor was leading us through the same discipleship program my very first counselor had used with me years earlier. And there it was again: the part about what we really "deserve"—the consequences of sin.

It hit me hard. Again. And something shifted. The moment I turned back toward Jesus—even just a half step—I started seeing what was right in front of me.

Amy wasn't just a little *off.* Amy was *completely* off.

We tried booking a few little getaways, hoping to reconnect. They didn't go well. I'd been asleep. I was still asleep. But something in me was trying to wake up. Spending just that little extra time with God, my senses were turning back on, my discernment coming alive.

She was overattentive to her phone. Cold and distracted. Maybe she'd been that way for a long time and I just hadn't

Spending just that little extra time with God, my senses were turning back on, my discernment coming alive.

noticed. I was too busy and stressed to see. But now I saw. I started to suspect another affair. And one night, I confronted her.

"Give me your phone," I said.

And there it was.

Chapter 8

The Mirage of Power and Pastures

THERE'S A BLINDNESS THAT COMES with judging other people. The self-righteous heart stops examining itself. No longer checking for the food in its own teeth, the fly left unzipped, the buttons misaligned—it feels justified, powerful, even untouchable. Pride convinces a person that being right is enough and that any method—shame, control, even abuse—is warranted if it proves the point.

But power wielded this way is always false power. It feels strong in the moment, but it corrodes everything it touches. Condemnation never produces life, and it certainly doesn't make you a winner. If you're "successful" at it, you end up convincing the condemned that you're right—they're terrible, horrible, awful. So why bother changing? Call someone a failure often enough and

Condemnation never produces life, and it certainly doesn't make you a winner.

eventually the response is "Fine. Then don't be surprised when I act like it."

And once that happens, apathy sets in. Hope dies. Why fight for change when the verdict is already written? Why keep trying when the outcome is always the same? That's judgment without grace, without Christ. It wins by crushing. Unlike Christ's judgment, it has no resurrection. Everything just dies around it.

Nobody can really live under that. A person under someone else's condemnation inevitably looks toward greener pastures. "There must be somewhere I can go to get free of all this pressure. Maybe someone else would see me, love me, choose me." The dream might be waiting just beyond this fence. The possibility of sweeter water always makes the thirst more intense. Once the promise of "something better" glimmers nearby, things can change rapidly.

Illusion lures the heart out into the open, where it feels wanted, chosen—yet in reality, it's a grand setup for a steep letdown.

But the person chasing that dream is still the common denominator. Every wound, every unhealed conflict, every piece of baggage is carried right into the next pasture. And what looked green from a distance quickly turns brown under the same old weight.

That's the danger of it. Illusion lures the heart out into the open, where it feels wanted, chosen—yet in reality, it's a grand setup for a steep letdown.

This is the truth: Love *is* what you need, but you don't secure it by force, and you don't find it by bouncing from one person to the next. It's all a mirage. The temporary highs of each encounter promise freedom but deliver emptiness. And it's all just avoidance of one thing: pain. Stop being afraid of pain, and everything changes.

The First Lockdown: Caught

That feeling of getting caught—if you've ever experienced it, you know. At the point, this was not the first—or even the second or third—time. Depending on your attitude or how justified you feel in this situation, you might panic, or you might shut down and tell yourself you don't care.

"Give me your phone."

I did a little of both. But at first, I was scared and panicky. *Oh no! How am I going to get out of this? What kind of story can I make up that will be believable?!*

I went into self-preservation mode.

Todd reached in to check my pulse, which was racing. I was caught. No story was getting me out of this. My own body betrayed me and gave me away.

"Quit your job now—or we're done."

I didn't bother telling him about the affair before this one. What did it matter? *It's all the same*, I told myself.

Under different circumstances, maybe I would've walked. Told Todd there was no real connection left between us and set us both free. But now we had kids. My boys. My everything. All I had left.

I didn't want to lose them, and I felt sure Todd would take them away from me. The risk was just too great. I was the wrong one. I was the one who had sinned. Maybe Todd was mean. Maybe he was distant. Maybe he was emotionally unavailable and failed to notice that I was hurting, dwindling, losing who I was.

But Todd wasn't in sin like I was. At least, I didn't think he was. Not compared to what I was doing.

Sneaking and lying. I felt unclean.

So I put my nose down and bowed. I had to do whatever he said. I immediately gave my two weeks' notice.

Did I believe that quitting my job would fix everything? No. But it was the only way I knew to say, *I'm still here. I haven't given up.*

When you betray your marriage, the people closest to you often feel betrayed too.

When couples suffer and their marriage takes a hit, everyone around them suffers with them. When you betray your marriage, the people closest to you often feel betrayed too.

The confession, plus quitting my job, crushed my best friend. And not just because she was disappointed.

What she never knew was that she'd been my alibi all along.

I would tell Todd I was with her and tell her I was with my parents, when I was really with the other guy. I let her think she was supporting me in my career, when really, I was using her as my cover. We were supposedly "besties," but I never told her what

I was doing. She was my closest confidante, but I never turned to her. Probably most offensive, I'd managed to completely hide this massive part of my life from her—expertly. How could she ever trust me again?

Oh, and she was also my boss. So having to give my two weeks'?

She was devastated. Not only did I lie to her face and use her, but I'd been one of her strongest managers, someone she could count on. And out of nowhere, I was going to be gone.

Of course, my family was hurt too. They were my lifeline during those Phoenix trips. When I wasn't off with the affair partner, I really did stay with them or sometimes with my best friend. It was our way of staying close now that I didn't live nearby anymore.

But I lost it all.

When would we see each other again? Would they still *want* to see me? Would they forgive me?

I cut everyone with that affair. It was one big lie!

I cut everyone with that affair. It was one big lie! And a whole web of people were left in the fallout.

Blame as a Rule, Shame as a Tool

Let's just say I didn't handle it well.

The first time Amy cheated, I yelled and screamed. I wanted everything out in the open, so I told her mom what she'd done. I wasn't thinking, *I want to shame her*—but of course that's what I did.

Do you believe shame can repair a relationship? Have you used it or allowed someone else to use it on you?

This time? I went all in.

Shame was no longer an accidental default—I used it on purpose. As a weapon. Against Amy.

I told her what a rotten a person she was—how she'd ruined everything. I deliberately attacked her self-esteem and self-worth, thinking maybe what she needed was to be cut down and crushed. Maybe that early desire that I'd noticed back while we were in premarital counseling—the desire to do whatever she wanted, to keep acting like a single even after we were engaged—maybe it had gotten out of hand. I'd been wrong to let it go. Independence had turned to rebellion—sneaking around—and maybe I should've locked her down much sooner.

Someone needed to show her that she was small. That she needed to be controlled. Otherwise, she might think too much of her "freedom" and do this again.

So I didn't hold back. I wanted her to feel the weight of what she'd done. I let my anger lead.

And control was my default. I wanted to know if she was serious about reconciling and staying in the marriage, so I demanded that she quit her job immediately. I also demanded access to everything—her phone, texts, emails, social media, you name it. If she went anywhere, I wanted to know where and with whom. My thinking was, *If she can't control herself, I'll do it for her.*

This wasn't new. But it was at a whole. New. Level.

Living Under House Arrest

For a year, I didn't work. I didn't move out either—and it was pure misery.

The boys knew something was wrong. There's no hiding that kind of tension in a home, no matter how hard you try. We told them, "Mommy and Daddy are having a hard time, but we're working through it."

And we were. Sort of.

We stayed. We started counseling. We joined a discipleship program called CTO—Called to Obedience. It was the first step forward. We were trying to work on our relationship, but there was just so much still unprocessed under the surface. We still didn't know what we didn't know—you know?

You try. You pick up the pieces as best you can. You do what you're told. You try to be "good."

Now I was home all the time. Todd was working seven days a week but no longer always at the airport. He'd worked his way up as a flight instructor. We even had our own plane. Todd wanted me to travel with him, so if he had to fly out to meet a client, I'd go too. I wanted to go with him.

We started doing more together—bike rides, hikes, even sailing.

But things were far from okay.

Todd was brutal. He didn't hit physically, but he *hurt*.

He called me names constantly: liar, cheater, betrayer, home-wrecker. But those paled in comparison to the names I was called during the first few days. Slut. Whore. Tramp. And once the name-calling stopped, he continued to shame me in new and creative ways.

Comments. Digs. I would tell him the truth about where I'd been, and he'd reply with, "Oh, I've heard that one before." Or I'd say, "You can trust me" and he'd respond, "Yeah, look where that got me. Nothing but hurt and misery."

My mind became saturated with self-condemnation.

We lived in our own self-imposed lockdowns.

I saw myself like a criminal on house arrest—with a big scarlet letter hanging from my neck. I would repeatedly say I was sorry and he would repeatedly reply bitterly, "You're only sorry because you got caught." "Our whole marriage has been a lie." "Are we going to run into someone you've slept with at Home Depot?" "Once a cheater, always a cheater."

And, not shockingly, he kept tabs on my every move.

"Who are you talking to? Show me your phone."

Even when I was out with friends, he didn't believe me. And I didn't fight back. *This is what you get,* I told myself. *This is what you deserve. You made your bed; now lie in it.*

He was angry and afraid. I was ashamed and dead inside. We lived in our own self-imposed lockdowns.

Power Struggle

We kept going to counseling, and Amy kept saying the same thing: "I need us to *do* things together. I need us to be a family."

I wasn't ready to take the blame for Amy's affairs, but I was hearing her. Not all the way—but one message was starting to sink in: Amy had a need that wasn't being met. And when that need went unmet for long enough, she looked elsewhere.

So with Amy home now, we made some changes. We got into kayaking down at the local lake. We started hiking again. We found out we loved sailing—so much so that we both became certified captains and joined a sailing club in San Diego. Mountain biking became a family thing—something all five of us could do together. We took annual trips to the beach.

We made a real effort to prioritize family time. And it helped.

Slowly, we worked on rebuilding trust. It wasn't overnight, and it wasn't perfect, but we made a real effort to prioritize family time. And it helped.

But then, something shifted again.

One of our boys was invited to join a competitive soccer team in Scottsdale. It was a big deal—a traveling team, with two-hour drives to and from practice several times a week and entire weekends booked with multiple games. All this on top of normal high school studies and responsibilities.

I didn't even have to think. It was too much. Too far. Too demanding—on him, on us, on finances and time and

What's
your
philosophy
on respecting
your spouse's
wishes—even
when you
don't agree?

everything else. But our son wanted it. So despite my clear no, he begged—and Amy said yes.

We had talked it through. I didn't agree. She let him do it anyway. And that was that. I felt burned. Once again, we were both holding on to our own opinions and will—letting go of that fragile trust we'd only just begun to rebuild.

Change Without Healing

Eventually, some things got better.

Through counseling and discipleship, Todd realized he hadn't exactly made things easy for me. He saw where he'd been cold, dismissive, and distant. He started to give a little—started saying yes to family time, yes to travel. We even took trips to Montana and Canada, and that was really fun. For a few years, it felt like maybe—just maybe—we had turned a corner.

But then? Over time, we got to coasting, and we started drifting again. And that's how we know the deep stuff never got touched.

We kept believing lies about ourselves and each other that never got uprooted.

We both had vows we couldn't see but that still controlled our actions—the same old fears, the same old reactions. We kept believing lies about ourselves and each other that never got uprooted. The same wounds plus the same lies equals the same choices.

And that's exactly what we did.

We'd made some outward changes. And things looked different for a while. But underneath, we still had all the same structural flaws as before living in Prescott—only now the cracks went deeper.

One of my sons wanted to join a competitive soccer team. I was all for it, and Todd was against it, but this wasn't exactly something new to me. No was his default, and frankly, I just didn't think he was capable of anything else. So when he refused to budge, swearing that if I went ahead he would "take no part in it," why would that have surprised me?

During his three-year stint coaching soccer, I loved watching him coach the kids. We really were making changes, but Todd was still using shame as a tactic. As you can imagine, that gets old.

And threatening not to help didn't exactly intimidate me. I'd spent years doing all the work, carrying all the kids' activities on my own. I shrugged it off and carried on.

So after a couple years, and as we gravitated back to our old ways, it turned out that nothing real, lasting, or substantial had actually changed.

Todd buried himself in work again. I jumped back into kids, school, activities, errands, and all the chaos. I got a pediatric job that I loved. Life carried on. And the connection we'd been fighting for slipped right through our fingers—again.

The Wrong Kind of Breakthrough

She made the call, went forward with our son's traveling soccer team without me. And I resented that.

I told her that she had no boundaries with our kids. If they wanted something, Amy made it happen. If I was not in

If we aren't careful to "choose" our battles, we become like the boy who cried wolf. Our cries stop being heard. A constant no loses its power. A blanket yes can do the same. Are you picking the right battles? How do you know which ones are truly worth it?

agreement, it didn't matter. I told her that since she'd gone ahead and chosen our son's will over mine—knowing full well how strongly I felt about it—I could not and would not participate.

It was the beginning of another unraveling, and we plunged headlong into it as if blindfolded.

I crashed. I didn't just stop coaching the kids or helping with soccer—I stopped being involved. I stopped pretty much everything outside work and ministry. Amy had to handle it all by herself, even to her own detriment. Even to the deterioration of our relationship. It was my way of saying, *You want the lead? Fine. Take it.*

I'd spent years trying to lead our family. Years trying to provide, hold things together, give everything I had. And when Amy completely overruled me—after I'd already told her *and our son* that my answer was no—I felt sidelined. Disrespected and pushed out of my own son's life. First, being Amy's husband meant nothing, and now being my son's father also meant nothing. So I backed away.

Did it ever occur to me that I might be winning a battle but losing the war? Or worse—that my kids might be losing something in the process? Yeah, no.

She was wrong—100 percent wrong. But I also handled it wrong. Of course I handled it wrong. Instead of fighting for connection, I went with the same old drill: withdrawal. And that withdrawal cost me everything we'd been working toward up to that point.

Instead of fighting for connection, I went with the same old drill: withdrawal.

Even though we weren't "there" yet, we were

moving forward. We were making progress. And then, with that one decision overruled, that one offense I let lodge in my flesh, I shifted back into isolation.

I wonder what might've happened if I'd leaned in instead of pulling away. If I'd said how much it hurt instead of shutting down. And I wonder what might've changed if Amy had slowed down enough to really hear me.

This time, it wasn't even about control; it was about respect—and making a point. Being the man and the father over my house. Protecting my wife and children. I wasn't an idiot. Maybe I had good reason for my position. For me, this was about *my son*—what was best for him—and having a say as his father.

I think for Amy, it was about our kids getting every opportunity.

But when we stopped honoring each other, everything else slipped too.

It was easy for me to say it was all her. It was dishonor and disrespect, all things considered. But I'd made a career out of dishonoring her. The problem with shaming someone for years, day in and day out, is they eventually come to agree with you. And then where does that leave them?

When we stopped honoring each other, everything else slipped too.

In all the abuse and all the distance, there was one thing I had never considered. One thing that had never crossed my mind. The one thing I had ignored the most. Not the house, not the money. Amy's physical well-being.

Red-Light Runner

Todd and I had become avid mountain bikers. One day, after riding fifty-plus miles, I got home just in time to shower and pick up the kids.

On my way, a red-light runner raced into the intersection, slamming into the passenger side of my car. Thank God my kids weren't in the car yet. If they had been, things might've turned out differently. I still think about how close we came to unthinkable loss. Instead of asking, *Why us, God?* I wondered, *Why* not *us?*

In that respect, we were spared.

If we're talking about deserving, we didn't *deserve* better than anyone else. I wasn't the red-light runner in this case, but I was running past the red lights in my marriage. I sped past every sign—and this time, it was my turn to get blindsided.

I was rushed to the ER with a broken leg and severe brain swelling. Todd came before they transferred me to a Level 1 trauma center in Phoenix. Neurologists reviewed my scans. The swelling would subside on its own—I wouldn't need brain surgery.

He called. He talked to me on the phone. But he wasn't there. Not really.

Whew! That was close—I almost had to shave my hair.

But I did need surgery on my knee, and I would remain in the hospital for several days. My best friend and family came. Todd stayed back in Prescott with the boys and didn't return until after the surgery.

"Someone has to take care of the kids," he explained.

I agreed. But that someone didn't have to be him. I had friends who would've stepped in without hesitation. I didn't ask Todd to come—but he didn't offer either.

And you know what? That hurt. It was more confirmation of what I was already coming to believe: I was on my own. Completely. Todd didn't "do" hospitals. For a long time, that's what I told myself to make peace with it. *It's okay. It's fine.*

"Todd had better be here when you wake up," my best friend said, eyes locked on mine. But deep down, I knew—he probably wouldn't be. *That's for normal marriages,* I thought. *Not mine.*

I made excuses for him. I didn't want anyone to think poorly of him—or of our marriage. But the truth was, it hurt. Bad.

He called. He talked to me on the phone. But he wasn't there. Not really. He came briefly after surgery—then left again until days later, when it was time to take me home.

It was lonely. And the truth kept pushing closer to the surface: *He doesn't want to take care of me.* Watching my grandfather care so attentively for my grandmother in their later years, I couldn't help but wonder, *Who's going to be there for me? What happens when I'm older, more fragile, more in need?*

When we got home, I was in a wheelchair. I couldn't walk. I couldn't work. I had a plate, screws, and pins holding my knee together. People graciously set up a meal train, so thankfully we had food for days.

Todd did what he could—but he wasn't happy about it. And he didn't hide it. He was frustrated, short-tempered. I felt like a

It was lonely. And the truth kept pushing closer to the surface: **He doesn't want to take care of me.**

problem and an inconvenience. So I did my best to wheel around, be useful, and not be too needy. Not ask for too much.

All the while, I was seeing the writing on the wall: He just wasn't the man I wanted him to be.

Déjà Vu: Patterns

I'd gone full throttle back into isolation, still deaf, dumb, and blind to the real cost of it. Married life was well into its slow drift back to the old, but as far as I could tell, the real slide didn't begin until Amy switched jobs again.

She'd been working part time at a pediatric facility when a new manager came in—and things got ugly. The whole staff was miserable. Every day, it was a battle just to show up. I urged her to find something else, and she wanted to—but it took almost eight months before she finally landed a new job.

She started at the beginning of 2019, and at first, it was a huge relief. I was genuinely happy for her. It was something new. She was now working with adults—which was never her dream, but at least she was out from under a terrible boss.

Things actually seemed kind of . . . happy again.

Then I noticed Amy spending more and more time with a new group of friends from work. *This is great*, I thought. *She's meeting people. Building community.*

But over time, it started to feel off.

The way she was behaving around the house reminded me of junior high. The group was becoming more like a clique. They had little nicknames for each other and had become inseparable. I'd come home to find my wife glued to her phone—texting nonstop, like a teenager. I could barely get a word in. And it wasn't just me who noticed. The kids picked up on it too.

She was so caught up in this new crowd—this new identity—that I started to feel suspicious, especially because there were guys in that mix. I couldn't prove anything, but this wasn't my first rodeo. I'd seen this behavior before. I'd seen these changes before—and I knew where they led.

She was so caught up in this new crowd—this new identity—that I started to feel suspicious.

Slowly, gradually, as I watched it all unfold, I started to feel increasingly upset, the old resentments rising.

Déjà vu. And a sinking, settling dread.

New Friends, New Me

Eventually, I made the leap—from the pediatric world to adults. I left the children's clinic for a job in adult case management. Part-time work with full-time perks: great pay, amazing benefits, banker's hours, no weekends, no holidays. I was nervous at first—I didn't have much experience in adult care—but by this point, I'd been a nurse for more than twenty-two years. I knew how to learn. I knew how to lead.

So I went for it—jumped at the chance to experience something new.

It was refreshing—empowering. A much-needed change.

And even more than the job, I loved the people. Most of them were thirty-somethings focused on their careers and starting families. They were fun, energetic, and smart. I found myself wanting to be like them. They inspired me, welcomed me, and made me feel special, appreciating my years of experience while I was invigorated by their youth.

And when I had questions, they didn't make me feel stupid. They taught me. They were encouraging. I felt seen, wanted, smart, and, most of all, valued.

Something was coming alive again.

Our marriage had drifted back into "business partner" mode.

Meanwhile, after the first few months, Todd barely noticed my new job—and we hardly talked about it. Our marriage had drifted back into "business partner" mode. We managed the house, handled the kids, ran like a team. But anything deeper? Emotional connection and intimacy of any kind were gone.

Honestly, I'd stopped expecting it.

After twenty-five years of marriage and countless ups and downs, I finally accepted the reality: *This is just how it is.*

So when I met someone new—a friend, at first—I wasn't looking for anything. But he was kind. Present. Lighthearted and thoughtful. One day he said, "You're the most beautiful woman I've ever seen."

"Wow!" I said with a laugh. "You need to get your glasses checked."

But it connected.

I didn't expect it. I didn't go looking for this friendship, but I welcomed it. For the first time in a long time, I felt so wanted—not as a nurse or a mom but as a woman. I kept it strictly at work in the beginning. But over time, the friendship grew into something more.

By then, our eldest was in college. Our middle son was a high school senior. The youngest wasn't far behind, and we'd just passed our twenty-fifth wedding anniversary. The empty nest was right around the corner.

I found myself asking, *Is this it? Is this all there is to marriage? To life? What now?*

I'd spent the previous eighteen years pouring myself out for our kids. And now they were building lives of their own. They didn't need me in the same ways anymore. And when I looked at Todd, I didn't feel needed there either.

Sure, we did things together—sailing, mountain biking, flying, exploring ghost towns. But those were *his* things. I gladly entered Todd's world; he rarely stepped into mine.

What about *my* ideas? The things that lit *me* up? Travel. Concerts. Disney. Game nights with friends or family.

We hardly ever did those things together. And if we did, there was always some sort of price I had to pay, some trade-off for the privilege. Usually, I just did them without him. I was unable to share my life with the person I loved. And that made my heart so very heavy.

> Your primary fun and recreation should happen inside your marriage first. Friendships and the occasional night out are healthy—but when "occasional" turns into "constant," pay attention. Have you noticed this pattern in your or your spouse's life? If so, don't ignore it. It will not end well.

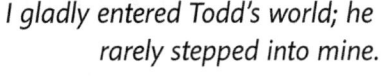

I gladly entered Todd's world; he rarely stepped into mine.

The Rage of Numbness

One day, Amy went for a bike ride with friends. I knew it was supposed to be her, another girl, and a guy. Later, I found out it was just her and the guy.

Excuses abounded.

"She was there at first, but, you know, she had to leave early. So then it just ended up being the two of us."

My heart sank.

Deep down, I knew I didn't believe her. But I couldn't even summon the energy to argue. I wasn't angry. I wasn't hurt. I wasn't feeling . . . anything. I was just . . . numb.

But is anyone ever really numb?

I remember coming home from my own ride, sitting on the edge of the bed, and praying. *God, am I ever going to feel again? Is this just . . . life now?*

Maybe a better question would've been *Will I ever feel* free *again? Free to love and trust?* Or even more simply: *Will I ever feel* good *again?*

After the bike ride with just Amy and the guy, I started asking more questions. Amy didn't like it. And her defensiveness only fueled my anger and suspicion.

Once again, I found that "numbness" quickly gave way to fury. I became even harder to live with—sharp, unsympathetic, and mostly checked out. At one point, Amy took a group of girlfriends from

Once again, I found that "numbness" quickly gave way to fury.

church up to our cabin. They planned to arrive early, and I snapped—mad that they'd wake me up on a workday.

I didn't lift a hand. Didn't support. We were arguing all the time—usually about her new friends—until it all came to a screeching halt.

A Day Late . . .

I was in that lovely stage of life when they recommend all the health screenings. *Time for a mammogram.* No big deal. I'd done them before—but this time, they found something. A lump.

A lump?? Really?!

"Oh, it'll be fine," I said, retreating into my usual "everything's fine" mode.

I reasoned away my fear: I had no breast cancer history in my family. I was under the usual age. There was no reason to worry.

They did a biopsy. And then we waited.

I kept insisting it would be fine—but we were both on pins and needles. And when the call finally came, everything was not fine. I had breast cancer.

I called Todd right away. "Oh, no! No. *No!*" he said. He was heartbroken. I was heartbroken.

We shared in that moment—and I was scared. But by then, our marriage was back in shambles. And I felt the wheel starting to spin: *Here we go around the hamster wheel again.*

When the call finally came, everything was not fine. I had breast cancer.

What's the
difference
between
being a fixer
and being
supportive?

Oddly, I didn't cry much. I just kept going—because I had to. And because, once again, I was on my own. Todd wasn't with me when I got the diagnosis. Wasn't there for the ultrasound. Wasn't there the one time I cried.

But once he found out, he went from zero to a hundred, immediately jumping into fix-it mode—which greatly irritated me.

"Okay, what do we need to do? Let's call this person—see that doctor—make that plan."

"Wait! Slow down! I've got this."

I'd been a nurse for twenty-two years. I knew where to find all the best people. I had the list. I had already made the calls.

I didn't need micromanaging—I needed support. And it was hard not to feel like this sudden engagement from him was more about *his panic* than caring about me.

Still, once I had my appointments booked, he came with me. He showed up. He stayed!

And that was . . . nice. *Really nice.*

But after twenty-five years, I was sick and tired of being sick and tired. Done with the hamster wheel. The ups and downs. *Nice,* I thought, *but too late.*

I wished he'd been like this when I broke my ankle. When I had the car accident. When I had my hysterectomy. When I had shoulder surgery.

I wanted him then. I needed him then. Now, it just felt confusing.

By this point, that sense of abandonment had become a canyon between us. It had started in childhood—my dad gone five days a week for work—and it carried into our marriage. Counseling helped, but the wound never closed. When I'd had medical issues back in 2013, I'd lie in a hospital bed and wonder, *How am I still in this alone?*

I reviewed the past.

Todd had dropped me off at urgent care with a broken ankle and told me to call when they were "done with me." He hadn't come when I had leg surgery. Hadn't taken me to my hysterectomy—said it was too early that morning. Hadn't picked me up after shoulder surgery—our sixteen-year-old had.

And I'd finally stopped wondering, *How's he going to take care of me when my kids aren't around? When my friends are all old and gone? How's he going to do it? He's* not.

So when he suddenly showed up with all this care and concern, I couldn't take it at face value. I didn't trust it. I couldn't let myself believe it would last. A day late and a dollar short, as the saying goes.

So when he suddenly showed up with all this care and concern, I couldn't take it at face value. I didn't trust it.

You had your chance. You had so many chances. Now you want in?

I didn't care. I was numb. Apathetic. Indifferent. Meanwhile, I had someone else—someone who made me feel known, wanted, and cared for.

So on January 2, I had surgery to remove the lump. Todd was there. He took care of me. He was kind. And I was grateful. But when it came time for radiation—twice a day, morning and afternoon—and he wanted to be there every single time, I'd had enough. He went from absent to smothering overnight.

"No thanks," I said. "I'm fine." I went with my mom or my best friend. And then, when the radiation ended, I told Todd I was moving out.

How I (Finally) Pushed Her over the Edge

The cancer diagnosis broke something in me.

It was no longer about something Amy had done wrong or a point I needed to make. All my years of neglecting her, avoiding hospitals, ignoring her exhaustion, her injuries, the stress she'd experienced from carrying all the kids' excessive activities—it all started hitting me at once.

I did the only thing I knew how to: I went into fix-it mode.

I had thought if I stayed steady, if I just kept working, it would keep everyone safe. When the turbulence hit my marriage again, it was nothing new. And if I saw her struggling, I kept up the same act.

Instead of comfort, I had given her interrogation. Instead of support, I had given her suspicion. And instead of love, I had given her pressure.

But now the turbulence was life and death, and it stunned me.

So I did the only thing I knew how to: I went into fix-it mode. Called doctors. Researched options. Tried to make plans. But the harder I pushed, the more she pulled away. I didn't know how to show her I was scared of losing her. I didn't realize I already had.

One night, I saw Amy texting some guy a video of our son.

"What's that about?" I asked.

"Oh, yeah, well . . . our son did this funny thing at school . . . and then someone else recorded it . . . then they showed it to me . . . and it started going around. And now I'm sharing it—"

I cut her off.

"Why are you sharing a video of our son with someone else before you even share it with his father?"

The writing was on the wall. I pressed harder—asking blunt questions and doubting her answers. She got mad and defensive. It escalated.

"I'm moving out," she said.

Once again—stunned.

"As soon as I finish radiation, I'm leaving."

When the Flesh Leads . . .

"I'm done, and I'm not doing this back-and-forth anymore. We rally for a year to two years, and we're good, and then it just fades away." I was done hoping. Done waiting.

We had passed our twenty-five-year anniversary, and our marriage was still in pieces. No number of doctor's appointments could stitch it back together.

Our kids were nearly grown. I had my own income with my own medical benefits. And I had someone else. I didn't need Todd's support—I was getting it elsewhere. *He* understood me. *He* related to me. *He* wanted to be there for me. I convinced myself that *he* was my true love—the one who *would* take care of me.

> When we lock away our shame and tell ourselves everything's fine, we end up living fractured double lives. The world promises comfort, but it only deepens the wound. Where are you tempted to run for relief—and how can you run to God instead?

Not Todd. Because that had never been Todd. And I didn't believe it ever would be.

After the first time I confessed and we separated? I stayed for love. The second? For the kids. This time? I wasn't staying at all.

What I didn't realize then was that I was leaning on my own strength, not God's. I thought I had already tried everything, turned to every possible option to rescue our marriage.

But I wasn't turning to Him.

I relied on myself—and the comfort of another person. I knew it wasn't right. Deep down, I knew I was making the wrong choice, but I kept letting my flesh lead.

To make it all work, to keep it all together, I started compartmentalizing again. I'd file away the guilt, tell myself, *Everything's fine.* Just yield to living a fractured life. Lock up the shame until later.

Then, I'd open the box, wallow for a while, cower under it—until I couldn't take it anymore. Having done my penance, I'd shut it again and step back into the other life, where it felt good.

And it didn't feel good with Todd.

What I didn't realize then was that I was leaning on my own strength, not God's.

He was trying; I'll give him that. But I was screaming on the inside. *You had your chance. My ankle. My accident. My hysterectomy. My surgeries. You had the chance, and you didn't want it. And now? Now I'm not giving up this other person for you. I just can't.*

Then COVID-19 hit. The world shut down.

I had no choice but to go to the doctor alone. By then, I was fine with that. I'd been doing it my whole life—terminating a pregnancy, surgeries, accidents. Always alone. So it was fine. Maybe it was even a sign: Time to move on.

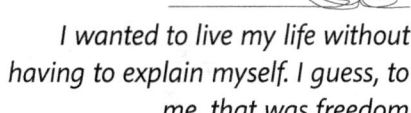

I told Todd I just needed space—a chance to find clarity. But that was a lie. I wanted "freedom," whatever that meant. What I really wanted was to carry on with the affair without Todd watching, asking

I wanted to live my life without having to explain myself. I guess, to me, that was freedom.

questions, and being in my business. I wanted to live my life without having to explain myself. I guess, to me, that was freedom.

So, with big dreams and big hopes for greener pastures, I left my husband of twenty-five years and got my own place. Free at last.

Growth, Change, Pain

We all come out of the womb selfish. A baby can't care for itself. Almost as soon as children can speak, their favorite word becomes "mine." Slowly we learn to share, but selfishness doesn't die easily. God has us on a lifetime journey of growing to be more like Jesus—the One who thought of others over Himself all the time.

Here's the hard reality: There is no growth without change, no change without loss, and no loss without pain. That's why growth hurts. Most of us won't change until the pain of staying the same is greater than the pain of changing.

Marriage is no exception. The Bible says, "But those who marry will face many troubles in this life, and I want to spare you this" (1 Cor. 7:28 NIV). But suffering isn't wasted. Romans 5:3 tells us that suffering produces perseverance, perseverance produces character, and character produces hope. We tend to learn the most when things aren't going well. Pain can be the very ground where God matures us.

That doesn't mean we enjoy the hurt—it means we shift our perspective. Out of our greatest pain often comes our greatest ministry. Paul writes in 2 Corinthians 1:3–4 (MSG), "He comes alongside us when we go through hard times, and before you know it, he brings us alongside someone else . . . so that we can be there for that person just as God was there for us."

Growth is never easy. But when we lean into God through the pain, He doesn't waste a single tear. He uses it to shape us into people of character, faith, and hope.

Accelerator

Take ten minutes to journal in three parts:

- A place in your life where you resisted change until it became too painful to stay the same.

- A place where pain you've walked through has given you new strength or compassion.

- One place right now where you're resisting change. Ask God what step of faith He's inviting you to take.

Close by praying Romans 5:3–5 out loud. Thank Him that suffering produces perseverance, character, and hope. Journal as you pray and listen.

Chapter 9

Eighteen Months and a Thousand Miracles

> *Saul, Saul, why do you persecute me?*
> *It is hard for you to kick against the goads.*
> *—Acts 26:14 NIV*

*T*HE "GOAD" REFERRED TO IN the Scripture was a long stick with a sharp point that farmers used to guide oxen. If the ox resisted and kicked back, it struck the goad and only hurt itself. In His words to Saul, Jesus was warning him that resisting God's call and direction for his life would only put him in a battle he could never win.

When God calls you to let go and you double down, gripping harder, you don't just resist Him—you wound yourself. You stress and strive, try everything you can to control a situation or soothe your pain, all the while blinding yourself to the cliff you're running toward.

When God calls you to let go and you double down, gripping harder, you don't just resist Him —you wound yourself.

Marriages in crisis often swing between two extremes: clinging in desperation or running for escape. Both feel like action. Both are just more of *you* doing your own thing.

Real transformation tends to happen when you stop. When you finally see that false freedoms are empty. Sometimes, especially in the beginning, it feels more like being dragged than led. Less like strengthening and more like stripping. After Saul's encounter with Christ, he went completely blind. But what looks like loss can be grace in disguise—the setup for a miracle.

Three days later, Saul regained his sight—and much more than that.

When you're in a hole you dug yourself, it makes sense that God's way feels wrong. You've been feeling fine all this time, doing what doesn't work—the very approach that got you in the hole. So when the right way comes, your reflex is to reject it.

That's why you let Him drag you. You take tiny steps. You move forward, even when you can't see where you're going. That's part of the process. You're no longer depending on what you think and how things look. And slowly, as surrender grows, hope glimmers through the dark maze. Eyes that were blind begin to notice—not only what He sees, but *how*. The restless heart begins to rest. In letting go—whether by choice or because life leaves us no other option—you catch glimpses of God's higher ways, His better design, the hidden threads He's been weaving all along.

Slowly, as surrender grows, hope glimmers through the dark maze.

WMWBM

"I think Mom will come home," one of our sons said.

I nodded.

Amy finished radiation on her birthday and, the very next day—as promised—she was gone. No long discussion. No big blowup. Just "I've rented an Airbnb for a month."

I'd braced myself, but nothing could prepare me for when she actually walked out. It felt like I'd been mugged and lost a piece of me. Like a cold rock had hit me in the chest and lodged there. Like something was really, really wrong.

Many times, I'd stared at a sheet of paper, writing my lists— on the left side, reasons to stay, and on the right, reasons to go. "Stay" always won.

I could've said, "Fine, don't come back." I didn't, because I didn't want her to leave. I never wanted her to leave. Even when I was mean on purpose, I was trying to keep her, not push her out. I don't know why, but somehow, I really thought that putting my wife down all the time was going to wake her up. Once she knew she was all those things I'd called her, of course she'd want to stay with me—*and only me.*

Major facepalm.

But this can't happen. This can't be real.

Amy. The boys. Me.

We were real. We were the Underwoods. This was our family. This was our identity.

And for the first time, I saw how much of my identity was wrapped up in *us*—what we'd built, what it meant.

I wasn't letting go yet. No way.

If it is to be, it is up to me. So I went to work—this time not to escape my marriage but to save it. I still wasn't really trusting God, but at least I wasn't running away and burying myself in isolation.

I jumped into WMWBM: Win My Wife Back Mode. Journals, devotionals, lists. I started looking for quick fixes—like patching drywall after a flood. It was damage control much more than seeking real change. It wasn't her I was trying to fool but myself. I was still blind to the deeper work God wanted to do in me. *Me? I* needed the deep work? Not even on my radar. I wasn't touching my trauma or wrong beliefs.

For the first time, I saw how much of my identity was wrapped up in us—what we'd built, what it meant.

I just wanted my wife back—so I made it about fixing Amy. If I could diagnose her, I could save us. That, I told myself, was love. I told myself I was being a good man. I called it ownership, acting responsibly—but I was still playing God.

What I didn't see yet—what I had absolutely no clue about— was that I'd reduced the woman I loved to a project.

God wasn't asking me to fix her. He was inviting me to let Him fix me.

God wasn't asking me to fix her. He was inviting me to let Him fix me.

False Freedom—and a New Daily Hope

Those days in the Airbnb were refreshing—and sad. For the first time in decades, I wasn't managing anyone's schedule. I could breathe. At first, I didn't know what to do with myself. After twenty-six years of managing a household, thinking and doing for everyone else, suddenly I was by myself. I could come and go as I pleased. I could eat breakfast for dinner—or not eat at all. In that sense, it was a much-needed break.

But the Airbnb also gave me space to continue my still-secret affair—time to hide, no eyes on me, no questions. I'd brought my *Jesus Calling* devotional and longed to feel God near. But I was impatient—grasping for anything to fill the holes in my heart.

Then, a new devotional email arrived in my inbox: *Daily Hope.*

Where'd that come from?

To this day, I don't know how that devotional found me, but it did, just when I needed it. "Don't Give Up on Lasting Love." I clicked, listened to the audio teaching. It made enough of an impression that I forwarded it to Todd.

"What do you think?" I asked in the email.

We both saw it as a godsend.

For a while to come, that devotional kept a thin thread between us. We listened almost every day. Some days we didn't talk, but I rarely missed an episode. And slowly, I began to feel God's presence again. He was with me. I could hear Him. I just wasn't ready to listen.

> Can you remember a time when God spoke to you through something simple—an email, a song, a word—that arrived exactly when you needed it?

He was with me. I could hear Him. I just wasn't ready to listen.

What's the difference between hearing and listening?

False Start

A month in—just like our son predicted—Amy asked to come home. And for a few weeks, I was happy.

We went back to our routines. Watched her shows. Had dinner together. Went on bike rides.

I still had suspicions—and information. We'd changed patterns without transformation before, but I ignored my gut and pretended things were better.

When COVID-19 hit, I was deemed "nonessential." Grounded. Amy, on the other hand, was essential. She was required at work. Shifts piled up, with long hours—twelves, sixteens— and the other guy was volunteering too.

Of course he was.

The extra shifts were a way for them to be together. She was over there building a life while I was home, holding the pieces of a life we were still pretending hadn't died.

One afternoon, while I was prepping for a mountain bike ride with Amy and our youngest, she called and said, "I'm not coming home."

I waited. Maybe it wasn't as bad as it sounded.

"What do you mean?" I asked. "We're supposed to go riding." It could be she had just forgotten, or needed space, or time, or something I didn't yet understand. I jumped to whatever was in front of

She was over there building a life while I was home, holding the pieces of a life we were still pretending hadn't died.

me. "I already got the salmon out for dinner. Where are you going?"

"I'm moving out again—and that's that."

She'd already arranged it with our eldest. She'd take his place; he'd move back in with me. No conversation. No explanation. Gone.

So I packed up the boys and went to the cabin. We'd stay for two or three weeks at a time. We cooked meals and made fires. The snow fell. The world around us got quiet, and life became simple. In some ways, it was healing—until the kids' anger surfaced. "Why did she leave again?"

I didn't want them turning against her. So I tried to give them another way to look at it, like Amy had done for me all those years when the boys would ask, "Where is Dad? Why doesn't Dad want to come?"

"Look," I said. "If Mom had broken bones, you'd bring her food, right? You'd take care of her."

They nodded.

"Just because it's not on the outside doesn't mean it's not real."

I told them what I was beginning to believe: that something had cracked inside her.

"She's got something going on," I said. "Maybe it's not physical. What if it's mental?"

That was the best I had. And honestly, it gave *me* something to hold on to.

If someone walked out on you tomorrow with no explanation, where would you turn first? What would you do?

I started putting the pieces together. A toxic job. A sudden career shift. Cancer. Twenty-five years. Empty nest. And she'd said it more than once: "Now I get why people divorce at twenty-five years."

It didn't make her wrong; it just made her broken.

I started reading books on trauma, betrayal, and shame. I journaled. I prayed. I listened.

So I started digging. I started reading books on trauma, betrayal, and shame. I journaled. I prayed. I listened.

Daily Hope became our one connection. We read and listened separately, sometimes talked. Without knowing it, I was already doing it: loosening my grip—letting God do the talking.

When the Switch Breaks

When the month ended, I moved home. It hadn't helped; if anything, I was deeper into the affair.

Trying to be wife and lover, Mom and escape artist, tore me in half. I couldn't do it. I couldn't be in that world anymore. After a few weeks, I left again—into my son's place, while he returned home.

Even then, I still half wanted to save the marriage—but not enough to give up the other relationship. I believed it was filling my needs

I still half wanted to save the marriage—but not enough to give up the other relationship.

that had been neglected for so many years. He made me feel wanted, valued, loved. He thought I was funny. He was interested in what interested me. He asked about my day and entered my world.

How could I keep that going while being back home?

Home meant single parenting again. It meant keeping up an act I was tired of. Work, work, work. My ability to flip the switch was starting to short-circuit.

Facing What's Underneath

Amy asked me to help her find a counselor. I found a CSAT—a Certified Sex Addiction Therapist who also specialized in trauma. She started. Handed me a bunch of books. "This is what I'm working through," she said.

I read them all—and then some. Still full throttle in WMWBM, I tried playing counselor too.

I wasn't chasing a marriage anymore; I was chasing a miracle.

"Do you think this [the serial cheating] has anything to do with what happened to you all those years ago?"

"I don't think so. That's all in the past," she said. "But maybe."

I grabbed that "maybe."

At this point, I'd take any sign of movement. I wasn't chasing a marriage anymore; I was chasing a miracle.

And God was chasing me.

Is there anywhere you are double minded right now? What can you do about it?

Sin Clouds Everything

The COVID-19 lockdowns were underway. Alone at my son's place, I was really hoping for that unmistakable *God moment*. A Red Sea splitting, a blinding light, and scales falling from my eyes. I longed for Him to do something dramatic—anything to make it crystal clear: *This is the Lord*.

But that's not what I got.

Everything was quiet. I kept saying I wanted to hear from God—but in truth, I didn't want a father's advice. I wanted confirmation. A stamp of approval.

That's being double minded: asking for truth but listening for permission. James 1 (NIV) says the double-minded person is "unstable in all they do" and "shouldn't expect to receive anything from the Lord." *The Message* Bible calls it "adrift at sea, keeping all your options open." That was me, asking for God's direction—as long as He was willing to bless mine.

Todd and I were still loosely connected. We'd still listen to the same *Daily Hope* devotionals. But *Daily Hope* started to clash with what I was doing. Who was I kidding? There was *always* a clash. I felt it. I knew it. I admitted to myself, *You're talking out of both sides of your mouth. You're double minded. You can't hear God like this.*

Sin clouds everything. Your judgment. Your clarity. Your words and intentions. Everything goes crooked.

On the surface, I was still trying; inside, I was done. Todd was all in. I wasn't—and he didn't know. And to make it more unfair, I was already deeply involved with someone else.

Dragged by Grace

Scrolling one night, a video kept resurfacing. I almost skipped it. *Just another guy trying to sell something,* I thought.

But one word grabbed me—a word that had been popping up for weeks: *community.*

What keeps you from seeking community—and when you do seek it, how do you know it's the kind God is inviting you into?

But I didn't like that word, so I ignored it. After a while, when you're praying and asking God for help and something keeps showing up despite your trying to ignore it, you have to consider if maybe it's God Himself nudging you.

I knew it was. But I didn't want community. I didn't think anyone else could relate.

I'd told God and counselors for years, "Find me one guy whose wife cheated multiple times, and I'll talk. Otherwise, screw this community stuff."

When you're praying and asking God for help and something keeps showing up despite your trying to ignore it, you have to consider if maybe it's God Himself nudging you.

What was I—a modern-day Hosea? He's not exactly the biblical figure I would've chosen if given the choice. How about David? A man after God's own heart. Or Elisha—double portion, no drama.

Can we reconsider this, God?

But God just kept laying it on my heart: *Community. Community. Community.*

I Googled "separated men's groups." Most looked scammy, offered on cheesy sales pages that scrolled forever.

Really, God?

Every time I tried to exit, they hit me with "Wait! Don't go! There's more!"

I'm not doing this.

But then I heard it loud and clear: *You* are *doing this.*

A million times, I wanted to check out and give up. But finally, in early May, I picked up the phone and made the call to Randy, the man on the listing, even though I didn't know him from Adam. He could've been in Zimbabwe or Antarctica for all I knew. Still, I sensed I needed to just *do it*. So, desperate, I waited to see who might be on the other end.

The man listened as I rattled off details. I figured he'd never heard a story like mine before—until he responded like a mind reader. *How does he know this stuff?!* He spoke my language—no religious clichés. He wasn't selling anything. After twenty minutes, I felt like he'd known me all my life.

"Reconciliation only works one way," he said. "And I'll tell you what that way is, but first—full disclosure—since you brought up Pastor Rick, Pastor Rick is my pastor. I'm one of the separated men's group leaders at Saddleback Church in California."

I had no idea God was planning to work the miracle in me.

For a moment, you could've heard a pin drop.

I was stunned. It was a God setup the whole time. A miracle.

The *Daily Hope* devotional. The one thread Amy and I shared. Pastor Rick. I was talking to one of his leaders! When I'd said

I was waiting for a miracle, I thought it was Amy's miracle.

I had no idea God was planning to work the miracle in me.

When does love mean holding on—and when does it mean letting go?

Before the group launched, Randy coached me one-on-one. We talked almost daily. He gave me reading assignments— *The Purpose Driven Life*, *Daily Hope* devotionals, books on marriage, psychology, and trauma. He helped me focus on "my side of the street." He walked me out of self-condemnation and taught me to notice and own my feelings before reacting.

He taught me *connection*—emotional presence, safety, partnership—what women really want. Not just being there. Not just buying things. Some days were a blur—there was just so much to take in. It was all so new.

It was the beginning of the end.

He walked me out of self-condemnation and taught me to notice and own my feelings before reacting.

If You Really Love Her . . .

In May, the COVID-19 lockdown lifted, and Amy started talking about *really* getting her own place.

I talked to Randy about it.

"If you really love her, you'll let her go."

Mic-drop moment.

It was brutal. I won't say it came easy. But eventually, I got to where I could say, "I don't want you to leave, but if this makes you happy . . . then I want you to be happy."

That was a 180 for me.

Before, I would've said, "No, you can't do that." I would've acted like I knew what was best. Like I was the Holy Spirit. But this time—I let go.

She called me on her way to sign the lease. It was traumatic. The yearlong lease meant this wasn't going to be over any time soon. So that sucked. But God apparently had more to strip away.

I even helped her move. Our sons pitched in too. We didn't want this or agree with her decision, but we served her anyway. Even if we were mad, we weren't mad enough. Amy was ours. We still loved her. Still wanted her. What else could we do?

I wasn't going to just drop everything God had given me, let my whole family fall apart, waste more than twenty-five years of life and investment—without a fight.

Days later, I got an SOS: The fridge in Amy's new condo had suddenly broken, and she was asking me to fix it.

The irony. In our first years of marriage, I felt disrespected and embarrassed because Amy's dad was her go-to, the guy she called on to fix everything, hang pictures, take care of her. Now it was me. In some ways, we'd come full circle.

I could've said, "Ask your boyfriend." But that wasn't my heart. It's not what God was leading me to. Now *I* was the one fixing things—the one she called on. That meant something.

If Jesus, the King, God Himself, could wash feet, I could fix a fridge.

If Jesus, the King, God Himself, could wash feet, I could fix a fridge.

But the ultimate irony of this moment wasn't just that I was fixing my wife's fridge in her new condo apart from me or that she was out building a life with another guy. The ultimate irony to me was that the only time I could do it was the exact time Randy had scheduled the very first separated men's group on Zoom.

It was the first day of community—the support I'd always needed but had resisted for more than twenty-five years, maybe all my life. And it all started in Amy's new condo. After repairing a broken fridge. When God would start repairing me.

I fixed the fridge and logged on.

On that call, I found out what I'd been telling myself all those years was totally untrue. I wasn't the only one after all.

Have you ever gotten exactly what you thought you wanted, only to find out it wasn't what you needed? What about the "better life" you're dreaming of today?

When a Desire Fulfilled Leaves You Empty

"Mom, where do you want this?"

"Over there. No—wait. Actually, by the window."

One of my sons moved it with a nod. No resistance. No shame. No guilt. My handsome men, helping me leave them.

The day I stepped into the condo should've been the happiest—my first official day of liberation. I'd thought about it a million times. Held it in my heart for years.

It was maybe the worst day of my life.

I don't think it helped that Todd and the boys moved me in. They carried all my things, including random pieces of furniture—from

In
moments
of regret
or second
thoughts,
*What do you do
with that inner
scream: what
am I doing?!*

our house—into the new apartment. I watched from a distance as the man I was abandoning found the strength to help me do it.

I'd inched closer to the life I thought I wanted—so why was I flooded with uncontrollable sobs as I picked up the keys?

The leasing agent took one look at me and asked from under his heavy brow, "You sure this is what you want to do?"

"Yes," I managed to say, as I swallowed the lump in my throat. "My husband and I are divorcing."

"I'm sorry," he offered sincerely.

I signed the papers and took the keys. Then I went to my car and cried and cried. I don't think I've ever cried that hard. It got so intense I almost threw up.

"What am I doing?!" I screamed inside, over and over.

I called Todd. Of course I called Todd. Who else knew me well enough to comfort me in that moment? It didn't make sense, but nothing did. Todd was at work but took my call. "We'll make it through, Amy," he said softly. "Everything's going to be okay."

I felt better. And somehow . . . I believed him. And then, just like that, like I'd done for so many years, I packed it all up and put it in a box. Turned off one switch and turned on another.

Eventually, I made my way back to the condo. Moved things. Opened boxes. Unpacked bags.

I met up with the other guy. Reminded myself, *This is the better life you keep asking for. So—here you go.*

Chapter 10

The Addict in All of Us

S CRIPTURE TELLS US THE SIN nature still lingers in our flesh, waging war against the spirit. It feels like a part of us, but it's alien—an intruder we overcome through our daily walk with Christ by the Holy Spirit (see Romans 7).

Addiction, as part of the sin nature, is a potential within all of us. The addict isn't just the one who drinks too much or can't quit the pills. It's all of us—turning to something, anything, to soothe, to numb, to fill. A quick hit that never heals the wound.

It's not who we are; it's a twisting of the deep worship we were created to give to God. And it shows up everywhere—not just in the bottle or the needle but in all the fixes we cling to: work, romance, money, control, performance.

We all have a medicine cabinet for the soul. The only remedy that truly heals starts with God—He alone knows what soothes and nourishes us. But often, we reach for the quicker fix. Something

We all have a medicine cabinet for the soul. The only remedy that truly heals starts with God.

immediately gratifying. Something that doesn't require trust, patience, or change. Whatever we crave—and what starts as comfort becomes a chain. The cruelest part? The fix always fails, while the failure is usually what ends up fixing things—ironically becoming the turning point.

But in Christ, failure itself becomes a doorway. The gospel doesn't deny the struggle—it redeems us in the midst of it. We may still wrestle with cravings, reach for the wrong thing, but we're just as loved as when we think we're at our best. He proved that when He died for His killers (you and me). We're never without a way of escape, a promise of freedom.

Sometimes, you fall into a pit and someone pulls you out. In a second, you're saved. Other times, it's a process. You're saved. Your rescuer is there with you, but the pit goes deeper, and it'll take longer to pull you out. There may be steps. You may need to go slow, so you don't fall back. You'll stumble—probably more than once. With Him, you can make it. But first, you have to see the pit for what it is: a big black hole that operates on the law of diminishing returns.

Every step of the way, the old distorted you who felt at home in the pit is dying off. Whatever's in there, the truth is you can do without. The first challenge isn't taking the step; it's seeing the pit for what it is and setting your sights on the light outside it.

The fixes will always fail. Addiction thrives in the dark, but grace is stubborn—it meets us there. Failure becomes the fix when it

Failure becomes the fix when it leads us to surrender what doesn't work.

leads us to surrender what doesn't work. And when the false fixes fall away, only then can the true remedy take hold.

Addicted to Love

"I think I'm an addict."

During our separation, I started counseling with two incredible trauma-informed EMDR (eye movement desensitization and reprocessing) therapists. For the first time in my life and for the next eighteen months, I focused solely on myself.

Not on what Todd had or hadn't done. Not on the state of my marriage. Just me.

I was a love addict: addicted to relationships.

We dug deep into my childhood, my trauma, my coping mechanisms and survival strategies. And eventually, we hit something I never expected. Even saying the word felt foreign.

An addict?

No way. Not me. I didn't drink. I didn't use drugs.

But the more we peeled back the layers, the more obvious it became.

I was a love addict: addicted to relationships.

"That's a *thing*?" I squinted and wrinkled my nose the first time I'd heard it.

But it was real. And I had it.

Are you aware of when you're craving connection? Could some of your "bad habits" actually be a hidden cry for something they can never satisfy?

At first, I fought it—hard. I mean, I *loved* love. I craved closeness, feeling wanted, being held. But did that make me an addict?

Wanting? No. Wanting doesn't make you an addict. But when your "drug" is people, when you keep "using" to the point of self-destruction, and when withdrawal feels unbearable—that's addiction.

The more I read about it—in recovery work, in the books my counselors recommended—the more I saw myself in every chapter.

The craving for connection. The panic when I was left alone. The compulsion to be desired. The need to feel chosen—even if it was by the wrong person.

If you know '80s pop music, you'll remember Robert Palmer's old music video for his hit "Addicted to Love": the slick-haired girls wearing scarlet-red lipstick, skin-tight dresses, pretending to play guitar.

Might as well face it . . .

And I was beginning—slowly—to see that no human being could ever love me into wholeness.

It played on repeat in my head—sometimes mocking me, sometimes grounding me in the truth. Because that *was* my truth. For decades, I'd tried to fill a void with people, romance, admiration, attention—anything that made me feel special.

But now, the old ways were unraveling.

And I was beginning—slowly—to see that no human being could ever love me into wholeness.

The Top Ten Test

"Write your wife's top ten favorite things," Randy once suggested, knowing exactly how the exercise was going to turn out.

Most men get through two—maybe three if they're really good.

I sat down, confident at first. I mean, I'd been married to this woman for more than two decades. I figured I could name ten things she loved.

I started writing:

1. Traveling

2. Disney

3. Time with the kids

And then I froze. What else?

Not what I thought *she should* like. Not what I liked about her. But what she actually loved.

It was eye-opening.

How had I lived with a woman this long and still didn't know what brought her joy? What made her feel alive? What comforted her when she was down?

That question haunted me: *What if I've never truly seen her?*

It was dawning on me: I didn't really know Amy because I didn't really connect. And I

I didn't really know Amy because I didn't really connect.

didn't connect . . . because I didn't know what connection meant.

I thought I did. I thought not solving problems was enough. But connection wasn't about fixing; it was about *listening*. Empathizing.

That took a while to sink in.

I used to hear her questions as criticism or, worse, an attack. "How was your day?" felt like a trap. I'd get defensive, shut down, or give the bare minimum. But once you realize it's not an attack, your whole perspective changes. I started to see: Amy wasn't interrogating me. She was trying to connect. She wanted in.

So I began a new approach: When we talked, I practiced staying still. I let her speak. And instead of reacting or solving, I'd just reflect.

"That must've been hard." "Wow. That sounds frustrating." "Sounds like you handled that really well."

It was simple. But she'd look at me like I'd given her a gift.

"That was awesome," she'd say.

And I'd think, *Really? That's it?*

Apparently, yes.

I was starting to get it. And thanks to Randy and the other guys saving me many times from sabotaging myself, Amy and I were still in contact. I still had

Thanks to Randy and the other guys saving me many times from sabotaging myself, Amy and I were still in contact.

chances to test what I was learning in real time—with the woman I loved.

Another shift: I stopped being outcome based.

I hadn't realized how many things I used to do "transactionally," meaning I gave in order to get. If I bought flowers, it was to earn points. If I said something kind, I expected a thank you. Everything had a hidden scoreboard.

Do you love to give—or to get? When you give, are there hidden strings attached?

But I started unlearning that. Randy called it "giving without strings": Do good—not because it gets you something but because it's who you are. Because you love the person.

That's when love started becoming real.

I realized I'd spent so much of our marriage loving her *my* way. I was doing what made sense to me: solving problems, providing, protecting. But I hadn't been curious. I hadn't studied her heart. Instead, I'd studied survival—provision, money, work, stability. Instead of her, I'd chased control.

Control was my drug. Control had been my addiction.

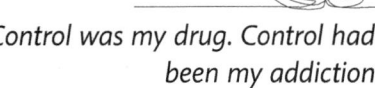

Control was my drug. Control had been my addiction.

Randy used to say, "You need a PhD in your wife." That line stuck with me.

So I went back to work—not to win her but to know her.

I started paying attention. Watching. Listening.

She lit up when I asked real questions—not just "How was your day?" but "What was the hardest part?" She liked when I noticed her smile, her outfit, her face when she was excited. She liked when I remembered something she'd mentioned three days earlier and brought it up again. She liked to laugh—deep belly laughs that made her eyes water.

And somewhere along the way, I realized I liked those things too.

Loving her like this wasn't a chore—it was a joy.

She was still distant. Still guarded. And I didn't know if we'd ever be together again.

But I knew this much: Even if I never got her back, even if the marriage never recovered, even if she married someone else—I would never again live my life asleep to the heart of another person.

I would never again live blind to the beauty in front of me.

I would never again live blind to the beauty in front of me.

Trauma Driven

In September, Amy told me she was planning a trip to South Dakota with friends from work. The night before she left, she wanted to go out for dinner. So at dinner, I asked her straight out, "Is he going too?"

He was.

I didn't hide how I felt.

"I'm really not okay with that," I told her. "I want you to do what you want to do, but I need you to know—that hurts."

She went anyway.

I unraveled.

Amy had started naming her addiction. I was staring mine in the face—that deep-seated need for control that only makes things worse. What I was about to feel was probably withdrawal. I felt raw. Without recourse. No strategy, no backup plan. No one else to turn to. There was nothing to grip. No plan to enforce. I was left with nothing but the pain, deep and inescapable.

I was angry. Disoriented. Thank God for the guys in the group. I had many late-night calls with Randy and the others, trying to make sense of it and not fall back into old patterns.

Amy texted me from South Dakota: "I love you," she wrote.

I didn't answer. I figured if I couldn't say something kind, I wouldn't say anything at all.

She texted again, this time saying she was hurt that I wasn't responding. I felt bad. So when I knew she was back in town, I went to Starbucks, picked up her favorite drink, and headed to her apartment.

Walking up the stairs, I heard her voice behind the door: "Hurry up! He's almost here."

She must have been following me on her locator app. A second later, he came down the stairs. Things got ugly after that.

Amy and I fought. We talked. For four nights straight, we stayed up, arguing, crying, asking questions. "We're just going in

How would you have responded in these situations? What response would reflect who you want to become, not just how you feel?

What I was about to feel was probably withdrawal. I felt raw. Without recourse. No strategy, no backup plan. No one else to turn to.

circles, Amy. How many more times are we going to ride this merry-go-round?" I demanded.

That's when I found out the affair had started not long after she'd gotten the new job, so by then, it had been going on for well over a year.

We started asking the question we hadn't wanted to face: *Should we just file for divorce?*

A Band-Aid® on a Broken Arm

Still reeling from catching Amy and for the first time seriously considering the d-word, I pulled out a book someone had given me way back in 1997—*Torn Asunder* by Dave Carder.

We started asking the question we hadn't wanted to face: Should we just file for divorce?

I wondered if the author was still alive. I Googled him. He was. Not only that, he offered free consultations. I got on his schedule. The whole phone call was strange.

"Hello, Todd! This is Dave," he said. "I don't want you to say anything. Just grab a pen and paper and start writing."

"Okay . . . "

"Your wife's a serial cheater. This is not a little issue. If you don't get to the core of the problem, it's never going to get solved. Nothing's going to change. Here's a book for her: *No Stones* by Marnie Ferree. Here's one for you: *Redemptive Divorce* by Mark Gaither. Now answer this—did your wife suffer any sexual trauma in childhood?"

"Yes."

"Well, that's what this is. It's all coming out now. Affairs. Strange behavior. You didn't cause it. You can't stop it. You can't fix it. She's not doing this to hurt you; she's medicating pain she doesn't even know she has. The behavior's called *ego-dystonic*—she's doing what she knows is wrong because it gives her a hit. Like a drug."

He kept going.

"Is she in counseling?"

"Yes."

"That's a Band-Aid on a broken arm. It won't do anything unless she gets to the root. She needs an intensive. I don't do this kind of counseling. I only work with one-time cheaters. This is different. Try Bethesda in Nashville. The book *No Stones* will explain everything."

And that was it. I hung up and sat there for a minute. And then I called Amy.

"I just had the strangest conversation. I'm not going to sugar-coat it. I'm just going to repeat what the guy said. You can do with it whatever you want."

I told her everything he'd told me.

She ordered the book.

Are there places in your life where you've settled for a Band-Aid instead of letting God touch the root and heal you?

"She's not doing this to hurt you; she's medicating pain she doesn't even know she has."

Staying Power

The problems that show up in marriage usually don't happen overnight. They develop slowly, almost without us noticing. Then one day, we wake up and wonder, *How did we get here?* The truth is, it took months or years of slow drift.

So, what do we do? We scramble for quick fixes—call the church, book counseling, sign up for a marriage retreat. We're looking for a pill, a shot, a weekend that can undo years of damage. And when it doesn't work right away, we blame the counselor, the program, or even our spouse.

If that's where you've been, it's okay. It's natural to want an easy answer, like taking ibuprofen for a headache. But marriage healing doesn't work like that. The truths we learn in counseling and retreats may be simple, but they take time to sink in. They take effort—consistent effort—to live out.

The key is staying power. Endurance. Refusing to give up. In our case, it took years of hard work to repair what had broken. But it was worth it. Every step forward mattered.

Don't worry about speed. Don't get discouraged if progress feels slow. Trust that God is teaching you something in the process. Galatians 6:9 (NIV) says, "Let us not become weary in doing good, for at the proper time we will reap a harvest if we do not give up."

Healing comes through consistency. Put in the work, stay the course, and don't quit. God will meet you in the endurance.

Accelerator

Plan one concrete way to invest in consistency this week. For example:

- Schedule a recurring fifteen-minute "marriage check-in" with your spouse.

- Block ten minutes each morning for prayer together.

- Commit to finishing one session of a book/counseling homework before the week is up.

Write it in your calendar *right now* so it doesn't slip.

Chapter 11

One More Try

---

*'Tis a lesson you should heed, try, try
again; If at first you don't succeed,
try, try again.*
—William Edward Hickson,
The Singing Master

WHAT MAKES ONE TRY AND try again after so many failures? Perhaps it's knowing that failure—ultimately—is not an option. We sense, deep down, when the problem isn't our circumstances but our unwillingness to let go. As long as we keep grasping, clinging, fastening ourselves to the old, we haven't really tried yet.

But in the middle of exposed weakness, another kind of strength is revealed. All the excuses run out. The exits are blocked. Running no longer satisfies; control no longer works. And what remains is the raw question pulsing in the silence: *Is God here?*

We sense, deep down, when the problem isn't our circumstances but our unwillingness to let go.

The answer comes, steady and unrelenting: *God is every-wnere.* In the heights and in the depths, in betrayal and in surrender, in the anger that rails and the whisper that calls—His presence fills even the darkest spaces.

This is the paradox of the breaking point: The end of ourselves becomes the beginning of Him. We don't have to wait for collapse. We don't have to stack up years of turmoil before letting go. At any moment, we can surrender—before the ditch gets any deeper. Whenever we choose to see, we'll find that the same invitation stands: to let go and to find Him already there.

No Stones

It was as if the author of that book had read my mail. Normally, I am not an avid reader, but I tore through No Stones cover to cover. By the end, nearly every page was highlighted. Stunned, I called Todd.

"This is me. I don't even know what to say. This is me."

The book exposed things I was living but oblivious to: "Trauma creates unhealthy coping mechanisms, which create trauma, which creates more unhealthiness. Without intervention, the cycle goes on and on"—just like I'd been doing. "The fear of being discovered in sexual sin makes it especially difficult for strugglers to ask for help." That line explained why I was always keeping secrets: "To be judged as nothing more than morally corrupt adds to the pain."

It was time for a change.

We looked up the intensive. Only one more was scheduled for the year—and it started *that week.* I said yes. God cleared the way: My boss approved the time off, and a sweet friend offered her beautiful home in the northern Arizona mountains. Away I went—just me, my computer, my Bible, and my dog.

For four days, I learned so much about myself—my choices, my patterns, the reasons behind them. I began to see how much of my adult life had been shaped by childhood wounds, past trauma, and the unhealthy choices that followed.

Both faith-based and deep therapy—it was eye-opening.

Throughout the intensive, I was silent. I needed the quiet to process.

I came home with secrets to reveal—telling the truth was a necessary part of the process. But I was also armed with insight and a new outlook. For maybe the first time, I believed I could rise above my past. I didn't have to keep repeating the same old cycles. And through it all, there was a whisper—reminding me who I truly belonged to and what I was really worth.

Full Disclosure

"What are you doing? This isn't right," Amy's dad would say. If her folks were taking sides, this time they were taking mine.

Up to now, they'd mostly stayed out of it. They didn't know about Amy's affairs or all of what we were going through. But when she came back from the intensive, she carried a recovery plan—and it demanded more disclosure. Full disclosure. For Amy, that meant telling immediate family nearly everything.

Whom in your life do you trust enough to hear your whole story—without judgment, without shame?

When she brought up the rape, the early pregnancy—things I had already shared after the first affair—it landed like they were hearing it for the first time. Anything that deep or heavy was out of their wheelhouse.

But if Amy was serious about recovery, it had to be done.

No secrets. No shame. Nothing left to hide.

So her dad would call now and then, confronting her the only way he knew—lecturing. Parenting.

We sat down with our kids—two in college, one in high school—and told them enough that they could understand the gravity of what'd been happening around them all these years.

Amy began naming her triggers and sharing them openly. "I'm going to go down this road," she told us. "I'm doing this recovery. I'm really going to try."

Letting family in didn't just impact Amy; it hit me too. I was uncomfortable with her parents' involvement. Their approach—the way they talked to her, tried to parent her—was the opposite of what I was learning in the men's group. But it wasn't my recovery; it was hers. And I was learning how to let go and trust the process.

The process . . . yeah, it was long. And brutal. I couldn't fix it. Couldn't stop her swings, her cravings, the pull toward someone else. All I could do was watch.

Until I broke.

I was learning how to let go and trust the process.

One Foot In, One Foot Out

I went back to my condo after the intensive. I was trying, but I was still living in two worlds.

Part of me wanted the marriage to work. I didn't want to be divorced. I wanted to say we'd made it. My parents had a fifty-year legacy of marriage. Why couldn't I?

And I didn't want to hurt Todd. But I was already hurting him—maybe more by staying than leaving.

I just felt so ready to move on. I'd already built a second life. I'd even convinced myself I was doing the "right thing"—managing both lives, keeping up appearances, holding on to the marriage so I wouldn't disappoint my parents, my friends . . . or God.

But by staying, I was lying—to Todd, to everyone, even to myself.

"Why don't you just divorce me?!" I'd say, lashing out at Todd. But he wouldn't. For a long time, he refused. And I wouldn't—couldn't—do it. In my mind, Todd had the biblical grounds. I didn't.

I knew I wasn't making any sense.

Oh, so you'll cling to that "biblical grounds for divorce" principle, I told myself, *but still go have affair after affair?*

> What are the biblical grounds for divorce? What was Jesus's attitude about it in Matthew 19:8?

By staying, I was lying—to Todd, to everyone, even to myself.

I felt so stuck. Still the double-minded person described in James 1:6-8: "That person should not expect to receive anything from the Lord. Such a person is double minded and unstable in all they do" (NIV).

Tell me about it.

Eyes Wide Open

How can boundaries protect both spouses when addiction or betrayal is involved?

Amy got a Christian sponsor. It lasted about a week—because she was still acting out, still sleeping with the other guy. The behavior wasn't changing, and her sponsor pulled away.

I stayed.

I leaned hard on my therapy sessions—and on my sister, who's a licensed addiction therapist.

"Stay off Amy's crazy train," she kept reminding me. "And stop catastrophizing." And the guys in the men's group held me accountable.

When I saw Amy's need—her brokenness, her distance—I had to fight the urge to step in. The guys constantly reminded me: Stay on my side of the street, stop being outcome focused, do the next right thing for the right reason, and quit worrying about ten steps down the road.

I devoured countless books—*Love and Respect; I Do Again; Love Must Be Tough; Love Focused; His Needs, Her Needs; Loving Your Spouse When You Feel Like Walking Away; Codependent No More; Prodependence; The Body Keeps the Score; Facing Love Addiction;* and more. I watched movies like *Fireproof, War Room,* and *Facing the Giants.* I was all in—from sunup to the wee hours of the morning.

When I saw Amy's need—her brokenness, her distance—I had to fight the urge to step in.

That Christmas, the boys and I planned a trip to Colorado. We invited Amy, and she came. Honestly, we had a good time. But I could see the frustration building. She was tired of the back-and-forth, the slips, the shame. She saw how much it hurt me.

It's not like I didn't know what was going on. I was no longer hiding in my work cave, ignoring everything around me. Eyes wide open, God was my escape now.

"You just need to file for divorce," she kept saying—mad that I hadn't.

But when we got back home, I could plainly see she was in a hurry to leave, to get to the other guy. I hit my limit.

The next day, I went to the courthouse and filed.

Everything about initiating the divorce was hard. I don't do courts, lawyers, judges. I handle them about as well as I do hospitals. I needed one of the guys on the phone with me just to get there and get through it.

Signed, Sealed, Severed

"I don't want to," he said, "but this will be my final gift to you."

Gift?

"If a divorce is what you want, I'll give it to you."

It was shocking. Sweet. Sad. And disorienting.

On one hand, I was relieved. *Okay. I don't have to do it now. This moves things forward. I can pursue the other relationship without feeling bad anymore.*

On the other hand, I felt like a complete failure. *I did this. This is my fault.*

Have you ever frozen when you thought you would run? What could that "freeze" be signaling?

The day I went to fill out the paperwork, I was a mess. Terrified. What a way to start the new year. Todd offered to go with me. Yes, still there for me. Still my fixer. Still holding me up.

Loving me.

Even when we got to the office, I physically could not bring myself to sign the papers.

I mean, I was there. I was fine. Everything seemed fine. This was the moment I'd been waiting for.

And my insides froze.

Even when we got to the office, I physically could not bring myself to sign the papers.

The office. The ugly lights. The papers. The people. I shut down.

"Want help?" Todd offered.

"Yes, please," I heard myself say.

Then I sat in a fog, going through the motions—signing dotted lines while Todd did everything else for me.

What God Hates

"That'll be $250," the woman behind the counter said.

Amy nearly collapsed.

Going to the courthouse once wasn't torture enough; now I was back—helping the wife I didn't want to divorce become my ex-wife.

But she was clueless. And I had promised her a gift. So when she asked me to fill out the forms for her—and then needed me to personally escort and support her—I did.

She heard $250 and nearly dropped. She didn't know there would be a cost.

A cost?

"'For I hate divorce,' says the LORD, the God of Israel" (Mal. 2:16 NASB).

Anytime you do something God hates, there's a cost.

Amy panicked, stepping aside, barely breathing, while I "landed the plane": completing the process, submitting the paper-work, walking through the door

Anytime you do something God hates, there's a cost.

that would finally, once and for all, finish what had been a slow death.

It was done. Twenty-five years of marriage: buried.

As we left the building, she looked at me. I looked back. A moment of silence. A beat. We could go our separate ways, never look back again. But we

It was done. Twenty-five years of marriage: buried.

stood there—as if something held us. Something good. Something outside us.

Amy wasn't being very decisive, so, naturally, I spoke first.

"Dinner?"

Divorce with a Side of Dinner

Was Todd being foolish? Or was he wise?

Naturally, after filing for divorce, we went out to eat.

It was surreal—sitting across from the man I had betrayed, talking, eating, just . . . calm. Maybe for the first time, I noticed something had changed in him.

What kind of man gives his wife a divorce as a gift—and still loves her?

I couldn't believe it. What sort of reality was this? Not only was he not lashing out—he still wanted to spend time with me, still wanted to be around me?

He could've told me to get out. He could've screamed. He could've said, "Don't you ever come near me again."

But instead, he took me to dinner.

Reconcili-what?

"Dad, we're going to Disney."

Disney. Always a big thing for the family—without me. It was Amy's thing. Her parents' thing. The kids' thing. Never mine. From the time we had started dating, I hadn't set foot in a Disney park. I even used to make fun of it with other guys.

In February, Amy and one of our sons had a trip planned to Florida. It was supposed to be his high school graduation trip, but COVID-19 canceled it. Of course, I had no plans to go. I gave my usual line: "Somebody has to work to

God had stripped away my need to make everything about me.

pay for it." Nine months later, he was in college—and I was going.

That's how much things had changed. How much *I had changed.*

God had stripped away my need to make everything about me.

So I decided to go. And not just as an exercise—I *wanted* to go. For our son. For Amy. For the family. Love was breaking through in places where fear used to grip me, keep me away. I'd been married to work. Now, with the divorce underway, I wanted to be present with them. Go figure.

So there I was, preparing for our first Disney trip together, when the next drama hit: Our son wanted a birthday dinner, and he invited me but not Amy.

This had nothing to do with me—but she blamed me. And whatever "reconciliation" was supposed to look like—well, *reconcile-what?*

This was our first family outing since filing. It wasn't about reconciling the marriage but at least reconciling the parts no divorce could take away. We were still parents. And we honestly still loved each other—even if the way that love showed up had to change.

Nevertheless, four and a half hours later, I was still hearing it: "I did all the work with our boys all these years! I did every-thing! And now you just step in—after doing nothing—*and you're the hero?*"

Oh, she dug in—on what a horrible father I'd been, on how I'd done nothing for their whole upbringing. I took it. Every word. I didn't defend. I didn't argue. I just sat there.

And for me, this marked a new day.

My son wasn't the only one celebrating a graduation. His was delayed months; mine, twenty-six years. But I felt like I'd graduated. Everything God was teaching me—this was the time to live it. I didn't need to fight back. I didn't need to defend myself. I knew her words weren't all true. I knew she was hurting. And I didn't need her to validate me.

There's a saying: You don't know God is all you need until God is all you've got. *That's exactly where I was.*

There's a saying: *You don't know God is all you need until God is all you've got.* That's exactly where I was.

Amy tried everything to get a rise out of me. I gave her nothing—no fuel for the fire. Eventually, she burned out.

And I got my answer to the questions I'd carried for years—through every betrayal, every sudden death, every shock that threatened to break my faith: *Is God with me? Is God my defender? Can I trust Him?*

Turns out, I could.

So we went to Disney—Amy, our son, and me. And it was awesome.

Why Now?

In the six months that followed the divorce filings, Todd kept showing up—fixing things at my condo, helping when I needed it, never asking for anything in return.

There were times he could tell I was still seeing the other person. And when he sensed it, he'd quietly back off. We wouldn't talk for a few days—but then he'd be back. Not pushing, not pleading, just . . . being present.

At first, I watched. I absorbed it. I didn't know what to make of it.

And then I got angry: *Why?! Why now?! Why are you doing this now? Why couldn't you do this before?*

That anger grew. And any time I let myself soften or wonder, I'd come right back to the phrase that, in some ways, comforted—and in more ways, haunted—me: *A day late and a dollar short.*

Four days after Lazarus died, everyone thought Jesus was late. Sometimes God's timing is meant not to disappoint but to set up a greater miracle. What situation in your life feels "too late" right now? Ask God to show you whether this is a place to keep waiting with Him or to take a faithful next step.

On the Flip Side

> *So they are no longer two, but one flesh.*
> *Therefore what God has joined together,*
> *let no one separate.*
> *—Matthew 19:6 NIV*

Well before the Disney trip, I had started showing up—soccer games, school events, all the things I'd ignored when I was married to work.

My youngest son was into stage and concert lighting design and trying to pick a college. The biggest school in the country for his interests was Full Sail University, in Florida. I told him to check it out—and if he decided he wanted to go, I'd move to Florida with him.

I told Amy she was welcome to come with us if she wanted, but either way, I was moving on. "There's nothing for me here. No reason to stay."

It wasn't about me anymore; it was about letting my son chase his dream. I wanted him to have what I wished I'd had—what I lost when my dad died and everything turned upside down.

For the first time in a long time, I started dreaming. I looked at places where I could build a simple life—just my son and me. A bachelor pad. Debt free. Carefree. Maybe I'd go into business. Maybe I'd go for broke, drop the big paychecks, and pursue ministry. I didn't know. But anything was better than the crazy cycle I was leaving behind.

In my mind, this was it—my last chance, after twenty-six years, to do what I should've done all along.

And while I was searching, Amy made another move.

"Can I come?"

Only she didn't just want to join me while I looked at mobile homes and cheap apartments. Amy wanted to look at houses—as if she intended to move with us.

So yeah. I dropped what I was doing, got us a realtor, and we looked at houses together.

It used to be that she would go and wish I'd joined her. Now the tables had turned. And honestly, I was just glad to spend time with her. I'd let twenty-six years disappear, paying almost no attention to the woman I supposedly loved—and vowed to love and care for.

That time was gone, and I could do nothing to get it back.

In my mind, this was it—my last chance, after twenty-six years, to do what I should've done all along. I planned to make the most of it. No matter what happened, what hit, what changed—I wouldn't make it about me.

So in addition to touring the university, we went to NASA. We went to the beach. We went to Disney. We did everything our hearts desired, and we had a great time.

I began to think we just might get a fresh start. My family would stay together.

Then we got back to Arizona.

We walked through the door, sat on the couch, and Amy said three words:

"I'm not going."

Awesome.

When You Get What You Want (and It Sucks)

After the first Disney trip, our youngest son decided to graduate from high school early and attend a college in Florida. The divorce was already in motion, but there was still a thread between Todd and me—we were still talking, still sharing *Daily Hope* devotionals, still listening to the same podcasts.

I was still wrestling with God.

But when we got back to Arizona, I made a decision: I was staying. Todd and our son would move to Florida without me.

I told Todd, straight up, "I'm pursuing the other relationship. I'm not moving to Florida."

I meant it. And for a minute, I felt free. Out in the open. No more secrets. I could live this new life fully.

Only nothing worked. Everything kept going wrong.

But I got what I wanted. It was all there—handed to me with chocolates and roses—and I was miserable!

The other relationship? Not so perfect after all. We weren't cohesive. We weren't getting along. It wasn't bringing the happiness I was searching for.

And Todd—the man I had begged to change for years—had actually changed. He was becoming the man I'd always hoped he'd be—now that I was letting him go. Was that all I ever had to do? Was that the kicker? The linchpin? The one thing I refused to do turned out to be the one thing that worked?

He was becoming the man I'd always hoped he'd be—now that I was letting him go.

I kept hearing the question: *Are you sure you don't want to give it one more try?* I knew that voice, that sound, that heart by now. It was me, but it wasn't just me. God was saying it too. I started to let His voice come through: *This isn't what I have for you.*

Kill Her or Kill Me

"Also," she continued, "I'm going public with the affair, and I'm going to throw myself into it fully."

Once again, I was blindsided and humiliated. Many angry conversations with God ensued.

You're God, and I'm not, remember?! You knew this was coming. You could've said something, and You didn't.

After a while, I got it all out and returned to the only place that made sense: *God, You know better than I do.*

I felt like Job.

First Hosea, now Job? Hey God, what happened to David? Why can't I have his story?

This time, I didn't need something to fall on my head to realize God probably had tried to tell me; I just wasn't listening.

After she left, I put it back in His hands.

I resigned myself to a realization: *I can control my responses. I can control my actions. But I can't control situations, circumstances, or other people.*

I cried. I screamed. I yelled at God. But I made my peace with it.

I've had enough. I can't take another moment of this, or my heart is going to explode! So this is it, Lord: You can kill her. I can kill her. You can kill me. Or I can kill me. Do You want to pick—or do You want me to pick? Because I'm done.

God loves you. You can come to Him raw. Sometimes the most desperate prayers—when we have nothing left to hide—open the way for Him to meet us most deeply. What is the raw truth you need to bring to God instead of carrying it alone? Where might God be inviting you to pray from the deepest, most honest place in your heart?

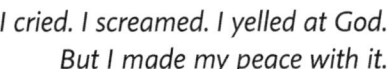

I cried. I screamed. I yelled at God. But I made my peace with it.

One prayer remained in my heart: "God, I ask You for this one thing: Be everywhere Amy turns—all the time, constantly."

If I Make My Bed in the Depths . . .

> *Is there anyplace I can go to avoid your*
> *Spirit? to be out of your sight? If I climb to*
> *the sky, you're there!*
> *If I go underground, you're there!*
> *If I flew on morning's wings*
> *to the far western horizon,*
> *You'd find me in a minute—*
> *you're already there waiting!*
> *—Psalm 139:7–10 MSG*

Suddenly, the voice I was learning to recognize in my heart wasn't just on the inside; it was everywhere I turned.

Everywhere.

Just like when Jesus said to His disciples in Matthew 28:20 (NLT), "And be sure of this: I am with you always, even to the end of the age."

I was the one sheep my Shepherd left the ninety-nine to pursue. He had never left me. I'd left Him.

The conviction was constant—gentle but unrelenting. The littlest things would pop out, all seeming to whisper, *One more try.*

I started reading Scripture again—for real this time. I stopped asking for signs and started asking to *see.* I leaned in and finally said it: *Okay, God. I'm listening. Where are You in all of this?*

I was the one sheep my Shepherd left the ninety-nine to pursue. He had never left me. I'd left Him.

And I heard Him.

Not in thunder or fire—but in a still, small voice: *I'm here. I've been here all along. But I can't pour into closed hands—or into a double-minded heart. I need your surrender.*

God had been gently knocking, asking me to surrender all the parts of my life—to turn to Him for connection, love, and relationship.

So I waved the white flag. And to the best of my ability, I surrendered.

Okay, God. I'm done. I'm done trying to control this. I'm done trying to make my life into what I think will make me happy. I'm done fighting You. You are God—and I am not. Not my will, but Yours be done.

I remembered His promise: "'For I know the plans I have for you,' declares the Lord. 'Plans to prosper you and not to harm you, plans to give you hope and a future'" (Jer. 29:11 NIV).

I wanted that hope. I wanted that future.

It wasn't long after that that I did the impossible—the previously unthinkable: I ended the affair.

As much as I wanted the fantasy, I wanted something more. More than anything else, I wanted to be obedient to Christ.

It wasn't easy. It wasn't clean. But it was real. I wanted that obedience more than I wanted control. I wanted God.

I didn't know what the future held. I didn't know what would happen with Todd. The only relationship I wanted to focus on was my relationship with God. And I made a decision to trust that everything else He had for me would fall into place.

Finally ready to stop chasing feelings, I surrendered to the One who had been chasing *me*.

I stopped making it about Todd . . . and started making it about Jesus.

I stopped making it about Todd . . . and started making it about Jesus.

So when Todd said, "I want you to come to Florida, and I want you in my life—but I don't *need* you," it woke me up.

For the first time, I asked, *Can you want someone and not need them?*

That night I told Todd, "If you'll have me, I want to try again."

Chapter 12

Death and Resurrection

THE END ISN'T THE SAME as the beginning. Yet every true beginning requires an end.

The gospel insists that every death holds within it the seed of resurrection. Can a man be born again? Can a marriage? The answer is the same: Not without first dying.

This is not just a marriage story—it's the human story. Man "fell from grace" because we tried to accomplish on our own what was already accomplished for us. "Be like God," we were tempted—by doing what God said not to do. From there, it was all on us. We abandoned our relationship with God and covered ourselves with fig leaves—as if protected by the works of our own hands instead of His love.

Thousands of years of human history did nothing to solve our problem. Humanity only got worse, just like our

We abandoned our relationship with God and covered ourselves with fig leaves—as if protected by the works of our own hands instead of His love.

marriages, our health, our finances, or our lives do when we cling to control and try to fix things ourselves.

Then Christ came to set it straight.

He showed us what real strength looks like: Not survival of the fittest, and not winning. But losing. Dying. Laying down our lives. Letting go.

Even Christ didn't fix His own broken, crucified body. When He laid His life down and trusted the Father to send the Spirit to resurrect Him, He demonstrated the ultimate trust. Even that happened in surrender—in letting go.

Our work is not to *fix* what's broken but to lay it down. Put it to rest. Give it back to God. Drop the weapons and surrender the need to win. All our fighting, fussing, self-torture, and intentional or unintentional abuse accomplish nothing.

Our work is not to fix what's broken but to lay it down.

The gospel calls us to a different fight: Fight for peace. Fight to keep the heart soft. Fight to love our enemies.

When we fight to have our way, life slips through our fingers. But when we finally let go, we find that the end is not the end. Letting go isn't losing—it's the beginning of the end, which leads to resurrection.

"For whoever wants to save their life will lose it, but whoever loses their life for me will find it" (Matt. 16:25 NIV).

Amy Moves Home

The end.

"I can't take it anymore!" Amy blasted.

"Huh?" I answered, genuinely curious.

"Everywhere I go—He's there. I get in the car, the radio's preaching at me. I open a devotional at work, and it's like it's written just for me. Even people around me bring up sermons or Scriptures—always the exact thing I'm trying to avoid. I can't outrun it. God's telling me what to do, and I know I have to obey."

We don't obey to earn God's love. But what if obedience is our part to play—our way of participating in His answers to our prayers?

It was the end of her self-reliance. And not only the end of *her* fight—it was the end of mine. The end of trying to make her get "there." The end of carrying her through it. Amy was finally hearing God for herself. And that's all I'd ever wanted.

Amy was finally hearing God for herself. And that's all I'd ever wanted.

I told her I still wanted her—but I didn't need her.

"If you'll still have me," she said, "I want to try again."

"Fine," I said. "You can come with us. We'll need to get a house."

I didn't care where we lived. I just wanted her out of Arizona—away from the guy, the job, the cycle. Her decision didn't mean everything came to a screeching halt. Even after she said she was ready to change, there were still slips. She'd still talk to him. Still get quiet. Still hold on to little mementos that I didn't want in our home.

Amy's lease ended in June, and she moved back in with us in July. By then, she'd already been looking for a job transfer for months—every other option had led to a dead end. But the Florida application? It went through fast. Doors flew open. We even found the perfect house and bought it—seamless, painless, without even seeing it in person. Suddenly, everything became crystal clear.

It wasn't because of anything we did, though. God was clearing the way. Making it obvious. And rewarding our obedience with miracles to help us.

Sometimes, when you've waited a long time for things to change—and then you *change—the* things *change fast.*

Sometimes, when you've waited a long time for things to change—and then *you* change—the *things* change fast.

Five Years to New

I knew it was God's will for me to stay in my marriage. Even though I'd given my heart to someone else, I decided I would be obedient to God—*even when I didn't feel like it.*

Was Todd 2.0 here to stay? Or would he retreat, like always?

Maybe he would, I reasoned. And if he does, that's okay, because I still have my relationship with God, and that's all that matters.

I didn't feel it yet. But I knew it was right. I wanted to be obedient. And I trusted that if I gave God my obedience, He would take care of the rest.

That July, the intensive Dave Carder had recommended opened back up, this time for in-person attendance. I wanted to do it again. There was more to receive face-to-face than I'd gotten from the online version during COVID-19.

Todd came with me and visited Travis, his high school buddy and bandmate. It was great for them to reconnect.

After the intensive, we added a few extra days and spent the Fourth of July in Chattanooga and then hit Asheville. It was good. But it was still hard, because the shift wasn't instant. I was still grieving the end of the other relationship, and Todd knew it. He'd notice when I got that far-off look. Sometimes I'd try to show him my phone, like I was trying to prove something. But he'd refuse.

"I don't want to control you. I don't want to be your dad—or your cop," he explained. "And honestly, I have no need to see something that's just going to wreck me."

During our separation, Todd's sister had kept warning him: "If this turns around, it's going to take a long time."

"What do you mean—how long?" he asked. "A few months?"

"More like five years."

She was right.

From my first counseling session to the last—it was five years.

It started in 2019, when I worked with the trauma specialist and finally began naming my traumas out loud. From there, it was layer after layer—Bethesda intensives, local counseling, books, hard conversations, setbacks, two steps forward and one step back. The work never stopped—and still hasn't.

By the end of 2021, our family was back together in Florida.

What if deep healing isn't quick—but it's still certain? Would you stay the course if you knew your breakthrough might take five years . . . or longer?

I was still grieving the end of the other relationship, and Todd knew it.

The affairs were over. The grief had loosened its grip.

We weren't perfect—but we were new.

And by then, we'd both soaked up more books on counseling, psychology, and marriage than we could count. Todd practically went through the intensives alongside me—reading all the content himself. We picked marriage counseling back up, this time with both of us showing up fully present.

And—crazy God thing—I reconnected with the Christian sponsor I'd lost during the affair.

And—crazy God thing—I reconnected with the Christian sponsor I'd lost during the affair. Turns out, she lived in Florida. We got to meet face to face.

When Delays Work in Your Favor

After a lot of searching, we finally found a church. At first, we were looking for one to pour into us—something with marriage groups and support. But we kept coming up empty.

Maybe that was the point. Maybe God was asking us to *start* the thing we were looking for.

So we did.

Now, I have seen more than one hundred men come through the separated men's group I started. The details of their stories differ—but the struggles? They're strikingly familiar: "We work too much. We miss the signals. We try to fix instead of connect. And sometimes, by the time we wake up, our wives have already said, 'Enough.'"

For Amy, trauma was part of the story. I don't know if she would've had the affairs otherwise. But when you've been wounded, you reach for the medicine you have. It was what worked. It dulled the pain—until it didn't.

Guys always ask me, "How did you do it? Why did you stay?"

Not every man gets the ending I did. One guy gave his wife the same book that helped Amy . . . and she threw it in his face. They divorced soon after.

The truth is, if Amy hadn't kept pressing in—kept showing up for counseling, kept pursuing healing—I don't know if we would've made it either. But she did. She wanted to get better.

As for me? In a strange way, I am grateful for the 2020 lockdowns. They broke the hold that work had on me. With everything shut down, I couldn't escape into busyness. I had to sit. Be quiet. Be still. Feel again. And open my life fully to God. Without that reset, I honestly don't know where I'd be today.

And whatever happened with the divorce?

It dragged out for nine months. Because we still had a minor at home, we were required to take a special parenting class, which delayed things even more. By the time the court date arrived, we'd called it off. The judge seemed almost as excited as we were when we called to tell her.

"The old marriage is divorced," I told her. "The old marriage is dead."

For the new one, I asked for a promise: "Every quarter, we do something to invest in our marriage. No coasting. No drifting. Always forward."

> God is not a genie in a bottle. Doing the right things doesn't guarantee the outcome we hope for. The real question is what will you do if you make all the right choices—and the outcome is still not what you wanted?

Out of our greatest pain often comes our greatest ministry. For us, that is proving true.

We began by hosting a handful of couples in our home, but the group grew so quickly that we soon had thirty people and no chairs left. Now we're part of the fastest-growing church in Florida, and there are far too many marriages in crisis for one couple to carry. So we teach marriage classes, lead small groups, and train leaders. We multiply.

Out of our greatest pain often comes our greatest ministry.

Pastor Rick used to say, "Humans can endure a lot of pain—if they believe there's a purpose."

Looking back, we wouldn't wish our story on anyone. But would we go through it again? Yes—though not because it was easy, and not because it turned out perfect, because neither is true. We learned that letting go was the key to holding on to our marriage. And no matter what we have to face, if it clears the way for God and draws us closer to Him—bring it on.

Part 2

Bring It On

*I*N PART 1, WE INVITED you into our story, our testimony—not just to show what we walked through but to help you feel seen in your own journey. Now in Part 2, we shift from storytelling to soul work—with Jesus.

Sometimes, He revealed Himself to us directly; other times, He guided us through people, community, books, devotionals, and other resources.

In this second part of the book, our goal is to pass along those insights—not as prescriptions but as reflections of what we've learned, as well as invitation for you to apply our reflections to your own situation and your own marriage.

While we wouldn't trade our journey for anything, we believe that knowing these principles sooner might have spared us some, or even much, of the pain we endured. We hope that by sharing what we have learned, we can help you avoid some of our pain points and move toward harmony more quickly!

These next chapters focus on the truths, principles, and revelations that helped us grow and heal—not perfectly but deeply. They're not a step-by-step manual, and they're certainly not a checklist. They're invitations. And we think they can help you in your journey.

At the end of each chapter, you'll find short reflections—five simple headings meant to help you pause and process:

1. **Something to Think About**—A few powerful thoughts or phrases to sit with. Read them slowly. Let them speak.

2. **Where Am I in This?**—Probing questions to help you identify your story within the topic. These are meant to stir honest reflection, not shame.

3. **Hold These Close**—A brief list of key ideas or themes from the chapter. You might want to underline them, pray through them, or share them in conversation.

4. **Word for the Journey**—A few Scriptures to meditate on. Ask the Holy Spirit to highlight the one you need most in this season.

5. **Prayer for the Road**—A short, heartfelt prayer to close the chapter and carry its truth with you into the next step.

This section is meant to be spacious. You can move through it quickly or slowly. You can do it alone or with a spouse, a counselor, or a trusted friend. However you use it, our prayer is that it leads to healing conversations—with yourself, with your spouse, and with God.

Chapter 13

Going Vertical

*M*ANY MARRIAGE BOOKS FOCUS ON tools for communication, finances, or sex. This isn't one of them. In fact, the first and most transformative lesson we learned was that our vertical relationship with God must come before everything else in life.

Growing up in conservative Christian homes, we were taught that God places the highest value on marriage and family. But while these "horizontal" connections are deeply important to Him, they're not above our personal intimacy and connection with the Father, Son, and Holy Spirit. God's foremost concern is our vertical relationship with Him—our salvation, sanctification, and daily union with His presence. This must be our highest pursuit.

The first and most transformative lesson we learned was that our vertical relationship with God must come before everything else in life.

Early in our separation, God spoke directly to me: I'd made an idol out of my marriage—out of winning Amy back. When we place marriage above our relationship with God, we turn it into an idol. Before He could rebuild us as a couple, He needed us to surrender everything and let Him become the foundation and centerpiece of our individual lives (see Luke 17:33).

It's nearly impossible to make progress in our horizontal relationships—especially with our spouses—when our vertical relationship with God is lacking.

During our separation, God revealed just how shallow our connection with Him had become. Before He could begin to restore us as a couple, He had to strip us down individually, breaking us to the point where He alone could become the center of everything. That process required us to release the preconceived ideas, expectations, and desires that once held the highest places in our hearts. Only after letting go could we begin to move forward. When we finally did, circumstances began to shift and, even amid the trials, we experienced the peace that only God can give (see Philippians 4:7).

He had to strip us down individually, breaking us to the point where He alone could become the center of everything.

Letting Go

The idea that "letting go" is the key to "holding on" reveals a powerful paradox at the heart of growth and transformation: When we release our expectations, attachments, burdens, and limitations, we make space to truly grasp what matters most. This is what Jesus was teaching in

Matthew 6:33 (NCV): "Seek first God's kingdom and what God wants. Then all your other needs will be met as well."

And again, in Luke 17:33 (TLB), He said, "Whoever clings to his life shall lose it, and whoever loses his life shall save it." When God calls us to surrender, this is what He means. The tighter we grip what we're afraid to lose, the more miserable and self-focused we become.

It's a lot like learning to swim.

When our boys were little, we taught them to swim in the backyard pool. At first, we let them get comfortable just being in the water, safely held up by their floaties. But then came the day they had to get in without that security. They clung to the edge with white knuckles, afraid to let go. Meanwhile, I stood behind them in the pool with open arms and a steady voice, saying, "I've got you. Trust me. You have to let go to be able to swim. I won't let you drown."

The tighter we grip what we're afraid to lose, the more miserable and self-focused we become.

Our towheaded boys would look up at Amy with wide eyes, as if to say, *I don't want to let go. I'm scared. What if I don't make it? What if I drown?* As their parents, of course we weren't going to let that happen, in the same way our heavenly Father knows He won't let us drown either.

Eventually, our boys would let go and swim to Todd—floundering and splashing the whole way, but they'd make it. And in the process, with their eyes fixed on their daddy, they learned how to swim.

In the same way, we have to let go of what's holding us back so we can move forward, even if it means floundering and splashing as we go. We'll make it if we just keep swimming—if we keep trusting and putting our faith in God. Sometimes it takes a daily decision; sometimes it's minute by minute. It's hard at first, but God will give us the strength if we ask for it.

A Three-Stranded Cord

God wanted our complete and total surrender, and He loved us so much that He used the very circumstances we'd created through our own sin to get our attention. We were the ones who made the mess, and He could have left us in it. But instead, He took what was broken and used it to draw us back to Him, making something beautiful out of it.

Romans 8:28 (NLT) says, "God causes everything to work together for the good of those who love God and are called according to his purpose for them." That means He can bring good even from the unwanted situations we'd ourselves caused. He doesn't always remove the consequences, but He redeems them for our

There's purpose in the pain.

good because He loves us that much. *There's purpose in the pain.* It's a signal. It gets our attention, so we can face the root issues and begin to heal.

As we healed and our individual relationships with God became firmly established, He wanted us to be anchored in Him as a couple, so we could thrive in that vertical connection together. Ecclesiastes 4:12 says that a three-stranded cord is not easily broken. That third strand is Jesus! When our marriage includes my spouse, me, *and* Christ at the center, it becomes something that can't easily come apart.

People often ask what that looks like in everyday life. For us, it means putting God first in everything. We start each day by praying together. We study the Bible and read devotionals together. We worship together. When problems arise, we go to God first—together. When we face big decisions, we seek His guidance—together.

We show each other grace and mercy, just as God does for us. *We listen to understand, not just to respond.* We forgive each other because Christ forgave us. We give each other the benefit of the doubt when we disagree. And we try to hear the emotions beneath the words instead of filtering everything through our own perspective.

We listen to understand, not just to respond.

Are we perfect at it? Not even close. Do we need to hit reset sometimes? Absolutely. But we read in Lamentations that His mercies are new every morning (see Lamentations 3:22–23). Because of that, we offer each other mercy and the grace to get up and try again when we fall short.

You Complete Me?

One thing we hear a lot is that our spouse is supposed to "complete" us, but that's simply not true. We need to be whole and complete in ourselves first. *Your spouse isn't meant to complete you but to complement you.* Too often, people go into marriage thinking it will fix their problems. In reality, marriage tends to reveal and even magnify those issues—not solve them. We should *want* our spouse, but we should never *need* them in the sense that our identity, healing, and happiness depend on them.

You may have heard the saying "You don't know God is all you need until God is all you've got." Nothing could be truer. During our separation, we lived that truth. God loves us so much that He will pursue us—even to the point of stripping away everything, if that's what it takes to get our attention. That's exactly what He did during that

God showed us that our control is only an illusion.

season. He called us to let go of the things we were clinging to so tightly. He did this not to deprive us but because He wants us to enjoy the peace and fulfillment of living in complete trust—having total faith in Him and Him alone.

We think we have control over our lives, our finances, our relationships, but God showed us that our control is only an illusion. So often, we as Christians will talk about how we have to give up control—but you can't give up something you never had in the first place. If we don't surrender that illusion to Him, the enemy is more than willing to take the reins, using our weaknesses and blind spots to wreak havoc in our lives. But when we let God take over, He leads us—even through the hard things. And while God doesn't micromanage everything we do or everything that happens to us, He *does* protect His people under His covenant. Ultimately, He has the final say.

> For Todd, trusting God to carry and provide for the family was really hard. For years, he had tried to control everything, to prepare for every what-if and worst-case scenario. Letting go and letting God take the driver's seat requires a leap of faith, but it's the only way to truly rest in Him.

We eventually discovered that when we don't fully surrender our lives to Jesus, instead of trusting Him, we let *fear* take the lead—fear of being hurt or losing something we hold dear. We worry we won't receive what we hoped for or what we believe we deserve. But the Bible says that perfect love casts out all fear (see 1 John 4:18).

He is our protector, our comforter, and our strength, and it's in His perfect love that fear is driven out.

We believe the opposite of fear is faith. Some say that fear is an involuntary feeling, while faith is a choice. That may be true—but when we choose to believe, when we choose faith, we're choosing to live in God's perfect love, trusting that He holds us in His hands. He is our protector, our comforter, and our strength, and it's in His perfect love that fear is driven out.

The Purpose of Marriage

So, why did God give us marriage in the first place? The primary purpose of marriage isn't our happiness—it's our sanctification. Sure, marriage can bring happiness. But it can also bring misery, even suffering. The Bible doesn't say *if* troubles come; it says *when* they come (see James 1:2–4). So, why get married at all if it's going to include seasons that are painful or difficult? Why walk into something that has the potential to hurt?

While we could quote Alfred Lord Tennyson—"'Tis better to have loved and lost than never to have loved at all"—we add that marriage is also valuable because God uses it to teach us. When we're born, we can't care for ourselves. And let's be honest—when we're kids, we're all about ourselves. Our kids' favorite word when they were little was "Mine!" We have to be taught how to think of others and how to share. As we grow and mature, we (hopefully) start thinking more about others and less about ourselves. But that's just the beginning—God takes that process much deeper.

As we grow in our faith, we're called to become more like Jesus.

As we grow in our faith, we're called to become more like Jesus. And Jesus was perfect—perfect in love, in forgiveness, in humility. God's ways are higher than ours, and His thoughts higher than ours (see Isaiah 55:8–9). He invites us to rise into His ways and mature in His character through relationship with Him.

Our spouses are also our brothers and sisters in Christ—God's son or daughter, placed in our lives to help us grow, just as we are placed in theirs. When we honor the covenant of marriage, it becomes a sacred space for transformation—a safe place where we work out our salvation with grace and truth.

Sometimes, your spouse might feel like the antagonist in your story, but it's been said that you can't learn how to love unless you have someone unlovable in your life. You can't learn how to forgive unless someone gives you a reason to forgive. A Christian marriage is a covenant between husband and wife—a sacred promise that says, "I'm not leaving just because we aren't getting along." "I'm not divorcing you just because you did something that requires

There's no better place than marriage to learn how to love like God loves, forgive like God forgives, and grow in the fruit of the Spirit.

me to forgive." "I'm not running away just because you're not making me happy right now."

Without that covenant, marriage becomes no different than the world's version of dating. But when both people are truly committed, marriage becomes a safe place to grow into the likeness of Christ.

There's a reason marriage vows include phrases like "through thick and thin," "in sickness and in health," and "for better or for worse." God knew exactly what He was doing when He created the institution of marriage. Marriage can bring happiness, but it can also bring sorrow. You will get hurt at some point—guaranteed. But if you're willing to put in the work, you'll grow in faith, character, and wisdom. There's no better place than marriage to learn how to love like God loves, forgive like God forgives, and grow in the fruit of the Spirit—kindness, gentleness, faithfulness, joy, patience, self-control, and peace that passes understanding. And in case that sounds like a Sunday school cliché, let's make it more real:

Marriage teaches us to love like God—when we're not being loved back.

- o To be kind—when we're met with unkindness.
- o To be gentle—when our spirit feels trampled.
- o To be faithful—even in the face of betrayal.
- o To be joyful—in the middle of trials.
- o To be patient—when mistakes keep happening.
- o To show self-control—when our flesh wants to lash out.
- o And to walk in peace that defies all logic—because only God can give us that.

Something to Think About

1. We often try to fix horizontal problems with horizontal tools. But when we go vertical first—seeking God before strategies—our posture shifts, and the conversation changes. You'll be a lot less disappointed in your spouse when you're not expecting

them to fulfill all your needs. In what ways have you expected your spouse to meet your needs?

_____

_____

_____

_____

2. When have you asked your spouse to complete you instead of complementing you? What is one way you can seek wholeness in Jesus first—and then bring that fullness to your marriage?

_____

_____

_____

_____

3. Before your next hard talk, what's one simple vertical practice you'll do (a two-minute prayer together, a single verse read aloud, a moment of worship)? When will you do it?

_____

_____

_____

4. In the tension you're facing, which Christlike trait
    might God be forming in you (patience, gentleness,
    self-control, faith)? How could you cooperate with
    Him this week?

_____

_____

_____

_____

Where Am I in This?

1. To what extent do you feel like God is front and
    center in your life and in everything you do? In
    what aspects of life do you already lean on God for
    strength and understanding? In what aspects do
    you still lean on yourself before God?

_____

_____

_____

_____

2. How much time daily or weekly do you set aside just to be with God? Are you intentional about spending time just *listening* to what God has to say to you?

_____

_____

_____

_____

3. How often do you fellowship with other believers who want to walk faithfully with Christ?

_____

_____

_____

_____

4. When something painful or unexpected occurs, are you more likely to turn immediately to Scripture, prayer, and/or praise and worship, or to something (or someone) else? Think about the exciting and stressful moments of your past week. What, or whom, did you turn to?

_____

_____

_____

_____

5. Walking with God—and learning to turn to Him for all things—takes both intention and practice. Where in your day could you create space for prayer, quiet reflection, Scripture, or worship? Don't stop at one moment. Consider

Walking with God—and learning to turn to Him for all things—takes both intention and practice.

choosing three, four, or even five times throughout your day to reconnect with Him.

_____

_____

_____

_____

6. What small things could help you stay anchored? (*Examples: Amy used Post-It notes. Todd practiced taking every thought captive.*)

_____

_____

_____

_____

7. What tools might help you stay connected with God? Here are some you can start with. Add your own as you think of them.

☐ Set a reminder on your phone to pray, read Scripture, or be still and listen.

☐ Create a worship playlist to listen to while running errands or doing housework.

☐ Listen to sermons or devotionals on your drive to work.

☐ Set a regular meeting or call with an accountability partner.

☐ _____

☐ _____

☐ _____

8. What might you need to surrender to strengthen your marriage? (Examples: Todd had to surrender control and striving for stability so he could rest and be present. Amy surrendered thrill seeking and

*entertainment so she could let God fulfill her and
enjoy true peace.)*

Hold These Close

It's nearly impossible to make progress in our horizontal
relationships—especially with our spouses—when our
vertical relationship with God is lacking.

When God is first, love has a source. His presence supplies
what conflict drains—patience, gentleness, self-control.
Before the talk, go vertical: Pray, invite the Holy Spirit,
and then speak. Alignment with Him steadies everything
else.

There's purpose in the pain.

Pain is a signal—not punishment. It's there to get your
attention, so you can fix what might be off. Ask God to
show you why you're hurting, to help you understand
what your spirit or soul may be crying out for. Pray for
wisdom. Know that He wastes nothing. He'll take what
the enemy meant for evil and use it for your good.

We listen to understand, not just to respond.

If you're fighting, arguing, or bickering with your spouse a lot, winning might be losing. Lay down the defenses and pick up curiosity. Ask, "Help me hear your heart," and wait. Listen intently. You may have to slow your breath, soften your tone, and calm down so you can seek the person—not the perfect comeback.

Your spouse isn't meant to complete you but to complement you.

Covenant is the guardrail that keeps us at the table when feelings fade and growth hurts.

Only Jesus makes you whole. When your identity is rooted in Him, you move from taking to giving—free to love your spouse without demanding them to fill what only God can. Wanted, not worshiped; partnered, not pedestalized.

When we honor the covenant of marriage, it becomes a sacred space for transformation—a safe place where we work out our salvation with grace and truth. Without that covenant, marriage becomes no different than the world's version of dating.

Covenant is the guardrail that keeps us at the table when feelings fade and growth hurts. It isn't an excuse to enable harm; it's a commitment to truth, repentance, boundaries, and mercy—so both can become more like Christ together.

Word for the Journey

Below, select the verse that stands out to you most. Read it slowly. Let it linger in your heart. As you hold onto the words, let them shape your thoughts. Whether you repeat the verse out loud, ponder it in silence, or explore it more deeply through further study, stay open to the Holy Spirit's leading.

"Seek first God's kingdom and what God wants.
Then all your other needs will be met as well."
—*Matthew 6:33 NCV*

"Whoever clings to his life shall lose it, and
whoever loses his life shall save it."
—*Luke 17:33 TLB*

"A triple-braided cord is not easily broken."
—*Ecclesiastes 4:12 NLT*

"Such love has no fear,
because perfect love expels all fear."
—*1 John 4:18 NLT*

"Trust in the LORD with all your heart, and do
not lean on your own understanding. In all your
ways acknowledge him, and he will make straight
your paths."
—*Proverbs 3:5–6 ESV*

Prayer for the Road

Father,

*I choose to go vertical first. I lay down my need to control outcomes and seek **Your** kingdom before everything else. Where I've been gripping tightly*

*to my life, teach me to release it to You—again and
again—trusting that in losing my way, I will find
Your way. Be the third strand in my marriage;
bind us to You so we're not easily broken.*

*In the places that feel confusing or heavy, I believe
You're working all things together for good as I
love You and follow Your purpose. Let Your perfect
love expel my fear and guard my heart and mind
with a peace that surpasses understanding.
Today I surrender my expectations, anxieties,
and idols. Center me in Your presence, align my
steps with Your will, and teach me to live from
union with You—day by day, moment by moment.*

In Jesus's name, I pray. Amen.

Grace in the Gray I

Truth vs. Love Thinkers

Most of us lean toward one of two ways of seeing the world—truth or love—but the Bible calls us to hold both together, "speaking the truth in love" (Eph. 4:15 NIV). The "gray" isn't about moral blur; it's the holy tension where truth stands firm yet love forgives, where love embraces but does not enable. It's conviction without condemnation—disagreement without divorce. Both conviction and compassion, truth and love, are vital, but when they slide out of balance, they can do real damage.

"Truth people," at the far end of the spectrum, see everything in black and white. It's right or wrong, yes or no. Out of balance, we can become perfectionists—justice seekers who feel every wrong must be corrected. Nothing gets overlooked.

In contrast, "love people," at the other end of the spectrum, tend to overlook almost anything, make excuses for behavior, and put compassion above conviction—peacekeeping above principle. Keeping the status quo gets valued over truth, even when it hurts in the long run.

In marriage, one spouse often leans more toward conviction and the other toward compassion—imbalances of truth and love that can collide when either side outweighs grace. For Amy and me, that was certainly the case. I leaned hard toward truth; Amy leaned toward love.

For me, everything had to have an absolute right or wrong answer. But the standard of "perfection" I held myself to wasn't God's—it was my own warped version. I thought perfection meant getting the project done, meeting the deadline, checking the box . . . even if it meant neglecting my kids or wounding my wife. Since I demanded that standard of myself, I demanded it of everyone else too.

At home, it showed up as constant correction and criticism. I created an atmosphere that felt more like boot camp than family. Looking back now, I can only shake my head.

I didn't see it at the time, but I was crushing the very people I loved most. Truth matters. Love matters. But when truth is stripped of love, it's no better than noise. As Paul writes, "If I could speak all the languages of earth and of angels, but didn't love others, I would only be a noisy gong or clanging cymbal" (1 Cor. 13:1 NLT).

Accelerator

- Write three or four strengths you see in your spouse.

- Ask God, "What words or Scriptures can I speak that build up my spouse?"

- Choose two or three life-giving notes or verses to declare over your spouse.

- The next time you feel tempted to fix (truth imbalance) or avoid (grace imbalance), *let go*—and speak words of life instead.

Chapter 14

———

Unmasking the Past

WE TEND TO PREFER LEAVING the past in the past. Some of us believe that opening up about it won't yield any good fruit. We think, *Why bother? It's all in the past.* So we sweep things under the rug, as if ignoring them will somehow make them magically disappear.

Nothing could be further from the truth.

Todd had found me a new counselor—this time a trauma specialist. I sauntered into her office and quickly explained that I had no significant trauma but that I was struggling in my marriage and needed help.

She looked at me—expressionless. I wondered what she was thinking.

"Okay," she said calmly. "So let's just talk."

No problem. I can talk. I love talking.

I spilled my list of marital problems as I saw them: What my husband did or didn't do, our recent separation, the empty nest ahead, and the fact that I'd just finished radiation for breast cancer.

A brief silence sat in the air.

"You've got a lot going on," she said.

"Yes," I replied, tears now rolling down my cheeks. "I do."

"Earlier, you mentioned not having any trauma."

"I don't. I'm here because my husband thought it would be a good idea. Your bio mentioned a specialization in trauma, and he believes I experienced trauma during my childhood."

"Really? What makes him think so?"

This time, no tears or flood of emotions. Like reading a grocery list, I told her about the rape, the promiscuity, the abortion, and the battering of my earlier relationships.

"And you don't think any of those experiences were traumatic?" she asked.

"Of course they were traumatic at the time, but they're all in the past. I'm fine. It's fine. Everything's fine. I've dealt with it and moved on."

"How did you deal with it?" she asked.

"Oh, I don't know. But it's over, and I'm past it. It is what it is," I stated resolutely.

And with that, my trauma counseling began.

From Trauma to Transformation

In her book *Denial: A Memoir of Terror,* Jessica stern writes, "Some people's lives seem to flow in a narrative; mine had many stops and starts. That's what trauma does. It interrupts the plot. It just happens, and then life goes on. No one prepares you for it."

Why do people who've been abused keep going back to the same situation? The answer is complex, but it begins with one simple root: trauma. Most trauma survivors are simply seeking the familiar. The situation may be dire, but it's what they know.

Are we therefore condemned to be stuck in the same ugly cycles? Is it possible to form *new* patterns and *new* attachments outside the trauma cycle? After or even amid trauma, can we develop healthy attachments to people, places, and activities?

One thing is certain: We can't just ignore it and expect things to get better. I was totally unprepared for how profoundly *not* dealing with the events of my early childhood would impact my adult life—or how unacknowledged trauma would resurface in silent and indescribable ways.

Why do we have to "deal with" our trauma? Because trauma makes it difficult to engage in intimate relationships. Whether it happened *to* you or was something you did, trauma damages trust—in both yourself and others.

How could I trust anyone who hadn't been through what I had? *They wouldn't understand,* I told myself. *They don't get it, so I don't trust them.*

But while it lingers unseen, unacknowledged, or simply ignored,

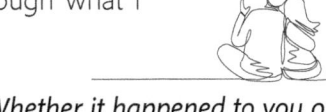

Whether it happened to you or was something you did, trauma damages trust—in both yourself and others.

the trauma tucks itself behind our masks while it keeps busy changing everything—rewriting mental programs to avoid dangers that may or may not exist and driving us blindly toward real and actual dangers.

Trauma reshapes our behavior and rewires our expectations. It filters how we perceive people, situations, and experiences. It impacts our thinking and behaviors from the subconscious level so that we are mostly unaware of its mechanisms. A traumatized brain tends to prefer the familiar—even when it consistently leads down the same destructive path. Trauma unchecked takes the driver's seat and steers our choices. It alters our beliefs and even our preferences, changes how we process information, and even affects the people and situations we're attracted to.

The early sexual abuse made it easy to continue seeking attention but difficult to surrender to real intimacy.

Many people assume that someone who's been sexually abused would avoid sex altogether. That isn't always true. I minimized what happened to me, somehow convinced that the rape part was my fault, but the craving to be desired was normal—a craving that had to be satisfied. I equated being sexually desirable with being valued—worthy of love.

The early sexual abuse made it easy to continue seeking attention but difficult to surrender to real intimacy. I kept everyone at arm's length to avoid getting hurt. I built walls—even though I desperately longed to feel close, safe, secure, loved, and worthy.

When Sex and Love Become the "Substance"

For a long time, I thought addiction applied only to substances like drugs or alcohol. I had no idea about "behavioral" addictions.

For me, sex wasn't the point. It was the necessary evil—the means to my fix. And my "fix," my "substance," was being in a relationship, because that was where I felt chosen and valued.

For me, sex became like a gateway drug. "Love," not unlike drugs or alcohol, gave me the temporary high I craved. It seemed to provide a sense of control, validation, even identity. I just didn't realize that it never actually achieved any of those things. The fleeting sensations were just that—totally fleeting.

I locked into a cycle—moving from one relationship to the next—until I eventually got married.

I didn't know that I'd buried deep shame inside. It was too confusing to acknowledge it, too hard to process it, too much to face. Inside, I was consumed by humiliation, angry at myself for the choices I'd made. I hated myself for allowing it all to happen in the first place. And because I didn't have any other tools, I buried the feelings with the very things that caused them.

Maybe you can relate. Or maybe you can see this happening in the life of someone you love. Maybe even your spouse.

"Love," not unlike drugs or alcohol, gave me the temporary high I craved.

After thirty-five years, disaster, desire, and a final thin thread of hope finally forced me to go back, to look, and to allow healing from the traumatic wounds of my childhood. This wasn't just about forgiving myself and feeling better, although those things are important. I had to rebuild my sense of self and self-worth.

In the process, I discovered that my true identity was not found in my past but in my lineage—as a daughter of the King. Jesus Christ redefined my worth. I had to relinquish any thoughts, ideas, values, and strongholds connected to being a wife, mother, nurse, friend, daughter, etc. Today, I know that *my identity is not shaped by my mistakes.* It is shaped by who God says I am. It's rooted in my inheritance and in the legacy I carry.

Through counseling, intensives, EMDR, tons of books, and self-education, I finally saw the truth: I had *never* truly experienced a stable relationship. Not even once.

If it was hard for me to trust in my husband's true and genuine love for me, it was even harder to trust in God's ultimate, undeniable, unimaginable, all-encompassing—even

My identity is not shaped by my mistakes. It is shaped by who God says I am.

reckless—love for me. I couldn't feel it. I didn't know how to see it. So I didn't receive it.

I might not have said this, but deep down, to me, "real" meant visible, tangible, gratifying, and within reach—all of which involve some ability to control the experience. God seemed to be none of these things. With God, you don't depend on a feeling but on faith. Sometimes, you have to wait to have some sense He is even there. How could I trust something—or someone—so impossible to grasp . . . to be *real*?

I finally saw the truth: I had never truly experienced a stable relationship. Not even once.

As a result of the trauma lens through which I viewed it all, I continued to seek love, attention, and affection through relationships—often sexual, including those outside my marriage.

The Memory of Pain

When we experience trauma, our bodies retain the memory of it.

Trauma triggers emotions, and emotions are energy. That energy doesn't just vanish. It has to go somewhere—inside our bodies.

The Body Keeps the Score, by Bessel van der Kolk, is a powerful book that explores this in great detail. It's worth the read. It explains how unprocessed emotional energy doesn't disappear but resurfaces—usually in destructive ways such as illness, emotional outbursts, or addictions.

For years, I medicated the pain from the sexual trauma that my brain, body, and heart were carrying through the **limerence** stage of relationships. This is the stage where you feel obsessive love and infatuation for a partner, thinking about them constantly and doing everything you can to get them to feel the same about you. I didn't know that's what I was doing. I didn't consciously recognize how much pain I was in.

How about you? It's vital that you look, because the pain will be there, whether or not you believe it is. It took me years of therapy and intensives to unpack it all and—surprise, surprise—it turns out everything wasn't fine. Things had never been fine.

Unprocessed emotional energy doesn't disappear but resurfaces— usually in destructive ways such as illness, emotional outbursts, or addictions.

If you're reading this and realizing that maybe things haven't been fine for you either, take heart. You're not alone, and facing the truth is not the end—it's the beginning of healing. It takes incredible courage to unpack the hard things you've carried for so long. But with God's help, the right support, and a willingness to keep going, freedom and wholeness are possible. What's uncovered can be restored. What's broken can be healed.

Keep going—you're worth it.

With God's help, the right support, and a willingness to keep going, freedom and wholeness are possible.

In my own case, the sexual abuse, the trauma, and the suppressed emotional energy eventually resurfaced as love and relationship addiction, destruction of my marriage and other relationships, and even cancer.

One therapy I highly recommend is called EMDR—eye movement desensitization and reprocessing. It helps reprogram incorrectly stored events and emotions. It's not quick, and it requires a significant amount of emotional work, but the healing it brings makes it worth the process. EMDR will be a unique process for each individual who moves through it.

Through EMDR, I revisited the events I had suppressed and repressed. From my healthy adult self, I was able to speak to the little girl who had been hurt. I let myself feel those emotions. I processed them. I reassured my inner child that she was safe now—that the hurting was over. I repeated this process for every major traumatic event I could recall, even the smaller ones. It was exhausting. But I came out healed. And I no longer live in shame.

One of the first books I read on this journey was *Facing Love Addiction*, by Pia Mellody. It gave me valuable insight into my choices, my actions, and the patterns in my relationships.

But what exactly is *love addiction*?

According to Mellody, a *love addict* is someone who is dependent on, enmeshed with, and compulsively focused on taking care of another person.[1] It might sound similar to codependency, but not all codependents are love addicts.

---

1. Pia Mellody, *Facing Love Addiction: Giving Yourself the Power to Change the Way* (HarperOne, 1992).

I had an obsessive quality about my relationships from early on. I poured an abnormal amount of time, attention, and energy into whomever I was with—often to the detriment of everything else in my life. I carried unrealistic expectations that they would love, affirm, and support me in just the right way. I wanted to be treasured and cared for, but I was terrified of being abandoned.

A love addict is someone who is dependent on, enmeshed with, and compulsively focused on taking care of another person.

So when I didn't receive what I longed for, I tried harder. I pushed and manipulated. And I constantly ended up disappointed because no one could ever live up to my insatiable need.

If you grew up in a household with an absent parent, a parent who was there but not very much, or a parent who was present but struggling with their own trauma, you may notice a pattern of similar challenges. Although I knew my dad loved me, his frequent work travel meant I didn't have a consistent male presence during my formative years. Mom's days were filled with work, managing a household, and raising three children, essentially by herself.

Dad was usually home only on the weekends. Dads play a role that only dads can. They speak to the child's identity without even using words. A father demonstrates what male affection should and shouldn't look like toward his daughter by the way he loves his wife and the way he loves her. When the father is absent or unhealthy, that example of love and affection isn't provided, leaving a child's developing sense of self lacking and open to be filled in ways it was never designed to be.

A father demonstrates what male affection should and shouldn't look like toward his daughter by the way he loves his wife and the way he loves her.

I was just a child when my trauma occurred. Why didn't anyone notice? At that age, I couldn't identify the signs of my own self-worth, much less recognize the effect those events had on me. Without guidance, there was no one to help me name it or address it. The silence around my pain allowed it to take root and quietly shape the way I viewed myself and my relationships.

All I knew was that I never wanted to be alone again. I craved companionship. I longed to be held, to be rescued from a pain I couldn't name. If I wasn't in a relationship, I didn't feel cared for, affirmed, safe—and I felt incomplete. That fear of abandonment and insecurity without a relationship drove me to jump from one to the next.

Living in a fantasy, I thought relationships rescued me from loneliness. I thought my "fix" was actually the answer, something that belonged in my life and brought fulfillment. Some people feel that way about alcohol, porn, food, work, or money.

Because of my past trauma, I longed to feel safe in the world—and in my fantasy, there was always *someone* who would come to my rescue. *Someone* who would love me, care for me, affirm me, and make me feel secure. With each new relationship, that fantasy would ignite. I'd experience a euphoric high that temporarily replaced my sense of abandonment—but I wasn't seeing the person in front of me.

I was seeing my fantasy. The image I had created in childhood.

True intimacy was therefore unachievable. I saw only what I wanted to see and tried to get the other person to do the things I had dreamed of. But it was never enough. And *that* is the mark of an addiction: It is never enough. It will never satisfy. It will always disappoint.

Ironically, the safer I felt, the needier I became.

Many love addicts are attracted to "love avoidants." I married one. A love addict chases affection from the love avoidant because finally earning that love creates an intense emotional high. The love avoidant, in turn, offers just enough attention to keep the pursuit alive, only to pull back again, trapping the love addict in a constant cycle of chasing what feels just out of reach. I wasn't aware of it at the time, of course, but once the limerence phase of our newlywed life faded, we settled into our routine—and distance.

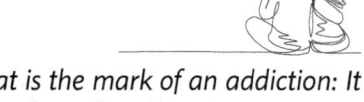

That is the mark of an addiction: It is never enough. It will never satisfy.

In those early years and throughout our marriage, I experienced abandonment over and over. As a love addict, that abandonment triggered a deep pain that I didn't know how to soothe. So I reached for my usual "medication."

After my confessions, Todd and I experienced brief moments of healing—but it was like putting a bandage on a broken arm. The deeper issues were never addressed. We didn't know then what we know now.

The only real shot at having a healthy relationship with my husband was not simply to confess and pray for forgiveness but to enter recovery so I could face my past hurts, habits, and hang-ups. It didn't really start with a book or an intensive.

I had to go vertical first. I had to get my relationship right with God.

James 1:22 (NIV) says, "Do not merely listen to the word, and so deceive yourselves. Do what it says." "Do what it says"—I longed for this more than anything. It wasn't enough to read devotionals, buy books and stack them on the shelf, meditate on His Word, or listen to podcasts. I had to start *doing*. This was, and still is, my sanctification process—and it won't ever be complete this side of heaven.

Withdrawal vs. Healing and Self-Care

For almost five years, I continued weekly personal counseling. The process meant confronting addiction, which didn't simply disappear. Going through withdrawal was a large part of my healing. Learning healthy responses to pain meant I had to sit with the deep aches I'd been numbing and ignoring for years through the cycle.

I yearned for an easy solution, like flipping a switch to turn it off. But it didn't work like that. I had to face my codependency and the ways I tried to cope with pain by acting out or seeking solace in external relationships.

Learning healthy responses to pain meant I had to sit with the deep aches I'd been numbing and ignoring for years.

Withdrawal can be brutal, as any addict will tell you. The symptoms alone were enough to keep drawing me back to the behavior—or person—I was trying to walk away from. Withdrawal isn't only physical but psychological. Physically, I was restless, headachy, and sleepless. Psychologically, the cravings intensified, bringing with them anxiety, irritability, and mood swings. I felt emptiness, heightened insecurity, and overwhelming vulnerability.

Cut off from the familiar chemical or emotional "reward," my brain fired distress signals nonstop, creating an almost unbearable state of unease. That mix of physical discomfort and emotional upheaval is what makes withdrawal so powerful and the "drug" so difficult to resist.

For me, most of it was emotional.

To stay "sober," I had to break ties and sever all communication with the other guy. I still had slips—old behaviors, poor choices—but over time, recovery got easier.

Learning to prioritize self-care—and to loosen my grip on others—was crucial. Self-care meant slowing down long enough to notice what my heart actually needed: sometimes rest, sometimes time alone, sometimes connection with someone I loved—even a hard conversation. Or it could be as simple as a bike ride or doing something creative.

I also had to revisit my past to address the events and places that had been holding me back. Setting healthy boundaries became essential. Thankfully, with God, you don't navigate these things alone; it's more like you allow yourself to process each thing as it arises. Your job isn't to "program" your life for healing but to notice when the cycle is calling you and choose something different. It wasn't just one but *all* of these actions that helped me finally begin moving forward.

It helped immensely when Todd stepped into the process with me. He didn't chase, try to control me, or shame me. Instead, he read books, attended groups, and engaged in his own therapy to understand the road I was walking.

Your job isn't to "program" your life for healing but to notice when the cycle is calling you and choose something different.

I was no longer alone, because we were navigating it together.

That made everything different—and better.

After we moved to Florida, Todd and I began marriage therapy again, both of us committed to the relationship and to improving our marriage.

But it wasn't easy. It was hard.

We had to be vulnerable and emotionally available in ways we'd otherwise learned to avoid or simply never knew. We made fresh commitments to prioritize our marriage—specifically our *connection*—even when it felt risky or uncomfortable.

We also attended a couple of three-day marriage intensives. Those were extremely helpful—even when we weren't in crisis mode.

We had to be vulnerable and emotionally available in ways we'd otherwise learned to avoid or simply never knew.

On my own, I completed two intensives focused on love addiction. I joined a Christian 12-step group for love addicts and diligently worked through the steps. I found an incredible Christian sponsor, who was immensely helpful in my recovery—holding me accountable, never judging, always there when I needed her. She taught me so much.

If you get nothing else from what I'm saying, get this: You need God. You need help. You need people—the right people who will stand with you, committed to your healing.

I also took antidepressants during that season—and they really helped. My mood swings were extreme, bouncing between highs to lows and everything in between. No one ever knew which version of me they were going to get. My family, friends, coworkers, husband, and kids were all at a loss.

But I've emerged from all this a new person. I no longer feel abandoned, shameful, or guilty.

It reminds me of a quote by an unknown author that someone sent me: "On the darkest days when I feel inadequate, unloved, and unworthy, I remember whose daughter I am, and I straighten my crown."

You need help. You need people—the right people who will stand with you, committed to your healing.

I am the daughter of the Most High King. I straighten my crown and remind myself of my worth.

The pain I've lived through and that I've caused has not been wasted. *There is purpose in the pain.* Out of it often comes our greatest ministry. I share all this with you to let you know this: You are not alone. You are worthy to be seen and heard. You are valuable, cherished, and deeply loved.

Straighten your crown. If I can do it, so can you.

Something to Think About

Most of us try to move on before we've truly healed. We say, *It's fine. I'm fine. Everything's fine.* But the body remembers what the heart buries. Unhealed trauma doesn't disappear—it hides.

Facing the past takes courage, but going back doesn't mean going backward. It means letting Jesus walk with you into the places you've tried to forget—so He can restore what was lost.

What have you buried that still needs healing?

Unhealed trauma doesn't disappear—it hides.

Where Am I in This?

1. Let's go deeper. What painful things have happened
    in your life that you've told yourself are "in the
    past"—even though you haven't allowed yourself to
    process what they left behind? Maybe some things
    are happening now, and you're already "stuffing."

    _____

    _____

    _____

    _____

2. Sometimes we're unaware of minimizing or
    dismissing pain. Is there anything that you've
    brushed off as "no big deal," told yourself didn't
    really affect you, or changed the subject when it
    came up? Write down whatever comes to mind.

    _____

    _____

    _____

    _____

3. When you start to feel restless, what do you reach
    for? What behaviors, substances, relationships, or

cycles have you used to numb or avoid emotional
pain?

_____

_____

_____

_____

4. How might you have built walls to protect yourself
    from being hurt again—like staying overly busy,
    keeping conversations surface level, or isolating?
    What might it look like to gently let one of those
    walls come down?

_____

_____

_____

_____

5. What would it look like to revisit your story with
    Jesus—not to relive the pain but to let Him show
    you what still needs healing? Maybe it's journaling,
    praying through a memory, asking someone to
    pray with you, or talking with a trusted counselor
    or pastor.

_____

_____

_____

_____

Hold These Close

Why do we have to "deal with" our trauma? Because trauma makes it difficult to engage in intimate relationships.

Unhealed trauma damages your ability to trust—both yourself and others. You may keep people at arm's length to avoid getting hurt. Trauma can shape how you think, what you do, and what you're drawn to—often pulling you back toward familiar patterns, even when those patterns are harmful.

My identity is not shaped by my mistakes.

Healing meant rebuilding a broken sense of self and self-worth. True identity isn't found in the past—it's found in being a son or daughter of the King.

When we experience trauma, our bodies retain the memory of it.

Trauma triggers emotions—and unprocessed emotions don't just disappear. That energy goes somewhere. It sinks into the body, resurfaces later, and can show up as anxiety, addiction, emotional reactivity, or even physical illness.

Learning healthy responses to pain meant I had to sit with the deep aches I'd been numbing and ignoring for years.

As recovery begins, new boundaries must be built. Withdrawal is a natural part of the process—it comes as you learn to be still, to feel what rises, and to replace old behaviors with new patterns. With tools, support, and consistent accountability, recovery gets easier.

There is purpose in the pain.

The pain we live through—and even the pain we've caused—doesn't have to be wasted. Pain is a signal. It tells us when something needs healing. It fills our hearts with compassion for others who hurt. Often, the same pain that once brought the most shame turns into our most powerful ministry.

As recovery begins, new boundaries must be built.

I am the daughter of the Most High King. I straighten my crown and remind myself of my worth.

When you feel unloved, unworthy, or not enough, it's easy to fall back into old patterns just to ease the ache. But the invitation of healing is to remember who you are. And the work is to rebuild a sense of self and self-worth—because Jesus Christ defines what you're worth.

Word for the Journey

Below, select the verse that stands out to you most. Read it slowly. Let it linger in your heart. As you hold onto the

words, let them shape your thoughts. Whether you repeat the verse out loud, ponder it in silence, or explore it more deeply through further study, stay open to the Holy Spirit's leading.

Often, the same pain that once brought the most shame turns into our most powerful ministry.

"He heals the heartbroken and
bandages their wounds."
—Psalm 147:3 MSG

"Forget the former things; do not dwell on the past.
See, I am doing a new thing! Now it springs up;
do you not perceive it?"
—Isaiah 43:18–19 NIV

"The LORD is close to the brokenhearted; he
rescues those whose spirits are crushed."
—Psalm 34:18 NLT

"There is therefore now no condemnation for those
who are in Christ Jesus."
—Romans 8:1 ESV

"Therefore, if anyone is in Christ, he is a new
creation; the old has passed away, and see,
the new has come!"
—2 Corinthians 5:17 CSB

"Do not merely listen to the word, and so deceive
yourselves. Do what it says."
—James 1:22 NIV

Prayer for the Road

Father,

*You see it all—every memory, every
moment, every ache I've tried to bury.*

*You know where I've minimized my pain
just to survive, where I've lost my voice, and
where shame has caused me harm.*

*Remind me often of what Psalm 139:23–24 (TPT)
says: "Examine me through and through; find
out everything that may be hidden within me. . . .
See if there is any path of pain I'm walking on,
and lead me back to your glorious, everlasting
way—the path that brings me back to you."*

*I invite You into the places I've hidden. Help me
name what still hurts and trust that You'll meet
me there with grace and mercy, not condemnation.*

*Teach me to rebuild what trauma tried to destroy.
Let Your love redefine my worth and help me
remember who I am: a child of the King. I want
to walk in truth, healing, and freedom. And I
trust You to lead me every step of the way.*

In Jesus's name, I pray. Amen.

Grace in the Gray II

No Condemnation

When Amy and I separated, God began peeling me back, layer by layer. In those first weeks, I started writing down all the things I'd done wrong to her. The list was long—and it kept growing. Every time I prayed, God showed me more. Soon I was buried under it. *What a horrible person I've been. No wonder she left.*

I felt condemned.

Then one morning, God reminded me of a verse I'd sung countless times as a worship leader: "There is now no condemnation for those who are in Christ Jesus" (Rom. 8:1 NIV). I knew the words, but until that moment, I hadn't lived them.

Instead of condemnation, God offered me grace. He showed me Proverbs 19:11 (NIV): "It is to one's glory to overlook an offense." Everything in me cried out for justice—for others to pay when they hurt me. But what about all the times I sinned against Him? I repeat the same failures over and over, and still He gives me grace. If not for that grace, I'd be eternally separated from Him.

That realization changed everything. For years, I'd been harder on myself than on anyone else, yet I was also quick to point out faults in others. God was teaching me a new way: to receive His grace deeply enough that I could begin to extend it to others.

Grace doesn't deny sin. It doesn't ignore wrong. But it reminds us that God doesn't condemn us—He forgives, restores, and invites us to be free as we walk forward.

Accelerator

Read and meditate on these verses on grace:

- Titus 2:11–12

- 2 Corinthians 12:9

- Romans 5:20–21

- Hebrews 4:16

As you read, consider:

- What's the theme of each verse?

- What does it teach you about grace?

- What have you learned about grace across all four verses?

- How would you define *grace* in your own words?

- Pray to God, *Help me understand grace more deeply.*

- Ask God, *What expression of Your grace do I most need to receive and live out right now?*

Chapter 15

The Offense of Forgiveness

THIS DISCUSSION MAY OFFEND YOU. Most people consider infidelity to be "grounds" for divorce. When someone passes up that opportunity and instead chooses forgiveness, it can offend those who would either rather not forgive or who had the chance and went for the divorce.

Forgiveness is not for the faint of heart. If you're new to it—really new to it—it feels impossible. Not just hard—*impossible.* Forgiveness can feel like you're letting the other person off the hook—like you're handing them a permission slip to hurt you again and again.

Here's the truth: Forgiveness is not for *them.* It never was. Forgiveness is for *you.* For *us.* It's the only way out of the pain. That's why God commands it—not to crush us but to set us free. He knew that if we didn't forgive, we'd be eaten up by bitterness and resentment.

Forgiveness is not for them. It never was. Forgiveness is for you.

Most of us find it difficult to forgive—it takes courage. It requires us to make a conscious choice to stop allowing past hurts to continue wounding us and start letting them go. It requires that we take charge and address the problem instead of defending it, ignoring it, or pretending it doesn't matter. For this reason, forgiveness is an *offensive* move.

In sports, *offense* is the strategy teams use to score points and defeat their opponents. In life, an *offensive move*, like forgiving someone, is a strategy we can use to defeat the hold that lingering bitterness and resentment from past hurts have on us. When we forgive others, we become more like Jesus.

We've seen what happens when people don't forgive. We've seen it in our marriage. We've seen it in the couples who come through our small groups. Bitterness doesn't just live quietly in the background—it *consumes*. It poisons. And eventually, it isolates.

Bitterness doesn't just live quietly in the background—it consumes.

God knew this. That's why He gave us a model in Jesus. "But God shows his love for us in that while we were still sinners, Christ died for us" (Rom. 5:8 ESV).

Jesus died for me while I was still betraying Him; while I was looking to my work, money, and financial stability for comfort; while I was emotionally unavailable, checked out, angry, and proud.

He died for Amy while she was tangled in a web of affairs, longing for someone else, and nearly walking away from our family.

Let me put it in marriage terms: We've all committed "adultery" against the One who married Himself to us forever.

He died for all of us while we shacked up with the neighbor next door; while we were scrolling the internet for pornography; and while we were ignoring Him—putting our friends, work, career, beauty, popularity, or success ahead of Him. He died for us while we were treating Him like Sunday-night leftovers—or worse, like dirt.

Jesus set the example.

He demonstrated that, no matter how egregious our sins, He forgives us completely and loves us enough to give His life for us.

The question was—could I love Amy like that? Could I forgive like that? Would I lay down my life like that—for someone who had just trampled my heart?

Spoiler alert: *I didn't want to.*

There was nothing in me that *felt* like forgiving. I didn't wake up one day thinking, *You know what? I should just let all this go like it never happened.* But Jesus kept bringing me back to the cross and to what He did for me—not just two thousand years ago but what He does every time I mess up.

Many times, I turned my back on Him in pride, fear, or selfishness. Still, He stretched out His arms and said, "I love you this much." His love isn't based on my behavior, because it's covenant love, and covenant love is not reactionary.

And that wrecked me.

When I think about what He's done for me, it really puts me in my place. It forces me to come back to my vows. *Did I really mean them? Or was I just reciting words I didn't understand?*

When I think about what He's done for me, it really puts me in my place. How could I expect to be forgiven but refuse to forgive?

"For better or for worse."
"In sickness and in health."
"Till death do us part."

How could I expect to be forgiven but refuse to forgive? Am I the exception to the rule? Do I get a pass because what happened to me is *just that bad*?

No. I don't think so.

Remember: Forgiveness is not for the offender; it's for the offended. It's not for the betrayer; it's for the betrayed. That's what God was trying to teach me.

He wasn't minimizing my pain; He was rescuing me from it.

That rescue started with humility. I stopped thinking about what was fair or what I was owed. I started thinking less of myself—and more of the other person. I chose to let go instead of constantly rehashing what Amy had done. I made a decision to *look the other way.*

Proverbs 19:11 (NIV) says, "It is to one's glory to overlook an offense." Does that verse irritate you? What does it even mean to "overlook an offense?" Just pretend it didn't happen?

That's not what it's saying. "Overlooking" is not pretending or excusing; it's refusing to let someone else's sin control your spirit. It's choosing peace over pain, honor over anger, glory over vengeance.

We want to believe we have the right to make the person who hurt us *pay*. We want justice—or revenge. We want to hold their sin over their heads. We want them to suffer the way we did.

But that's not forgiveness.

The idea of the "Golden Rule" might take you back to grade school, but it still rings true. Jesus Himself said, "In everything, therefore, treat people the same way you want them to treat you" (Matt. 7:12 NASB).

Would you want every person you've ever hurt or wronged—knowingly or unknowingly—to come after you with the full force of vengeance, seeking to cause you the pain you caused them?

Forgiveness doesn't say, "You didn't hurt me." It admits, "You did hurt me. But I won't let your sin become my prison."

Forgiveness is not about what *they* deserve. It's about what God offers *us*. Freedom. Peace. Healing.

Forgiveness is not about what they *deserve. It's about what God offers us. Freedom. Peace. Healing.*

I wanted those things more than I wanted to be right.

Surrendering Again—and Again

Forgiveness is the first step toward letting go. It's the first step of freedom. It's the only path to peace.

That might sound backward. Peace should come from *justice*, from being *heard*, from *getting closure* . . . right? That's rarely how it works in God's kingdom.

"'For my thoughts are not your thoughts, neither are your ways my ways,' declares the LORD. 'As the heavens are higher than the earth, so are my ways higher than your ways and my thoughts than your thoughts'" (Isa. 55:8–9 NIV).

His ways stretch us. They humble us. But they always lead to life. That's what I had to learn: After an offense, the way forward is almost always the opposite of what I *feel* like doing.

Truly forgiving is not a one-and-done event. You don't say it once and it's over. We're not wired that way. There's a moment when you decide to forgive, and that's a good start. You pray. You say the words—maybe out loud, maybe in front of others. But that moment is only the beginning. The pain doesn't vanish just because you prayed it off. Triggers still come.

Truly forgiving is not a one-and-done event.

A word, a tone, a memory, a dream—something random can knock the breath out of you when you least expect it. And when it does, you might feel like a failure. *I thought I forgave! Why is this still bothering me?* I had to come to terms with the fact that forgiveness is a process. It is a repeated, intentional, ongoing surrender.

Not because you're weak, but because you're human.

Even after reconciling, Amy and I had to forgive each other again and again—not necessarily because we were still hurting each other but because the old hurt kept resurfacing. Some days, it came in waves. Other days, it was a low ache in the background. Either way, we had to let it go as many times as it came up—until, little by little, the waves would come less and less often.

As Lysa TerKeurst explains in her book *Forgiving What You Can't Forget*, forgiveness is both a decision and a process.[1] That insight gave me so much freedom, because when the pain came back, I no longer felt like a failure or that I would always be stuck with it. I learned to see each recurrence as an opportunity to forgive again—one more layer, one more healing. And when I couldn't do it on my own, I turned to the only One who could. I asked the Holy Spirit to help me forgive the way He does. The power of Jesus's sacrifice covers the gap between what I *want* to do and what I *can* do. He always meets me there.

Forgiveness is an ongoing process because we are human and, unfortunately, we never really forget. Something will trigger us again in the future, and when it does, we have to make the decision to forgive *again*. In 2 Corinthians 10:5 (NIV), Paul said, "We demolish arguments and every pretension that sets itself up against the knowledge of God, and we take captive every thought to make it obedient to Christ."

When I couldn't do it on my own, I turned to the only One who could. I asked the Holy Spirit to help me forgive the way He does.

---

1. Lysa TerKeurst, *Forgiving What You Can't Forget: Discover How to Move On, Make Peace with Painful Memories, and Create a Life That's Beautiful Again* (Thomas Nelson, 2020).

In this Scripture, Paul is trying to teach us to bring our thoughts under the authority of Christ. The concept of "taking every thought captive" conveys the action of actively seizing and controlling our thoughts. And, of course, this is not just a one-time choice; it's ongoing.

In many cases, it's something we have to do minute by minute. The more we do it, the better we get at it. It just like going to the gym. We can't just instantly bench three hundred pounds; we have to work our way up. It's the same with taking every thought captive: The more we take those thoughts captive and give them to Jesus, the easier it gets.

We could never do this on our own. It's not within our human capacity apart from God to forgive offenses this deep. And that's the beauty of grace. God doesn't ask us to forgive from our own strength. He gives us *His*. *It's through Him that I've been given a renewed mind, a softened heart, and a new perspective on Amy*—not as the woman who betrayed me but as the woman God entrusted to me.

Just as with bitterness, if we let unforgiveness take hold, it won't just sit quietly; it will consume us.

And with His help, I can let it go. I can move forward. I can forgive . . . and keep forgiving.

I've lived this many times over. Just as with bitterness, if we let unforgiveness take hold, it won't just sit quietly; it will consume us. *The tighter we cling to the offenses, wrongs, betrayals, and abandonments, the more miserable we become.*

Do I still get triggered? Absolutely.

Sometimes it's a memory. Sometimes it's a dream. Sometimes I wake up in a fog, unsure of what's real, and I wonder, *Will I ever be free from this?* But here's the answer I come back to every time: "Yes, I can, and I will—with Jesus's help."

It always takes longer than I want, and that's okay. This goes even beyond marriage. This is sanctification. It's how God grows our character, makes us the new creation we are in Christ, teaches us His heart, and draws us close. And if it brings me closer to Him? Then bring it on!

The Next Level

People hear "next level" and think about a financial upgrade or a badge of achievement. The real next level is this: learning to love. It's marriage through thick and thin, learning to care for someone else and see them as Christ sees them.

Marriage has been one of the hardest things I've ever done, but it's also been the most spiritually refining. It's reshaped how I see life, love, and myself. It's maturity. It's finding out what trust in God really means. It's walking through fire and knowing you're still held. It's having awful things happen to you and still believing you're okay because you're in covenant with the God who takes His cheek to your cheek and holds you, as a loving Father.

Marriage has been one of the hardest things I've ever done, but it's also been the most spiritually refining.

"I led them with cords of human kindness, with ties of love. To them I was like one who lifts a little child to the cheek, and I bent down to feed them" (Hosea 11:4 NIV).

That's where I want to live. Held. Fed. Safe. Not because life didn't hurt me—but because grace wouldn't leave me in the pain.

Only when we truly let go, when we truly forgive, will we begin to experience the peace that passes all understanding. Only then will we step into the freedom God has for us. We're created and called to love like God loves, and He loves us for who we are, not for what we do or don't do. No amount of good behavior or right words could add to or subtract from His love because His love isn't based on our performance; it's based on who He is. Thank God, because if it were any different, I'd fail every time.

Only when we truly let go, when we truly forgive, will we begin to experience the peace that passes all understanding.

Maybe you're thinking, *That all sounds nice—but I can't do it. You don't understand. My situation is different. What my spouse did is inexcusable.* I hear you. I thought all those things. I've felt that kind of pain—the kind that takes your breath away and makes you want to walk out for good. I mean, how many affairs should one person have to forgive? One was more than enough, but after a while, it just seemed ridiculous.

Yet . . . Jesus's words kept ringing in my spirit: "Then Peter came to Jesus and asked, 'Lord, how many times shall I forgive my brother or sister who sins against me? Up to seven times?' Jesus answered, 'I tell you, not seven times, but seventy-seven times'" (Matt. 18:21–22 NIV).

It sounds crazy, but then again, how many times do I want Jesus to forgive *me*? I urge you to really think about that.

So how do you forgive when you don't think you can? There are plenty of books out there that walk through this topic in great depth—but I'll share what God taught me personally.

Forgiveness is not for the other person; it's for you. It doesn't let them off the hook. It doesn't condone what they did. It doesn't pretend the offense never happened. And it definitely doesn't pretend you weren't hurt.

I thought forgiving meant I had to act like it never happened or, worse, open the door for it to happen again. But none of these things are true.

Real forgiveness isn't denial; it's *release*. Denial is thinking we can control what other people do. Actually, the moment we step into control, it stops being a relationship and becomes manipulation.

> *Real forgiveness isn't denial; it's release. I started valuing our relationship more than the illusion of safety.*

That realization shifted everything for me. I stopped trying to control Amy's decisions. I started valuing our relationship more than the illusion of safety.

After being hurt so deeply, I sometimes wondered if I'd survive. It was only by the power of the Holy Spirit that I could let go, only by God's help that I could move forward, and only by His grace that I could forgive—as many times as the wounds tried to rise again.

It hasn't been easy, but it has been worth it.

This is next-level maturity. Not financial success. Not spiritual showmanship. Next level is learning to see through pain with the eyes of Christ, and the only way to it is forgiveness.

Something to Think About

We often think forgiveness is for the other person. It feels unjust to let someone "off the hook"—especially when the pain they caused still lingers. But what if forgiveness isn't letting them off the hook . . . but taking yourself off theirs?

Forgiveness isn't a one-time event—it's a repeated surrender. And it's not about pretending nothing happened; it's about refusing to let someone else's sin have the final word over your spirit.

Forgiveness isn't a one-time event—it's a repeated surrender.

Jesus didn't just model forgiveness; He gave us the power to walk in it.

What would change if you saw forgiveness not as weakness—but as freedom?

Think of someone who hurt you. What's one small step you could take today to release that pain and move toward freedom?

Where Am I in This?

1. Have you ever felt that forgiving someone meant excusing what they did? How has that belief shaped your ability to move forward?

    _____

    _____

    _____

    _____

2. Have you ever said, "I could never forgive them for that"? How does it feel in your body when you think or say those words?

    _____

    _____

    _____

    _____

3. When pain resurfaces—through a memory, a trigger, or a feeling of injustice—what's your first response?

    _____

    _____

_____

_____

4. You may have heard the saying "Let go and let God."
   What does "letting go" mean to you—and what
   might it look like to let God into that place?

_____

_____

_____

_____

5. Have you ever asked the Holy Spirit to help you
   forgive where you feel stuck or numb? What might
   it look like to do that today?

_____

_____

_____

_____

6. Think of a person who has hurt or offended you. How does Jesus see him or her? Write down anything He shows you.

_____

_____

_____

_____

Hold These Close

Forgiveness is not for them. It never was. Forgiveness is for you.

Holding on to someone else's sin doesn't protect your heart—it burdens it. Forgiveness brings freedom. It's not erasure or excusing—it's detoxing the poison. The gift of forgiveness is often more for the wounded than for the one who wounded.

Forgiveness is a process. It is a repeated, intentional, ongoing surrender.

It's not weakness to feel pain after deciding to forgive. Healing happens in layers, and surrender is often required more than once. When old wounds get triggered, it's not a sign of failure—it's a fresh

When old wounds get triggered, it's not a sign of failure—it's a fresh opportunity to let go again.

opportunity to let go again. Forgiveness happens one surrender at a time.

The tighter we cling to the offenses, wrongs, betrayals, and abandonments, the more miserable we become.

If you're holding a cactus and it's piercing your skin, is it better to get angry and grip it tighter—or to let it go? Unforgiveness grips the cactus. It's not just painful—it's self inflicted. The release might feel costly, but it's also where peace begins.

He wasn't minimizing my pain; He was rescuing me from it.

God doesn't ask us to forgive so the pain will be ignored; He invites us to forgive so the prison of bitterness can be dismantled. His heart isn't indifferent—it's fiercely committed to justice and to restoring what was broken. Every act of forgiveness is a step of trust in His ability to make things right.

It's through Him that I've been given a renewed mind, a softened heart, and a new perspective on Amy.

True forgiveness is not something we conjure up—it's something we receive and pass on. God provides the strength we don't have, the grace we didn't think we could offer, and the vision to see someone differently. A renewed mind leads to a softened heart—and that's where freedom begins.

A renewed mind leads to a softened heart—and that's where freedom begins.

Word for the Journey

Below, select the verse that stands out to you most. Read it slowly. Let it linger in your heart. As you hold onto the words, let them shape your thoughts. Whether you repeat the verse out loud, ponder it in silence, or explore it more deeply through further study, stay open to the Holy Spirit's leading.

"But God shows his love for us in that while we were still sinners, Christ died for us."
—Romans 5:8 ESV

"A person's wisdom yields patience; it is to one's glory to overlook an offense."
—Proverbs 19:11 NIV

"Get rid of all bitterness, rage, anger, harsh words, and slander. . . . Instead, be kind to each other, tenderhearted, forgiving one another, just as God through Christ has forgiven you."
—Ephesians 4:31–32 NLT

"For if you forgive other people when they sin against you, your heavenly Father will also forgive you."
—Matthew 6:14 NIV

"Bear with each other and forgive one another. . . . Forgive as the Lord forgave you."
—Colossians 3:13 NIV

Prayer for the Road

Father,

You see the places in my heart where I've been holding on. You know the pain I've carried, the offense I've rehearsed, and the justice I've wanted.

Help me release what I've been gripping so tightly. Help me forgive—not because they deserve it but because You've forgiven me. Show me where bitterness has taken root, and gently pull it up by Your Spirit. I don't want to be stuck in the past. I want to move forward—free, clean, and whole. Teach me to forgive again . . . and again . . . and again. Thank You that I don't have to do it alone. You are the One who strengthens me, heals me, and teaches me how to love like You.

In Jesus's name I pray. Amen.

Chapter 16

What We'd Do Differently

Before we got married, I imagined life with Amy: Just the two of us—together all the time, snuggling on the couch, going on vacations, holding hands while walking our dogs in the park, and making love in the most wild and special places. I pictured us conquering the world together, gazing into each other's eyes. She would think I was the greatest thing in the world and hang on my every word, just like when we were dating.

Then we had kids—and suddenly everything changed.

I felt like I disappeared. Like I was no longer important. I felt used, overlooked, and unnecessary. Babies were made—my contribution to this whole thing called marriage was done and over. The best I could do for everyone was get out of the way.

Amy could handle the kids—I wasn't needed in that depart-ment, or so I thought. And to

I saw no other way to add value but to bring home the almighty dollar.

be honest, I felt helpless. She was home caring for all three boys, running errands, keeping the house. Meanwhile, I felt sidelined. Benched. Worse, I felt like the water boy—but bringing a paycheck instead of water. Raised in a conservative Christian home, I'd learned early that providing was my highest God-given role. I saw no other way to add value but to bring home the almighty dollar.

Unfortunately, our society has taught us that the standard measure of a man is what he provides for his family. Bringing home the bacon became the ultimate metric for a good husband. I'm not saying providing isn't important; it is. But over the years, I've learned it doesn't rank number one. Not even close.

But at the time, I didn't know what to do, and I had no one to talk to. My parents were gone. No older, wiser men noticed how I was doing or spoke into my life. So I did the only thing I knew how to: I worked. Yeah, I could fix cars, mow the grass, and kill the bugs, but beyond that, I built businesses and generated cash. That's what I was good for.

Men want to feel important to their wives. We want respect. But I felt like a third wheel at home. I couldn't help with the kids. I couldn't stop them from crying or get them to go to sleep. With my parents gone, I didn't know who I could ask for help. So I looked for validation in my career, believing that if I worked hard there, people would want me. They'd look to me for advice. They'd see me as someone of value. I wanted to feel like I mattered.

Men want to feel important to their wives. We want respect. But I felt like a third wheel at home.

So I sought to make money and rise to the top.

That led to one of the biggest mistakes of my life: My wife was no longer number one, no longer second only to God. My kids weren't number two. Instead, work and career filled every slot. My identity was wrapped up in my job—in who society and my upbringing said I was, not in who God said I was.

Connection

Amy and I became managers of the household rather than lovers and companions.

Amy and I became managers of the household rather than lovers and companions.

Slowly, we drifted apart, connecting less and less, doing little more than managing day-to-day tasks together. While I was seeking fulfillment in my work, Amy was searching for connection, first with me and then wherever she could find it—with the kids, friends, other family members, and even coworkers. Connection and intimacy between us had gone out the window. At the time, I didn't even know "connection" was a thing.

On the surface, Amy said things like, "I don't want money or stuff; I just want you." But I didn't believe her. She used to say, "I'll go anywhere with you," but I didn't believe that either. She never said it outright, but the story I told myself was that she'd go anywhere with me—as long as I had all the "things" and all the money. So I put my nose to the grindstone and worked harder. In my mind, I was meeting all the family's financial wants, desires, and needs—I was doing what I was supposed to be doing.

I was wrong. God didn't create me just to work and make money for my family. He created me to be with them—to love them, connect with them, be present with them, and lead them. Providing isn't the same as leading. Providing alone is not enough.

It took me more than twenty-five years to finally get this. Sure, I met Amy's and the kids' financial needs, but I missed their most important needs—the connection and intimacy they longed to have with me.

I met Amy's and the kids' financial needs, but I missed their most important needs—the connection and intimacy they longed to have with me.

Connection does not equal providing. In fact, the two are not related at all. *Connection* involves truly listening and showing empathy—something I didn't do.

Amy would often say, "I wish you would come into my world." What did that even mean? I thought I was already in her world.

She was talking about *connection*. She wanted me to listen as she talked about her day, without trying to fix her problems. She wanted me to put myself in her shoes, understand all she was going through, and show that I empathized with her. It meant *telling* her I loved her, not just thinking it. It meant telling her she was beautiful every time the thought crossed my mind.

I wasn't good at these things. Yes, I thought them, but I didn't say them out loud—and boy, was that a mistake. It's a common problem men face: We figure that thinking counts, but it doesn't. If we don't say it—if we don't verbalize it so our wives can hear it—it doesn't count.

Looking back, it's silly to think otherwise. It's like saying, "I won the lottery—because I thought about playing, even though I never bought a ticket." You can't win if you don't play.

The same was true in my marriage. It didn't count if I didn't say it. Amy is not a mind reader! Neither am I. No one is.

It's a common problem men face: We figure that thinking counts, but it doesn't.

For my kids, *connection* meant seeing their accomplishments and praising them. It meant being there to watch them reach their next goal and encouraging them when they thought they couldn't. It meant seeing them at their best and letting them know I noticed. It meant hanging out and sharing important moments—watching airplane shows on TV, enjoying their favorite movies with them, or joining them as they played with toys.

I failed at all these things. It's easy to say that from where I am in life now, but I never would've admitted it back in those days. I thought I was doing the right things, and no one could've told me otherwise.

My identity is found in Jesus.

What I Would Do Differently

If I knew then what I know now, what would I have done differently? What have I learned?

My self-worth is not found in my work, my job, or my career. It's not based on what others think of me. I don't need their respect. My identity is found in Jesus.

During our separation, I learned that you don't realize God is all you need until God is all you have. That was exactly my experience. Now I look to God to sustain and fulfill me—not my wife, my kids, my job, or anyone else. I used to seek from others what only God can provide.

So if I could do it all over again, here's what I would do: First, I would let God meet all my needs by spending more time with Him—reading His Word, worshiping Him, and seeking Him in my everyday life. I would let Him hold me to His cheek, just as He said in Hosea: "That I lifted

All those years I'd thought I was in control were nothing but an illusion. God is in control.

him, like a baby, to my cheek, that I bent down to feed him" (Hosea 11:4 MSG).

I'd realize how fruitless the pursuit of respect, recognition, and money truly is. I'd put far less effort into my career and devote maximum effort to my relationship with God, my wife, and my kids.

I'd encourage Amy—without dictating—to prioritize our relationship above the kids.

I'd remember always my identity as a son, covered and cared for by a trustworthy Father, and I'd lead my family by setting the example of putting Him first in everything.

On flights, we're taught to secure our own oxygen masks first to avoid passing out and being unable to help others. In marriage, we need to put our relationship first—before kids, careers, finances, or anything else that tries to come between us, and second only to our vertical relationship with God.

Feelings

As men, we try to control our world—to dodge pain, boost output, and grow our income. But during my separation from Amy, God showed me that all those years I'd thought I was in control were nothing but an illusion. God is in control. Period. And now, at this point in my life, I wouldn't want it any other way.

There are certain things I wish I could go back and tell my younger self—armed with what I know now. I would have learned how to identify what I was actually feeling—not just the usual happy, mad, or sad, because that doesn't cut it. I would have used my feelings wheel to dig deeper and get to the root of my emotions. I would have learned to communicate my actual feelings to my wife and, later, to my children. I would have learned to be vulnerable with them. I would have gotten over myself—and much earlier.

Work is no substitute for relationships—especially with our spouses and kids. It's a common mistake, born from a deep need in many men. We use work to avoid facing relationship problems directly, to excuse ourselves from getting involved. It feels easier and, in our minds, more rewarding, to throw ourselves into work than to face the challenges at home.

In hindsight, I can unequivocally say that the reward is far greater when we invest time in our relationships over a job or career that won't last.

In hindsight, I can unequivocally say that the reward is far greater when we invest time in our relationships over a job or career that won't last. Respect from my wife and kids is immeasurably more rewarding than any short-lived respect at work.

Back then, I just didn't know how to get it from my family. How could I command respect when I didn't give connection?

When I'm on my deathbed, my work and career will not be there for me. I can only hope to have my wife and children by my side. I barely put my mom ahead of my work when I got the call that she was dying. Glory to God, He got my attention and pulled me away from my music studio when my mom was going downhill. Had God not intervened, I wouldn't have been there to say goodbye. That's not something I want to repeat.

Today, I make an effort to connect with Amy and my kids—not only figuring out my true feelings but also sharing them.

Am I perfect? No—but I'm on a short leash with God, and I like it. When I stray from the path, I allow God to get my attention and yank me back.

I wish I had done that back then.

Something to Think About

Sometimes the damage in a relationship doesn't come from a single blowup or event but from the slow drift of disconnection.

It's easy to assume that showing up physically or paying the bills is enough. But as I shared, *"While I was seeking fulfillment in my work, Amy was searching for connection."*

When one spouse is emotionally checked out, the other often feels unseen, unimportant, or alone. Whether you've been the one leaning away or the one left waiting, this chapter reminds us: Being present matters.

What might it look like to reengage with your spouse—not just with your time but with your heart, your soul, and your whole being?

Where Am I in This?

1. Have you ever felt unseen or overlooked in your marriage—even though you were trying your best to contribute? Describe.

   _____

   _____

   _____

   _____

2. Your spouse may or may not be fully aware of how you feel—or may have only heard glimpses in moments of conflict or heightened emotion. Take a moment to jot down a few words or sentences that describe how you've felt about being overlooked, disrespected, or misunderstood. What would it sound like to express that with honesty, vulnerability, and grace?

   _____

_____

_____

_____

3. Is it possible your spouse just doesn't know how to
    show you that they sees and appreciate you? What
    are some specific things you could ask for—simple
    gestures or words—that would help you feel more
    connected and valued? How can you communicate
    those to your spouse?

    _____

    _____

    _____

    _____

4. Even when things are hard, a small word of encour-
    agement can soften the atmosphere and begin to
    melt the ice. What are some things you genuinely
    appreciate about your spouse? Write down a few
    things they do well—whether it's making people
    laugh, handling logistics, offering spiritual insight,
    keeping the kids on track, or just making an excel-
    lent cup of coffee. Speaking those things out loud
    might mean more than you think.

    _____

_____

_____

_____

Hold These Close

While I was seeking fulfillment in my work, Amy was searching for connection.

When emotional needs go unmet, it's easy for couples to drift in different directions. One may pour into work or parenting, while the other longs to feel chosen and known. Both are trying—but often in different ways. Reconnection begins when we recognize not just what we've given but what we've missed.

Amy and I became managers of the household rather than lovers and companions.

Many marriages slowly slide into survival mode. The daily grind takes over, and intimacy fades—not from crisis but from neglect. Remembering how it started—and what made you feel like a team—can help reignite connection where routine has taken over.

Providing isn't the same as leading.

Providing may be honored, but it was never meant to be the whole story. Emotional presence, spiritual leadership, and shared vulnerability matter just as much or more. True connection isn't built by contribution alone but by care, attentiveness, and intentional love.

You can't win if you don't play. The same is true in marriage. It doesn't count if you think it or feel it—you have to say it.

Love can't live on assumptions. Disengagement may feel safer than risking rejection—but intimacy requires expression. Presence rebuilds trust, and connection grows where words are spoken, not just felt.

Presence rebuilds trust, and connection grows where words are spoken, not just felt.

Our identity is found in Jesus.

Self-worth is not found in work, a job, or a career. It's not based on what others think. Real identity doesn't come from output, income, or reputation. Our identity comes first and foremost from Christ! It also comes from being known and loved apart from performance. No amount of external success can take the place of internal peace and relational connection.

Word for the Journey

Select the verse below that stands out to you most. Read it slowly. Let it linger in your heart. As you hold onto the words, let them shape your thoughts. Whether you repeat the verse out loud, ponder it in silence, or explore it more deeply through further study, stay open to the Holy Spirit's leading.

*"Husbands, love your wives, just as Christ loved
the church and gave himself up for her."*
—*Ephesians 5:25 NIV*

"You cannot serve both God and money."
—*Matthew 6:24 NIV*

*"If it is possible, as far as it depends on you,
live at peace with everyone."*
—*Romans 12:18 NIV*

*"Gracious words are a honeycomb, sweet to the
soul and healing to the bones."*
—*Proverbs 16:24 NIV*

*"However, let each one of you love his wife as
himself, and let the wife see that she
respects her husband."*
—*Ephesians 5:33 ESV*

*"Marriage is the beautiful design of the Almighty, a
great mystery of Christ and his church. So every
married man should be gracious to his wife just
as he is gracious to himself. And every wife should
be tenderly devoted to her husband."*
—*Ephesians 5:32–33 TPT*

Prayer for the Road

Father,

*Thank You for Your covenant with us—Your
Church, Your Bride—and that You are teaching
me not only how to love but how to be loved.*

*You see every part of me: the places where
I've felt invisible and the places where I've
chosen distance over connection. You know
where I've been trying, where I've grown
tired, and where I've simply missed it.*

*Thank You that You're not asking for
perfection—You're asking for presence.*

*Teach me to love well—not just through duty or
in hopes of getting what I want but with Your
kind of love. Help me see others the way You
see them. Help me notice—and appreciate—
the ways my spouse is trying, even when it
doesn't come out right. And if I've been the one
waiting, help me speak my needs with grace, not
resentment. Restore what's grown cold. Soften
what's become harsh. Reignite what's been
quenched. Remind me often that this marriage
is meant to reflect something holy—and that
with You, it's never too late to begin again.*

In Jesus's name I pray. Amen.

Chapter 17

Grief

G RIEF IS TYPICALLY UNDERSTOOD AS a natural emotional response to loss, marked by deep sadness and sorrow. No one steps into life expecting to be hit with grief. It often catches us off guard. In many cases, it's also a form of emotional trauma. As we've discussed, our brains perceive trauma as a threat and activate the body's survival response—fight, flight, or freeze.

Once that involuntary response fades, we tend to move through what are commonly known as the five stages of grief. They aren't necessarily linear—we may go back and forth among them.

Elizabeth Kübler-Ross's book *On Death and Dying* explores these stages in depth. Here's an overview:

1. The first stage is *denial*. In this stage, we struggle to accept the reality of the loss. We may feel shock, disbelief, or emotional numbness.

2. Next comes *anger*. We might get mad at God, the person we lost, or ourselves for not being able to prevent the loss.

3. Then comes *bargaining*, where we imagine ways to "undo" the loss—making internal deals or replaying scenarios in our minds.

4. The fourth stage is *depression*, when the weight of the loss settles in. Sadness, loneliness, and hope-lessness can take hold.

5. Finally, we come to *acceptance*. This doesn't mean forgetting—it means learning to live with the loss. We embrace the reality of what has occurred and accept its finality. We find our way forward.[1]

Acceptance is the goal—coming to trust that God is in control. By this stage, we believe all things work together for the good of those who are in Christ. We know God's got us, and we can find peace even in the pain.

When the Floor Dropped Out

I remember the day my dad died like it was yesterday. It wasn't the first time I'd experienced grief like that. I'd already lost a great-grandparent, two grandparents, an aunt who

1. Elizabeth Kübler-Ross, *On Death and Dying: What the Dying Have to Teach Doctors, Nurses, Clergy, and Their Own Families* (Scribner, 2003).

died by suicide, and an uncle who suffered a sudden, para-lyzing stroke.

But none of that prepared me for this.

I was getting ready for something I had dreamed about for years—cleaning my plane at the airport, preparing for a show where my dad would finally see me fly. And then the call came.

He had collapsed in the music store. No signs. No warning. Just—*boom*—gone.

My dad was only forty-nine. He was healthy, doing his thing—and then he just dropped dead.

At first, I told myself maybe he was just unconscious. This couldn't be real. But deep down, I knew. It was like the floor had dropped out from under me. Everything after that moment is a blur.

To make matters worse, the loss came at a time when I was riding an emotional high. I had just gotten engaged five days earlier to an incredible woman. I was deeply in love and full of hope. It was a whirlwind of emotions—what had been a joyful, hope-filled season was suddenly clouded with shock and heartbreak. I felt utterly lost—completely unsure how to move forward in the middle of so much joy and sorrow colliding.

I remember the initial stage of denial, though it didn't last long. I moved quickly into anger—an emotion that stuck and consumed me for a long time. Sure, there were tears. But I never sought help. No counseling. No therapy. Just me, trying to function while anger erupted at random moments throughout the next year.

I had dreams where my dad was still alive—so vivid that I'd wake up convinced his death was the dream and I could expect to see him later that day, working at the music store. Sometimes I imagined he'd escaped to a tropical island. Other times, I dreamed of ways I could have saved him.

But falling apart wasn't an option. My mom and sister still needed me. The business still had to run. I was getting married. So I buried everything.

Emotions are energy. When we suppress them, they don't disappear; they pop up later—and usually not in a good way. It's like that old arcade game Whac-A-Mole. (Yeah, I know that totally dates me—but that's exactly what it felt like.) I'd pound one emotion down, only for it to pop up somewhere else—in some random moment I couldn't control.

Emotions are energy. When we suppress them, they don't disappear; they pop up later—and usually not in a good way.

What we resist persists. What we don't express, we suppress. What we don't deal with, we repress. What we don't work out, we act out.

I had a hard time connecting with Amy. Honestly, I had a hard time connecting with anything on an emotional level. I know now that I wasn't even connecting with *myself*. Aside from moments of happiness, emotions meant pain and suffering. So I tried to keep things on the happy side. But anger still crept out, and yelling became my default whenever things got serious.

They say time heals all wounds—it doesn't. But it can soften the sharpest edges.

After the first year, the dreams started to fade. I thought about my dad less often. But the anger? It still showed up—unexpected, misplaced, and almost always too loud. Looking back, I'm certain there were times I snapped at Amy—not because of her but because I hadn't dealt with my father's death. The pain from losing my dad was still living in me, looking for a way out.

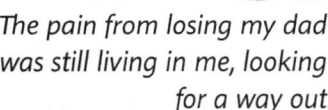

The pain from losing my dad was still living in me, looking for a way out.

Déjà Vu

Three years later—*whac!*—it happened again. Total déjà vu. Because Dad died so suddenly, I never got to say goodbye. I'm so grateful I was able to get ten minutes with my mom before she passed. Still, I was suddenly losing another parent. My mom was just fifty-one. I was twenty-seven—and now I was living without both my parents.

At first, I felt relief. She had seemed so unhappy without my dad. But within the hour, I had to call my grandmother—my mom's mom—and tell her that her daughter was gone. That was one of the hardest calls I've ever made.

My grandmother reacted in complete denial. She kept telling me to go back in and tell the doctors to wake my mom up.

If I thought my dad's death sent me reeling, this was another level entirely. It was like every old wound in my life had split wide open. Childhood trauma I'd buried deep—which I thought I'd dealt with—came rushing out like a geyser.

The fear. The sadness. The panic. The guilt.

I went completely numb. For months, my body and brain stayed in self-protection mode. I just couldn't take the pain. I didn't cry much. I didn't feel much. I just kind of . . . shut down. I turned into a big, walking blob of flesh that didn't have much to say and didn't feel much of anything.

I turned into a big, walking blob of flesh that didn't have much to say and didn't feel much of anything.

And once again, I didn't go to therapy or counseling—I just figured I needed to power through, that time would be my healer.

In the meantime, Amy didn't know what to do to help me, but I certainly wasn't present with her. I had emotionally abandoned her. There was no connection. No warmth. No awareness. I didn't even notice that she was hurting from the loss of her mother-in-law. I had no idea that in the near future, she'd be looking to get her needs met elsewhere.

I started writing songs left and right. I pulled a few people together, formed a band, and started playing shows. The emotional release of playing music felt good—so that's where I went. I should have shared all that with Amy, but I didn't. I didn't even know what was going on inside me. In retrospect, I don't think I was aware at all.

I needed help—and I didn't get it.

Betrayal

I plugged along like this for a couple of years, until Amy's first affair confession—yet *another* traumatic emotional blow. Anyone who's ever been betrayed knows what I mean. I skipped right past denial. There was no denying this. I went straight to anger—my go-to emotion by then—and stayed there for months, viciously venting to anyone who would listen.

Amy took my anger. She took my verbal abuse, even though she didn't have to.

I thought it was okay to be angry and let her have it—after all, she had betrayed me. I believed yelling would make an impression, that it would somehow keep her from doing it again.

But I was wrong.

This time, I went to counseling—but not to deal with my emotions. I was focused on how to salvage the relationship.

> This time, I went to counseling—but not to deal with my emotions. I was focused on how to salvage the relationship.

Once again, I missed a big opportunity to get to the root of the anger that had overtaken my life. My counselor reminded me of what Jesus had done—and continues to do—for me through His forgiveness. His mercy is so great. It quelled a lot of my anger.

But not permanently. Things got better for a while. We reconciled. The anger faded. But it didn't stay gone. It came back.

The next blow came around ten years later—another confession.

Because anger hadn't worked the first time, I figured I needed a different response. So this time, I went with shame. I became intentionally vindictive. I tried to *guilt* Amy into not having another affair, thinking maybe that would fix it. Little did I know, all I was doing was feeding her shame cycle and fanning the flames of her addiction even more.

I could have left, but I loved Amy. I didn't want a divorce.

With this confession, I sank into another deep depression that lasted for months. I couldn't comprehend how I had ended up in this situation. I told myself I must have done something profoundly wrong and was paying the consequences. Or maybe the enemy was just relentlessly attacking me for some reason. I had no answers.

I felt sorry for myself and sought guidance from a church counselor who urged me to find community. I told him, "I dare you to find me one other man whose wife has had even one affair—let alone multiple. I'll talk to him." He never did.

I yearned for resources, for someone who had lived through what I was living—but I found no one.

I yearned for resources, for someone who had lived through what I was living—but I found no one.

And even though I still didn't want to lose my marriage—despite everything Amy had done—it was getting harder and harder just to function. Getting up was hard. Going to work was hard. I quit shaving regularly for a few months. I just didn't care anymore. And with me in that state, as you can imagine, Amy got nothing from me. Instead of connecting and moving toward her, I shut down. She tried to pursue me, but I was cold.

One Change

Again, I figured time would do the healing. And while I did slowly come out of the depression, the pain, the hurt, the emotion, the energy—it was all still there. It wasn't always conscious, but it lingered beneath the surface. Amy and I worked through things. We made some major changes. And for a while, things were really good.

So you might think that, years later, when *another* confession came and this time we separated, I'd have been crazy to stay. In fact, I've been labeled by many people as a modern-day Hosea.

But one thing—one single, simple, monumental thing—had changed.

God had been working on me—little by little. And without me realizing it, all the pieces were lining up to finally break

God had been working on me— little by little.

through to my seemingly impervious heart. Quietly beyond my notice, God was ordering every step. He knew exactly what it would take to get me to finally deal with my stuff.

First came Amy's cancer diagnosis—yet another blow.

At the time, I wasn't in a good place. Anger was popping up again. Things between Amy and me weren't going well, and I was going numb. I remember asking God, *Will I ever feel anything again?*

A cancer diagnosis has a way of resetting things. It yanks you back to what's real, what's truly important in life, and what can be discarded. The moment I heard her diagnosis marked the first softening of my heart, the beginning of a deep preparation for what was coming.

Then Amy announced she was moving out. It was another blow. Another rupture. Another ripping open of my heart. Another jolt back to reality.

A cancer diagnosis has a way of resetting things.

COVID-19 hit—quarantines, financial strain, loss of work, and the fear of catching and possibly dying from an unknown disease. God wasn't messing around. He was tearing open my hardened heart and stripping out the years of emotional nastiness I'd let build up because I had never properly dealt with my grief.

Finding Brotherhood

Finally, I realized that the people who had told me I needed community were right. That's when I found a separated men's group—a bunch of other guys who'd been through, or were going through, the same stuff I was. It was such a relief to know I wasn't alone. There's just something about realizing others are in the same boat—it calms the chaos inside.

One of our group's most helpful exercises was also simple: We were challenged to become experts on our wives. We had to make a list of ten things our wives loved. Most men got stuck after two or three. It was eye-opening—and humbling. I realized how little I actually knew about Amy's heart—not just what she needed, like food and shelter and all the staples of stability, but what made her feel truly loved and understood.

This wasn't about keeping score or gaining brownie points for the occasional show of affection by way of flowers or a night out. It was about learning to tune in. To pay attention. To get curious. That list wasn't just an assignment—it was a mirror. It showed me how much I'd missed over the years—not because I didn't care but because I didn't know how to look.

There's just something about realizing others are in the same boat—it calms the chaos inside.

One of our group's most helpful exercises was also simple: We were challenged to become experts on our wives.

That group helped me reframe what it meant to be a man—not just someone who provides or protects but someone who sees. Someone who listens. Someone who gets it wrong and keeps showing up anyway.

At last, I not only knew I needed therapy and counseling—I actually wanted it!

At last, I not only knew I needed therapy and counseling—I actually wanted it!

I found an amazing therapist trained in EMDR and spent nearly two years diving deep into myself.

Unlocking the Past

EMDR felt strange at first, but over time, it helped me unlock memories and emotions I didn't even know were still in me.

One day, during a session, something wild happened—I remembered falling off a baby bed while in the hospital nursery when I was barely a year old. The whole thing came rushing back: Me as a baby in the hospital, scared and helpless. The sharp fear. The disorientation. The sense of abandonment I couldn't possibly have understood at the time.

I didn't even know that memory was there. But it was. And it had been running in the background for decades—unprocessed.

That one moment explained a lot.

I finally realized that's why I've always hated hospitals—couldn't stand the smell, the lights, the helplessness of it all. Of course, that wasn't an ideal aversion, considering that Amy's entire life was in hospitals.

That memory also helped me understand my lifelong need for control. Somewhere deep inside, I'd learned that if I didn't stay in control, something terrible might happen.

Remembering that moment cracked something open—like a key turning in a locked door.

Through my men's group, I was learning what my wife had really been longing for: connection.

At the same time, through my men's group, I was learning what my wife had really been longing for: connection. And through therapy, I was beginning to understand why I'd never been able to offer it. My emotional wiring was atypical to begin with, but all the added grief and loss I'd buried had only made things worse. By the time I got help, I was a hot mess.

I had to reset and start over.

I realized there were more than three emotions—even if part of me still wanted to deny their reality. I had to learn to identify and understand what I was feeling. I couldn't keep living like Spock.

This is crucial—because in a relationship, you can't ask for your wants or needs to be met if you can't even figure out what they are. God created us as emotional beings. Our emotions aren't sidenotes—they show up every day and affect everything. We need to feel them, name them, and process them in healthy ways. We need to express them without suppressing or stuffing them down.

One day, my counselor looked at me and said, "I just want to thank you for showing up."

"What do you mean?" I asked.

"It's just that . . . not many men do this," she said.

I didn't get it at first. By then, I knew I had issues. I knew I needed help. And I had figured out where to go to get it. So to me, it seemed perfectly logical that I was there seeing the

In a relationship, you can't ask for your wants or needs to be met if you can't even figure out what they are.

"doctor." But then she told me, "I have about eighty clients. Only four of them are men. And you're the only one who's kept coming back. Most men, if they come at all, only come once or twice, and then I never see them again."

There are a variety of reasons men tend to avoid counseling—such as emasculation, emotional suppression, lack of an emotional vocabulary, and cost. For most of us, when our fathers saw us crying as we were growing up, they told us, "Stop crying, or I'll really give you something to cry about." We were taught to suck it up and suppress emotions, starting as little boys. This led to a complete lack of emotional vocabulary, which unfortunately has made it nearly impossible for us to talk about feelings.

That hit me. I used to be *that guy*. But not anymore.

Strangely, in this new state of mind, I couldn't understand why a man *wouldn't* seek help. But then I would think back to my own mindset for the first twenty-five years of my marriage—I never went to therapy. Looking back now, I realize that I needed it badly. I just didn't think I did. But I was wrong.

Lessons from the Other Side

Another big change I would make to the first twenty-five years of our marriage is this: I would've gone to therapy right after my dad died—and kept going as long as it took. I would've returned after every emotional blow. I would've learned how to identify and express my emotions in healthy ways instead of stuffing them down.

I would've realized that anger wasn't the root issue—it was a signal. A sign that something deeper was going unaddressed. I would've learned that anger is rarely a *primary emotion*, which is our immediate and natural response to a situation. Anger is more often a secondary emotion that is hiding a deeper and more difficult primary emotion.

For example, our spouse may put family or a friend before us, and that hurts because it makes us feel unvalued and lonely. In that case,

I wish I had seen how important it is to identify that deeper emotion rather than reverting to the easy way out—anger.

hurt is the primary emotion. Feeling unvalued and lonely is hard, so we often express our hurt in a much easier way: anger, a common go-to emotion to cope with pain. Of course, this is not greatly helpful and only avoids the real issue: the true primary emotion that triggered the whole thing. I wish I had seen how important it is to identify that deeper emotion rather than reverting to the easy way out—anger.

I would've learned how to connect with Amy emotionally—not just over our to-do list but in a real way.

Who's to say how things would've or could've been different in my marriage if I'd made those choices earlier? Maybe things would have been different. Maybe not. We'll never know.

But here's what I do know: There's no avoiding grief. You have to walk through it.

Sometimes we try to outrun grief by pushing forward, avoiding hard conversations, or stuffing down emotion.

And time is not my healer. Jesus is.

Something to Think About

Grief is a natural emotional response to loss—marked by deep sadness and sorrow. But in many cases, it can also come with emotional trauma. And trauma doesn't just stay in the past—it lingers in the body and spirit until it's named and tended to. Sometimes we try to outrun grief by pushing forward, avoiding hard conversations, or stuffing down emotion.

But suppressed pain doesn't disappear—it just goes underground, where it waits to resurface later in unhealthy ways.

Was there ever a time in your life when you felt deeply disappointed or let down—but never really talked about it? (Maybe it felt too small to mention or too big to touch.)

Can you think of a moment that changed you and made you tougher, quieter, more guarded, or more driven? (Often, grief is hidden in the moment we stop being fully ourselves.)

Did someone's words or actions leave a lasting impact— maybe a parent, coach, teacher, or friend? (Sometimes buried pain comes from what was—or wasn't—said.)

Where Am I in This?

1.   Grief doesn't always come from a single defining loss. Sometimes it builds quietly—through repeated misunderstandings, chronic stress, unmet needs, or simply carrying too much for too long. In marriage, unprocessed grief can show up as silence, distance, or defensiveness—and often, neither person realizes what's really going on. Have you found yourself shutting down, snapping quickly, or feeling disconnected but unsure why? Describe.

_____

_____

_____

2. Have you ever told yourself, "I'm fine," just to avoid the flood of emotion that might come if you admitted you weren't? Describe a situation when that happened.

_____

_____

_____

_____

3. Could something deeper lie beneath your frustration—not just current tension but pain from another season that hasn't fully healed? Take a moment to pray and listen. Journal what comes to mind.

_____

_____

_____

_____

4. Are you carrying stress or sorrow about things outside your marriage—health, parenting, finances, global unrest—that's affecting the way you show up at home? Write down those other matters that are concerning you.

_____

_____

_____

_____

5. Are you carrying grief? What would it look like to invite Jesus into that space—not to rehash the pain but to begin healing what you've been carrying alone?

_____

_____

_____

_____

6. What would it look like to begin naming the small and unspoken griefs with your spouse? How will you listen—not to fix but to hold your spouse up?

_____

_____

_____

_____

Hold These Close

Grief is typically understood as a natural emotional response to loss. In many cases, it's also a form of emotional trauma.

Grief often runs deeper than sadness—it can tap into unresolved trauma that shapes how we respond to pain and connection. It can activate deep survival responses, especially when the loss feels sudden, violent, unjust, or unresolved. In many cases, grief and trauma overlap, affecting not just how we feel in the moments immediately following painful events but also in our ability to connect, trust, and feel safe.

Stuffed feelings don't disappear—they resurface in sarcasm, mood swings, sudden outbursts, or numbness.

Emotions are energy. If we suppress them, they don't just go away. They pop up later—usually not in a good way.

What's buried isn't gone. Avoided grief doesn't vanish. And stuffed feelings don't disappear—they resurface in sarcasm, mood swings, sudden outbursts, or numbness. They can show up as resentment, fatigue, or even physical symptoms. Emotional energy demands an outlet. If we don't express it honestly, it will express itself destructively.

In a relationship, you can't ask for your wants or needs to be met if you can't even figure out what they are.

Emotional awareness is key to connection and effective communication—especially when things get heated. Healing begins by recognizing and naming what's happening inside.

A quick temper or ever-present frustration is rarely about the present moment.

As we grow in emotional honesty, we grow in relational intimacy. The more we understand our internal world, the more we can invite others into it.

Anger is rarely a primary emotion; it's a secondary emotion that is hiding a deeper and more difficult primary emotion.

When anger shows up in marriage, it's often pointing to something deeper—something unhealed, unspoken, or still grieving. Beneath the anger, there may be fear, sadness, guilt, or hurt. A quick temper or ever-present frustration is rarely about the present moment. It's a signal that something still needs attention. Until we uncover what's underneath, anger will continue to hijack our relationships and block real connection.

There's no avoiding grief. You have to walk through it. And time is not my healer; Jesus is.

The journey through grief becomes holy when we let Him lead us through the pain, step by step, bringing comfort, wisdom, and wholeness along the way.

True healing isn't found in time alone. Time may dull the ache, but only Jesus can transform it. He doesn't ask us to deny our sorrow; He meets us in it. The journey through grief becomes holy when we let Him lead us through the pain, step by step, bringing comfort, wisdom, and wholeness along the way.

Word for the Journey

Below, select the verse that stands out to you most. Read it slowly. Let it linger in your heart. As you hold onto the words, let them shape your thoughts. Whether you repeat the verse out loud, ponder it in silence, or explore it more deeply through further study, stay open to the Holy Spirit's leading.

> *"You're blessed when you feel you've lost what is most dear to you. Only then can you be embraced by the One most dear to you."*
> *—Matthew 5:4 MSG*

> *"Jesus wept."*
> *—John 11:35 NIV*

> *"He'll wipe every tear from their eyes. Death is gone for good—tears gone, crying gone, pain gone—all the first order of things gone."*
> *—Revelation 21:4 MSG*

> *"The LORD is close to the brokenhearted and saves those who are crushed in spirit."*
> *—Psalm 34:18 NIV*

*"He heals the heartbroken and
bandages their wounds."*
—Psalm 147:3 MSG

*"Let him have all your worries and cares, for
he is always thinking about you and watching
everything that concerns you."*
—1 Peter 5:7 TLB

*"You keep track of all my sorrows. You have
collected all my tears in your bottle. You have
recorded each one in your book."*
—Psalm 56:8 NLT

Prayer for the Road

Father,

*Thank You that You see what no one else
sees. You understand the weight I carry—
even when I've buried it beneath anger,
silence, or busyness. You don't rush my
healing. You walk with me through it.*

*I invite You into the places I've hidden—griefs
I never named, disappointments I tried to
outrun, and pain I didn't know how to process.
Help me to be honest, not just with You, but
with myself and with my spouse. Teach me to
recognize what I'm feeling and bring it to You
instead of stuffing it down or lashing out.*

Restore my connection—to my heart, to
my marriage, and, most of all, to You.

Thank You that time is not my healer—You are.
I trust You to lead me through this grief and
into the kind of wholeness only You can give.

In Jesus's name I pray. Amen.

Grace in the Gray III

I Am Not the Holy Spirit

One of the hardest truths God showed me was how often I treated Amy like a child instead of an equal. Without realizing it, I'd stepped into a role that wasn't mine—I thought it was my job to convict, correct, and fix her. In other words, I tried to be her Holy Spirit.

But God never asked me to play that part. My role wasn't to point out Amy's faults or force her to repent. My role was to love her, honor her as an adult, and trust that she had her own walk with God. She had to make her own choices, just like I did.

That realization set me free too. I didn't need to police her. I didn't need to "be right." What I needed was to step back and love her as Christ loved me.

It reminded me of the Pharisees who were so obsessed with rules that they missed the heart of the law. Jesus healed on the Sabbath, allowed His disciples to pick grain, and constantly put people before regulations. I was acting more like a Pharisee than a husband.

Galatians 6:1-2 (MSG) says it best: "If someone falls into sin, forgivingly restore him, saving your critical comments for yourself. . . . Share their burdens, and so complete Christ's law."

My job wasn't to play Holy Spirit. My job was to share burdens, extend grace, and love my wife.

Accelerator

- Pray: *"Lord, help me release control. Show me how to love my spouse without trying to be their Holy Spirit."*

- Write one practical way you can honor your spouse as an equal this week—without correcting, fixing, or controlling. Share that commitment with your spouse if it feels right, or simply live it out quietly as an act of love.

Chapter 18

The Heart's Compass

O NE OF THE MOST SIGNIFICANT lessons God has taught us is the distinction among a want, a need, and a desire. For instance, over the next three to five days, I'll *need* water to survive or I'll die. I might *want* a certain outfit or *desire* sexual intimacy, but lacking either won't kill me.

During our separation, we wrestled with these distinctions. We asked God to reveal what was truly essential, what was simply wanted, and what only He could supply. We also asked the Holy Spirit to teach us where and how the desires of our hearts were meant to be fulfilled.

Most importantly, we learned to express our feelings honestly and clearly, acknowledging that we cannot read each other's minds.

When Head and Heart Collide

For me, the deepest transformation began when I started naming my actual wants, needs, and desires.

I had an unspoken list of things I believed were essential in my relationship with Todd—not just love, affection, and happiness but also help around the house, involvement in our boys' sports, family outings and vacations, travel, meaningful conversations and laughter, regular date nights, a successful career, and a sense of security. I expected him to be emotionally available, spiritually engaged, and somehow able to pick up on what I needed without my having to say it.

I expected him to pick up on what I needed without my having to say it.

I also had deeper needs—like being seen and heard—that were harder to name and even harder to fulfill, mostly because I didn't know how. I believed I had to control or manipulate Todd to get what I wanted—or what I thought I needed.

I didn't yet know how to let Christ be the one to meet those deeper needs. I knew the truth in my head but struggled to get it to take root inside my heart. That disconnect was hard for me. I also held the mistaken belief that Todd was obligated to give me all these things. I had confused wants and desires with true needs.

The more time I spent in prayer and studying God's Word, the more I began to see that my most essential needs—love, security, and fulfillment—were already met in Christ; I was just learning how to receive them. When I felt lonely, overlooked, or unloved, I learned to turn to Him. I had to let Christ become the source of my satisfaction.

I had to let Christ become the source of my satisfaction.

I'd sit with the following verses, reading them again and again, repeating His promises out loud until they started to sink in:

"Who shall separate us from the love of Christ?
Shall trouble or hardship or persecution or
famine or nakedness or danger or sword? ...
For I am convinced that neither death nor life,
neither angels nor demons, neither the present
nor the future, nor any powers,
neither height nor depth, nor anything else in all
creation, will be able to separate us from the love
of God that is in Christ Jesus our Lord."
—Romans 8:35, 38–39 NIV

"Set your minds on things above,
not on earthly things."
—Colossians 3:2 NIV

"God will fight the battle for you.
And you? You keep your mouths shut!"
—Exodus 14:14 MSG

"Let us not become weary in doing good,
for at the proper time we will reap a harvest
if we do not give up."
—Galatians 6:9 NIV

"The LORD appeared to us in the past, saying: 'I
have loved you with an everlasting love; I have
drawn you with unfailing kindness.'"
—Jeremiah 31:3 NIV

"Take delight in the LORD, and he will give you the
desires of your heart."
—Psalm 37:4 NIV

"And God is able to bless you abundantly, so that
in all things at all times, having all that you need,

you will abound in every good work."
—*2 Corinthians. 9:8 NIV*

*"His divine power has given us everything we
need for a godly life through our knowledge of
him who called us by his own glory and goodness.
Through these he has given us his very great and
precious promises, so that through them you may
participate in the divine nature, having escaped
the corruption in the world caused by evil desires."*
—*2 Peter 1:3–4 NIV*

We can't expect our spouse to meet needs that only God can fulfill. But that's exactly what I was doing—looking to Todd for satisfaction, acceptance, and security. It wasn't fair to him. Honestly, it wasn't fair to me either. In marriage, we don't complete each other—we're meant to complement each other. Marriage works best when two whole people come together, already anchored in God.

Marriage works best when two whole people come together, already anchored in God.

As I grew in understanding and in relationship with God, I began to notice when I was looking to Todd to be my source. In those moments, I learned to surrender my need back to God—just like Scripture says: "Casting all your cares on him, because he cares about you" (1 Pet. 5:7 CSB).

He Should Just Know

For years, I tried to get my needs and desires met without saying them out loud. I read books, attended marriage conferences, and did everything I could to steer or influence Todd instead of just being honest with him. If I casually mentioned something I liked or wanted a few times over the years, I believed he should *just know.*

After twenty-five years of marriage, I still struggled to say simple things like, "I'd like some flowers" or "I'd like to go to this concert." I didn't feel like I could say, "I want to plan a trip with our friends" or "It would mean a lot to me if you came to the boys' game." So instead, I dropped hints, gave meaningful stares, and waited for his telepathic powers to kick in. Classic.

I dropped hints, gave meaningful stares, and waited for his telepathic powers to kick in. Classic.

We can't expect our spouses to be mind readers.

I spent years in counseling—individual and marital. Every therapist told me the same thing: "Amy, you can't expect him to have a crystal ball. You have to *tell* him."

But I would always respond, "It doesn't mean as much if I have to say it. He should just know."

I was wrong. And that mindset only caused more pain—for me and for us.

As I grew in maturity and started letting God meet my core needs, something shifted. I stopped relying on hints and silent frustration, and I began telling Todd what I actually wanted—things like travel, Disney passes, or simply going to bed and waking up together.

And you know what happened?

Todd started listening. He started engaging. He didn't try to fix everything—he just showed up.

Now we laugh together more than I ever imagined. He cooks! We share household chores *and* recreational companionship. We go to bed and wake up—together. We have date nights, meaningful conversations, family time with our boys, and we travel regularly—with friends and by ourselves. I never thought I'd convince him to go on a cruise, but we find ourselves on one at least once a year. We've also made it a weekly tradition to go grocery shopping together.

Almost every time, before we check out, we end up in the flower section. Todd will turn to me and say, "Would you like some flowers this week?" And I get to choose. Sometimes I say yes. Sometimes I say no. Either one is okay with him. And every now and then, he still surprises me with a premade arrangement delivered to the house—because he knows how much I love the thoughtfulness behind it.

However . . . I do wish I could trade in the massive collection of vases we've accumulated. Anybody need one?

Act Your Way into a Feeling

The way we think determines the way we feel, and the way we feel often determines how we act. But it's also true that we can act our way into a feeling. For example, you may not wake up every morning brimming with affection for your spouse. Thank God love isn't just a warm emotion—it's a choice, an action, a verb. When we choose to act in love, even when we don't feel it, our emotions can catch up.

When we move our thoughts in the direction of love, our emotions will eventually rise to the occasion and support the life we're envisioning.

You've probably heard the phrase, "I love you, but I'm not *in love* with you." That can—and will—change when we're willing to change our actions, because when we move our thoughts in the direction of love, our emotions will eventually rise to the occasion and support the life we're envisioning.

The Bible tells us to take every thought captive (see 2 Corinthians 10:5). Why? Because God knows that when we change the way we think, it starts to change the way we feel. There's a pattern here. In wholeness, feelings don't lead—they follow.

Still, for years, we let ours lead. We didn't know another way.

Our culture is overflowing with phrases like "You do you!" and "Follow your heart!" and "Go with your gut" and "Do what feels right." But here's the problem: All those inclinations can fluctuate wildly—depending on how much sleep you've had, whether you're hangry, or even if you're just having a bad hair day.

Feelings are not truth.

I first heard this from a mentor I trusted deeply. At first, the idea puzzled me. I mean, I *loved* the good feelings—happiness, joy, optimism, affection, and hope. I chased after them and avoided anything that brought on sadness, guilt, shame, loneliness, or disappointment. I thought that was wisdom.

But she kept saying it: "Amy, feelings aren't truth."

It stuck with me, even when I didn't like it. When I found myself doing things I swore I wouldn't, Paul's words in Romans 7:15 (MSG) felt like a mirror: "What I don't understand about myself is that I decide one way, but then I act another, doing things I absolutely despise."

That was me. I would decide one way and then go the other. My emotions often had the final say.

I struggled to let go of whatever—and whoever—made me feel special. I craved God's presence. I longed to align my life with His will. But the God I was still getting to know couldn't hold me in His arms. I wanted something physical to soothe my flesh—something I could see or feel. I didn't yet realize it was my spirit that was truly thirsty. Maybe I struggled to let go of both the things and the people that made me feel special. I struggled to bridge the gap between what I knew in my head and what I felt in my heart.

I didn't yet realize it was my spirit that was truly thirsty.

I wasn't truly feeling it when I told people I wanted to stay in my marriage, but my mentor would gently say, "The feelings will come."

I wanted that kind of faith—the kind that doesn't need to feel strong to take the right step. So once again, I chose to follow Christ. I didn't feel brave. But I chose obedience. I was learning to trust. I stayed close to His Word and kept taking small steps. Psalm 139 reminded me that God knew me inside and out. I leaned into that, trusting His ability to guide me into freedom—from emotional chaos, from people-pleasing, from letting my well-being rise and fall with someone else's actions.

I had to realize: I'm not called to be feelings led; I'm called to be Spirit led. So even when I didn't feel like reading my Bible, I did. The enemy did everything he could to keep me discouraged. But I kept showing up. I wanted to be a sponge. I wanted His Word to soak in.

Godly feelings usually follow obedience.

Jesus said in John 14:21 (NIV), "Whoever has my commands and keeps them is the one who loves me."

I was learning to persevere in obedience—even when I didn't see immediate results. I clung to Galatians 6:9 (NIV): "Let us not become weary in doing good, for at the proper time we will reap a harvest if we do not give up."

And let me tell you—I *wanted* my harvest. But I wasn't sure what that would look like after every-thing I'd done wrong. I thought my actions disqualified me.

Godly feelings usually follow obedience.

I wrote out Scriptures on sticky notes—Matthew 10:38-39, Proverbs 3:5-6, and Matthew 11:28-30—and stuck them everywhere: the fridge, the mirror, the dashboard . . . basically everywhere but on the dogs.

I needed God reminders: God's got me. He's all I need. He's the only one I can truly count on.

So I kept aligning myself with His Word, taking every thought captive "to make it obedient to Christ" (2 Cor. 10:5 NIV). When my emotions rose up, I met them with truth. This became my daily practice: to believe, to trust, and to obey, no matter what I felt (see Proverbs 3:5-6). Not every day was easy, but that was the road to healing.

I drew strength from God's power (see Philippians 4:13), rested in His grace (see 2 Corinthians 12:9), and fixed my eyes on Christ (see Romans 6:6-7). Over and over again, I whispered, "Not my will, but yours be done" (Luke 22:42 NIV). Even when I didn't feel like it, I *chose* to follow. I was learning to live by faith—not feelings.

I was learning to live by faith —not feelings.

Emotional Energy

When I was younger, I thought I had three emotions: happy, mad, and sad. Maybe four if you count tired. That was about it.

As I got older, I learned only certain emotions were acceptable in certain situations. And the rest? Off-limits. So I stopped feeling them. Or at least I stopped showing them.

My emotional intelligence was basically nonexistent. You can imagine how that played out in marriage. Amy would ask how I was feeling or what I thought about something and I'd freeze—not because I didn't want to answer but because I genuinely didn't know. I couldn't give her something I didn't have language for.

I couldn't give her something I didn't have language for.

It took years of therapy to even start unraveling this mystery. Whenever something emotionally traumatic hit—like losing my parents or discovering another affair—I would shut down. And it wasn't conscious; it was instinct. There's a part of the brain called the amygdala that controls our trauma responses: fight, flight, or freeze.

I used to freeze. Every time.

It felt like getting hit in the head with a baseball bat. My thoughts vanished. Feelings disappeared. Everything went numb.

When my mom passed away, I went months without feeling much of anything. I didn't reach out for help. Didn't talk to anyone. Didn't even know how to start.

But then, something surprising happened: Music started pouring out of me. I wrote songs. I recorded an album. Looking back, I realize my emotions were looking for a way out.

Emotions are energy. What we resist persists. What we don't express, we suppress. What we don't deal with, we repress. And what we don't work out . . . we act out.

Emotional energy doesn't disappear. It has to go *somewhere*. It builds. It leaks. It shows up in all kinds of ways—sometimes creatively, but too often through anger, addictions, affairs . . . you name it.

Learning to Speak the Language of the Heart

My resistance to emotion impacted everything—my marriage, my job, my kids, even my own sense of identity. I needed help, but I didn't ask for it until *twenty-five years later.*

During EMDR therapy, I uncovered something huge: My parents had trained me not to feel. Not only was I discouraged from expressing emotions—I was never taught the words. It's no wonder my emotional responses in marriage boiled down to just two: angry or exhausted.

No wonder nothing changed.

Learning to figure out what we're feeling is the beginning

Learning to figure out what we're feeling is the beginning of healing.

of healing. One of the first tools my counselor gave me was a feelings wheel—a diagram of a circle with seventy-two emotions built around six core feelings. To most guys, a "feelings wheel" probably sounds ridiculous. But honestly, once I started using it—really using it—I realized something: Having words for what was happening inside me helped me understand myself. Once I had the words, I could express them. And once I could express them, I could connect.

I can't tell you how much relief that brought. I didn't feel stuck anymore. I wasn't trapped in some emotional desert where all I had to offer was "I'm fine" or "I'm tired." I had language. I had understanding. And from that—healing.

I'm still practicing, but it's already reshaped how I see, how I respond, how I live. And I'm a better man because of it.

In the separated men's group, I heard something that wrecked me (in a good way): "All my wife ever wanted from me . . . was connection." But to connect, I had to *feel*. And to feel, I had to *identify*. Only then could I share.

Now I welcome her questions. I even initiate conversations.

I used to think when Amy asked me, "How was your day?" she was setting a trap. I genuinely felt that way. Part of that came from my frustration—I didn't know how to give her what she was asking for.

Now I know better. Now I welcome her questions. I even initiate conversations. Amy knows this process doesn't come naturally for me, so she's patient. She listens. She helps. And her empathy gives me courage to say, "Hey, I don't know what I'm feeling—can you help me figure it out?"

I only wish I'd known this thirty years ago.

Something to Think About

When you don't know what you need, it's easy to expect your spouse to figure it out—and to feel disappointed when they don't. But what if instead of seeing that disappointment as their failure, you saw it as an invitation to self-discovery?

Your heart has needs. So does your spouse. But not every desire is a need—and not every need is theirs to meet.

What are you really longing for? Are there any places where you've expected your spouse to play a role only God was meant to fill?

Where might God be inviting you to communicate more clearly . . . and to trust Him more deeply?

Where Am I in This?

1. What is the atmosphere of your marriage and household, and what does it reveal about what's growing beneath the surface?

   _____

   _____

   _____

   _____

2. How would you describe your home? Write down five to seven words or phrases that describe how it usually feels and five to seven that describe how it occasionally feels. *(Refer to your feelings wheel for guidance.)*

Usually: _____

_____

_____

_____

Occasionally: _____

_____

_____

_____

3. What emotions do you tend to feel while you're alone? What emotions tend to fill the room when you are with your spouse? *(Use your feelings wheel to help name them.)*

Alone: _____

_____

_____

_____

_____

With your spouse: _____

_____

_____

_____

_____

4. What creates disconnect and avoidance in your
    marriage? *(For example, Todd felt disrespected,
    while Amy felt ignored.)*

    _____

    _____

    _____

    _____

5. What is your spouse processing, excited about,
    or struggling with? Name one or two significant
    events that happened in their life over the past
    week.

    _____

_____

_____

_____

6. How did your spouse feel when that happened? What do your answers reveal about your attention, awareness, and connection?

_____

_____

_____

_____

7. Are feeling or moods creeping into your marriage— resentment, withdrawal, silence—weakening the fruit you're meant to produce? Name any that resonate.

_____

_____

_____

_____

8. What might you be prioritizing above your spouse? Are you telling yourself, *It's just for a season* or *This will fix itself later*, while something "small" is slowly spoiling your connection? *(For example, Todd believed his overworking would go away when the kids were older—but the damage was already growing.)*

_____

_____

_____

_____

9. What in your marriage feels alive right now?

_____

_____

_____

_____

10. What feels like it's slowly fading, being neglected, or drained of life?

_____

_____

_____

_____

Hold These Close

We can't expect our spouse to meet needs that only God can fulfill.

We often confuse wants, needs, and desires—expecting our spouse to fulfill things only God was meant to satisfy. Disappointment isn't always their failure; sometimes it's our expectations that are off.

We can't expect our spouses to be mind readers.

Unspoken expectations breed frustration and can fuel false stories. Clarity—not hinting—opens the door to deeper connection. Give your spouse a real chance to succeed by communicating with love and respect.

Feelings are not truth.

Feelings are real but not always true. When we let God's Word lead, our emotions begin to follow—and healing begins.

What we resist persists. What we don't express, we suppress. What we don't deal with, we repress. And what we don't work out . . . we act out.

Unprocessed emotion doesn't disappear—it leaks. Left unspoken, it builds beneath the surface, often showing up through disconnection, outbursts, and a slew of other unhealthy patterns. Healing begins when we stop stuffing and start naming what's really going on.

Learning to figure out what we're feeling is the beginning of healing.

Emotional intimacy starts with emotional language. When we put words to what's happening inside, we give our spouse the chance to understand us—and this opens the way to being fully known and fully loved.

Word for the Journey

Below, select the verse that stands out to you most. Read it slowly. Let it linger in your heart. As you hold onto the words, let them shape your thoughts. Whether you repeat the verse out loud, ponder it in silence, or explore it more deeply through further study, stay open to the Holy Spirit's leading.

"The LORD is my shepherd.
I have everything I need."
—Psalm 23:1 GNT

"Seek your happiness in the LORD,
and he will give you your heart's desire."
—Psalm 37:4 GNT

"Happy are those whose greatest desire is to do
what God requires; God will satisfy them fully!"
—Matthew 5:6 GNT

*"For he satisfies the longing soul, and the
hungry soul he fills with good things."*
—*Psalm 107:9 ESV*

*"Set your minds on things above,
not on earthly things."*
—*Colossians 3:2 CSB*

*"And God will generously provide all you need.
Then you will always have everything you need
and plenty left over to share with others."*
—*2 Corinthians 9:8 NLT*

*"Everything that goes into a life of pleasing God
has been miraculously given to us by getting to
know, personally and intimately, the One who
invited us to God. The best invitation we ever
received! We were also given absolutely terrific
promises to pass on to you—your tickets to
participation in the life of God after you turned
your back on a world corrupted by lust."*
—*2 Peter 1:3–4 MSG*

Prayer for the Road

Father,

*Thank You for knowing my heart
more deeply than I do.*

*Teach me to name my needs honestly—and to
entrust them fully to You. Help me release every
expectation that was never mine to carry. Where*

I've looked to my spouse for what only You can provide, gently realign my heart. Help me to communicate honestly, lovingly, effectively, and with humility. When my feelings waver, anchor me in Your Word. When I'm tempted to hide, draw me toward connection. Fill the spaces of longing with Your presence. You are the only One who satisfies. And I trust You with every part of me.

In Jesus's name I pray. Amen.

Grace in the Gray IV

Love Believes, Bears, Endures, Hopes

During our separation, I spent many nights wide awake at three a.m., my mind spinning with regret and pain. Again and again, I recited 1 Corinthians 13:4-8 (NIV), clinging to what love really is. Most of us know the first part—"Love is patient, love is kind"—but the end of that passage hit me the hardest: "It always protects, always trusts, always hopes, always perseveres."

Another translation (ESV) says it this way: "Love bears all things, believes all things, hopes all things, endures all things."

Love believes all things, even when someone hasn't been honest but is trying to be truthful. Even when they haven't followed through but now say they will. Even when the odds are against something working out, but God has told us to have faith. Love bears all things, even when it hurts, even when it's not right, even when it's happened before, even when it's breaking a rule. Love endures all things, even when the other person isn't doing the right thing, even when it gets really hard, even when our wants and needs aren't being met. Love hopes for all things, even when it looks like there's no hope, even when we don't see a way out, even when we feel sad, lonely, and left out.

That's how I'm called to love my wife—not with naive optimism or blind denial but with a love that sticks, carries, hopes, and stays.

This is living in grace. This is living in the gray. And it's not wrong—it's the way of Jesus.

> ## *Accelerator*
>
> - Read 1 Corinthians 13:4–7 slowly, out loud.
>
> - Circle or underline word(s) that challenge you most right now.
>
> - Ask God for one concrete way to show "1 Corinthians 13 love" to your spouse this week. Then do it.

Chapter 19

The Sacred Order

WHEN THERE ARE NO PRIORITIES—OR when the right priorities are in the wrong order—everything becomes chaos.

Priorities don't just determine *what* comes first but *who*. They bring clarity to confusion and simplicity to difficult decisions. If we're faced with the choice between getting revenge or extending grace and mercy—and Christ is our top priority—then no matter how hard it is or what we're feeling, we will choose to give grace and extend mercy.

Choosing our priorities can definitely be challenging.

Should we be more focused on earning enough money to buy the next greatest thing—and giving our kids the best of every*thing*—or making sure they have the best of *us*? Sometimes, we can have both. But we need to know which one matters more.

Is it more important to take your child to every classmate's birthday party or to have a date night with your spouse?

Priorities don't just determine what *comes first but* who.

There *is* a sacred order. And when our priorities are in this order, we begin to experience guidance and blessing in places we didn't even know we needed it. This sacred order is revealed to us in the Bible, and the Holy Spirit empowers us to walk it out. But even when the foundation is clear, it still takes both discernment and discipline— discernment to know when and how to pivot based on God's direction and discipline to actually follow through.

That's often easier said than done.

Over the years, we've had plenty of opportunities to try— and fail—at both. But through it all, God has graciously met us with correction, encouragement, and wisdom. We want to share with you some of the strategies we used to get on the right path and what they taught us.

Through it all, God has graciously met us with correction, encouragement, and wisdom.

Leaving and Cleaving

My parents are among my closest friends. I went from living at home—seeing and talking to them every day—to getting married at the young age of twenty-one, even before finishing college. I had spent only one semester at university before getting married, and even then, I lived alone.

Living with someone other than my parents and brothers was completely new to me.

The Bible is clear about the concept of leaving and "cleaving" (adhering firmly and closely) in marriage. Again, Genesis 2:24

(NASB 1977) says, "A man shall leave his father and his mother, and shall cleave to his wife; and they shall become one flesh." God has a great purpose in this command—and for good reason. But let me tell you: It's not always easy.

Growing up with a close bond to my parents made it hard to transition from depending on them to depending on Todd. He was supposed to be the one I shared everything with, but I didn't know how to stop turning to my parents.

I talked to my mom *a lot*. Early in my marriage, we had daily conversations—sometimes multiple times a day. I was in nursing school, and I would call her after every test to tell her how I did. When I didn't know how to cook something, I'd call her for advice. I had never kept a house before, so I'd ask her how to clean the carpet or get stains out of shirts. She was my go-to for everything—my resource and my model.

Growing up with a close bond to my parents made it hard to transition from depending on them to depending on Todd.

Todd would come home from work and find me still on the phone, talking and sharing things with her. A lot of times, I wouldn't even get off the phone; I'd just keep chatting away, without a second thought.

That habit slowly created a wedge between us. Still clinging to my mom, and maybe to my childhood, I wasn't as emotionally or physically available to Todd as I should've been. He didn't feel like he could share things with me, and I don't see how he could've, because I was always on the phone. We'd miss walks with the dogs and eat dinner late because I was preoccupied. It frustrated him, and, honestly, I was oblivious.

When we moved into our first home, things didn't change. If something broke—like the garbage disposal—or if we needed a ceiling fan installed, I immediately called my dad. It wasn't even a question. My dad had always been the one to handle those things. Todd's dad had passed away, so I just defaulted to what I knew.

I thought it was harmless at the time. After all, who wouldn't *want* help? But I didn't realize I was undermining Todd's confidence as the man of the house. He was trying to step into his role as the leader of our home, and I unknowingly sidelined him. My dad stayed the main guy, and Todd was called in only when a second set of hands was needed.

He was trying to step into his role as the leader of our home, and I unknowingly sidelined him.

That pattern lasted longer than I'd like to admit. And it didn't stop at chores. I also shared intimate details of our marriage with my mom—especially when things weren't going smoothly. I didn't have anyone to turn to for marital advice. She was whom I knew. I didn't have married friends to talk to yet—I was one of the first in my circle to get married. Like most young couples, Todd and I were figuring out how to live together. So when Todd would say something that bothered me or use a tone I didn't like, I vented to my mom.

My parents were my example; I wanted a marriage like theirs. But there was a problem: By sharing too much with them, I skewed how they saw Todd. They didn't like seeing me hurt or upset, and hearing all those private details made it harder for them to fully support Todd—or our marriage.

Love and Respect

One of the most important lessons we've learned throughout our journey is the principle of love and respect from Ephesians 5. There's a great book about it by Emerson Eggerichs called—you guessed it—*Love & Respect*.

Scripture is clear: Women primarily need love; men primarily need respect. When I kept leaning on my parents instead of my husband, I wasn't showing Todd respect. He felt like I was choosing them over him. And it made him feel lonely, inadequate, insecure, and insignificant.

When we got married, I knew we were a team, but I didn't trust him yet. We were young. We had never done this before. I didn't know he *could* lead. How was I supposed to trust this boy—who had never owned a home—to fix the garbage disposal? Or install a ceiling fan? I never gave him the chance.

Ladies, don't make that mistake.

It's you and your spouse against the world. You're on the same team. Stop relying on your parents, friends, or family as your primary source of strength. Look to your husband. Instill confidence in him by believing in him; God already does. You'll learn together. Grow together. Make mistakes *together.* And if you fail, so what? At least you did it side by side. And twenty years from now, you'll laugh about it.

Stop relying on your parents, friends, or family as your primary source of strength. Look to your husband.

Eyes on Me, Mommy!

When a woman prioritizes her husband, it demonstrates respect—our most fundamental need.

This is a good place to talk about what respect truly entails and why it holds such deep significance for men. In nearly all our coaching sessions with couples, we've noticed that this is one of the most misunderstood or overlooked dynamics in a marriage.

Contrary to what culture might suggest, most men have surprisingly delicate egos and are deeply affected by even subtle forms of contempt. What we crave—far more than being told what we're doing wrong—is the confidence that we're capable. That we're good at something. That we can do great things. Deep down, we yearn for someone who believes in us. We want a cheerleader. And that need starts early.

The first and most significant woman in a boy's life is usually his mother. As little boys, we seek her attention constantly—whether we're hitting a ball, riding a bike, or jumping off the bed. I'll never forget the time one of our sons was at bat during a T-ball game and saw Amy talking with a friend in the stands. He stopped the game, walked to the fence with his bat in his hand, and shouted, "Eyes on *me*, Mommy! Eyes on *me*!"

There's nothing more powerful you can do for your husband than to build him up, encourage him, and remind him how much he is valued.

That same desire doesn't go away when we grow up. When our wives build us up, we feel like we can take on the world. We can overcome anything. It literally doesn't matter what anyone else thinks. What matters most is what the one we love—the one we chose—thinks. There's nothing more powerful you can do for your husband than to build him up, encourage him, and remind him how much he is valued. Tell him how good he is. Tell him what a great job he's doing.

On the flip side, if you want to damage your marriage, there's almost nothing that will do it faster than tearing him down. Criticizing him. Letting him know he's failed.

Tiny Humans

A major season in many marriages is the child-rearing years. As we all know, children can't care for themselves for a long time—and most often, the primary caregiver is the mother. Women tend to be in this role for a mix of biological and emotional reasons. Biologically, women are equipped for pregnancy, birth, and breastfeeding, which creates an immediate and necessary dependency between mother and child. That early bond fosters a deep emotional connection and naturally places us in the nurturing role as our children grow.

When you combine that with the qualities many mothers embody—like compassion, patience, and selflessness—it's easy to see how the children can quickly become the center of everything, including the marriage. That's exactly what happened in ours.

We had three boys in just three years—and they were busy. They outnumbered us, and like any well-meaning mom, I wanted to give them the world. I wanted them to have every opportunity, be exposed to everything, learn everything, and participate in everything. But almost every one of those opportunities came with a price—whether time, money, or both.

I remember thinking our firstborn son could be the next Gerber Baby, so I bought modeling photos. We had yearly memberships to the science center and the zoo. I wanted to create fun, enriching experiences—things that would stimulate their minds and create memories. We did "Mommy and Me" playtime at the library, "Moms in Touch" at church, Gymboree gymnastics—you name it. I'm getting tired just remembering it all. I enrolled them in every activity I could think of, partly to keep them active and partly because I was secretly hoping they'd pass out from exhaustion, so I could get a full night of sleep.

Raising three kids that close in age was so much fun, but also exhausting.

As they grew older, so did the list of extracurriculars. Todd was working hard to keep up financially, and I was pouring everything I had into the boys. What I failed to realize during all this was that I was slowly placing my children above my spouse. I had picked them over Todd. I justified it to myself—Todd was an adult, but they *needed* me. They couldn't drive themselves to their activities. They needed help with homework. They couldn't cook their own meals. They wanted to go on vacation during school breaks. And while all that was true, I could have done much of it without sacrificing Todd's place in our family.

Todd was working hard to keep up financially, and I was pouring everything I had into the boys.

Todd felt neglected. All my attention was focused on the boys, and resentment began to build in him. I was feeling it too. The more he worked, the more I felt like a single mom. We were in different lanes carrying heavy loads—loads no doubt we could have shared. And the imbalance of it all slowly created first emotional distance and then conflict. I wish someone had told me this sooner: Prioritizing your spouse doesn't take anything away from your children. If anything, it preserves the emotional intimacy—the bond—that holds the family together. I just didn't know.

Children are undeniably a cherished and central part of any family. Prioritizing your spouse as number one—second only to God—is crucial for the long-term health of your marriage and your family, especially during the child-rearing years.

Of course God comes first. That's the vertical alignment we talked about earlier. But right after that, it's your spouse. Even with tiny humans pulling at you, needing you, crying for you, and depending

Prioritizing your spouse as number one—second only to God—is crucial for the long-term health of your marriage and your family.

on you—your spouse comes next. Then come your children and extended family, followed by work and career. This doesn't diminish your other relationships but safeguards them.

Your marriage is the cornerstone on which your family is built. Scripture emphasizes how important the marital bond really is. Again, Genesis 2:24 (NIV) says, "That is why a man leaves his father and mother and is united to his wife, and they become one flesh." We're not only called to leave our parents and cleave to our spouse—this principle also highlights that the marriage relationship comes first, even before the parent–child relationship. Prioritizing God and your spouse teaches children what healthy relationships look like.

Unfortunately, our boys didn't see that modeled in our home until much later, in their teen years. Kids grow up. They leave home. But your spouse is meant to stay. How you prioritize your marriage now will shape how your kids approach their future relationships.

Todd and I eventually realized *there's no such thing as coasting in marriage.* You're either moving forward or moving backward. We thought we were coasting during those years after the kids were born, but we were slowly drifting. By the time our kids started leaving the nest, we were so disconnected that we found ourselves separated—sitting in divorce court, about to throw away more than twenty-five years of marriage. We don't want any couple to end up where we did.

How you prioritize your marriage now will shape how your kids approach their future relationships.

If you take away one thing from this chapter, let it be this: Investing time and energy in your marriage is the smartest investment you could make. The health of that sacred bond ensures healthy fruit in everything you do together, including child-rearing—and then when the nest is empty, your relationship will still be vibrant and deeply fulfilling.

Raising children is a sacred responsibility, but it should never come at the expense of your marriage. Prioritizing your spouse strengthens your home, models love and commitment to your children, and lays the foundation for lasting connection.

A strong marriage isn't just a gift for you—it's one of the greatest gifts you can give your children.

Remember, a strong marriage isn't just a gift for you—it's one of the greatest gifts you can give your children.

Today, Todd and I are hopeful that our boys see God first in our marriage. We hope they see that our priorities are finally in the right place and can feel the difference.

Neglecting your spouse in favor of parents, children, friends, or work creates a space for resentment, distance, and conflict. Protecting the love and bond with your spouse creates a space for your children—and everyone—to see God and develop emotional maturity. A strong marriage is the foundation for a strong family, whether you have children or not.

Today, I have an amazing relationship with my parents, and so does Todd. And we have a deep, growing relationship with all three of our boys. We're a team—against the world. Together, we can accomplish anything.

May your marriage grow strong roots, bear rich fruit, and sow seeds that carry blessing into every place your lives touch.

Something to Think About

What happens in your marriage becomes the building blocks of your home and then determines the seeds you sow and the fruit you'll bear together. A healthy apple produces a healthy seed, and a depleted apple produces a depleted seed.

What kind of seed is your marriage creating right now? What kind of fruit have you been seeing in your children, projects, work, family relations, friendships, church life, finances, physical health, and mental health?

Where Am I in This?

1. Whatever consumes the bulk of your time and
    money reveals your true priorities. What do your
    calendar and bank account say you value most?

    _____

    _____

    _____

    _____

2. How much quality time do you spend with your
    spouse on an average day or week? How much do
    you think would be ideal?

    _____

    _____

    _____

    _____

3. What do your daily routines center around? Work?
    Kids? TV? Friends? Sports? Phones?

    _____

    _____

_____

_____

4. What's the first thing you and your spouse do when
    you wake up? And the last thing before bed? Who
    or what gets your time—your phone? The TV? The
    news? Your spouse? Your kids? God?

_____

_____

_____

_____

5. What do you argue about most—time, money,
    attention? What do you usually agree about?

_____

_____

_____

_____

6. How often do you set aside intentional time to
    connect, pray, or check in emotionally? Do you

ever take time together just to hear God? What would it look like to do more of this?

_____

_____

_____

_____

7. Based on your answers to the previous questions in this section, what do you think you're prioritizing in your marriage right now?

_____

_____

_____

_____

8. Is there something you're cherishing more than each other—something that actually belongs to God? *(Examples: Todd wrestled with the pressure to provide. Amy clung to her need for attention and comfort.)* Identify and describe it, and explore how this might be damaging to your relationship.

_____

_____

Hold These Close

There is a sacred order.

When the sacred order is in place—God first, and then your spouse—everything is protected. Your children, business, and calling benefit most when your marriage bond is strong.

There's no such thing as coasting in marriage.

What feels like "coasting" is often slow drifting. By the time disconnection becomes obvious, the gap can feel wide. Marriage needs regular attention—time, care, and intentional connection. Investing in your marriage isn't extra; it's the smartest investment you can make.

It's you and your spouse against the world. You're on the same team.

Marriage works best when you face life side by side—not from separate corners. Choosing outside voices over your spouse's slowly erodes trust. But when you believe in one another, instill confidence, and keep learning together, you become stronger together. Unity doesn't happen by

Unity doesn't happen by accident—it's built through everyday choices to believe in each other, show up, and stay in it together.

accident—it's built through everyday choices to believe in each other, show up, and stay in it together.

Prioritizing your spouse as number one—second only to God—is crucial for the long-term health of your marriage and your family.

Misaligned priorities slowly create emotional distance and conflict. Prioritizing your spouse teaches your children what healthy relationships look like. Tend your marriage, and you tend your whole house.

Word for the Journey

Select the verse below that stands out to you most. Read it slowly. Let it linger in your heart. As you hold onto the words, let them shape your thoughts. Whether you repeat the verse out loud, ponder it in silence, or explore it more deeply through further study, stay open to the Holy Spirit's leading.

> *"That is why a man leaves his father*
> *and mother and is united to his wife,*
> *and they become one flesh."*
> *—Genesis 2:24 NIV*

> *"However, let each one of you love his wife*
> *as himself, and let the wife see*
> *that she respects her husband."*
> *—Ephesians 5:33 MEV*

> *"Two are better off than one, because together they*
> *can work more effectively. If one of them falls*

*down, the other can help him up. But if
someone is alone and falls, it's just too bad,
because there is no one to help him."*
—*Ecclesiastes 4:9–10 GNT*

Prayer for the Road

Father,

*Thank You for the gift of my marriage. Help
me to keep You first and to honor my spouse as
second only to You. Where my priorities have
drifted, realign them with Your heart. Heal the
places that have grown distant, and help us
grow together in love, unity, and strength. Let
our marriage reflect Your goodness and grace,
for our family and for generations to come.*

In Jesus's name I pray. Amen.

Chapter 20

Tidbits and Truths

W'RE SO GLAD YOU'VE MADE it this far in our book, and we commend you for being here. Marriage isn't easy—but it can be one of the most rewarding journeys life has to offer. And God has so much for us in this thing called marriage. In this chapter, we'd like to share some of the tidbits and truths we've picked up along this difficult journey. We pray they bless you and your marriage, right where you are.

Intentionality

At some point during the first few years of our marriage, we attended one marriage conference and then never went again. But over the past three decades, we've learned the value of investing in our marriage through conferences, retreats, and other events and resources that help us grow as a couple. There's no coasting in marriage: You either progress forward or drift backward. Growth doesn't just "happen"—we have to be intentional.

Once Todd and I understood this concept, we started creating systems to ensure our marriage continues to evolve.

For example, we've made it a habit to engage in an activity that enhances our marriage every quarter. That might mean attending a conference or seminar, reading books together, or diving into an intensive workshop.

We also strive to have a weekly date night—something we neglected for years. It's important to set some boundaries for date night, though. This time is about you and your spouse—your thoughts, your dreams, your emotions. It's a chance to connect. It's not the time to talk about the kids, your calendar, or the to-do list. No business allowed!

Marriage has to be made a priority—not above our relationship with God but certainly above the worldly noise.

We're intentional about keeping our marriage vertical, with Jesus at the center. As mentioned before, we pray together daily, do Bible studies most days, attend church, worship, serve, and seek God first in everything. When we miss a day—and sometimes we do—we feel it. But we don't beat ourselves up about it. We just pick back up and keep going.

We know now that marriage has to be *made* a priority—not above our relationship with God but certainly above the worldly noise. We can't let work and busyness take over to the detriment of our relationship. We have to grow—together—with intentionality and commitment.

Encouragement

During our separation, I learned one thing that changed *everything*: I should speak things as though they *can be*, not as they *actually are*. I never used to do this. I considered myself a realist. As far as I was concerned, anything other than telling it "like it is" was lying. But wow, was I wrong. It's actually biblical.

Romans 4:17 (TLB) says "And this promise is from God himself, who makes the dead live again and speaks of future events with as much certainty as though they were already past."

Words are powerful. When we speak about our spouse as they *can be*, rather than by what we see now, they begin to rise into that vision.

For example, I helped Amy study through nursing school. When I made comments about how easy it was, or wondered why it was taking her so long to grasp the knowledge, I made her feel small. If I could go back, I would tell her what a great nurse she was going to be, how she was going to change lives in her job, how much I believed in her, and that she should never give up. Inside every one of us is a little boy or girl who needs to know that they're seen and heard, that we believe in them, that they're special, and that we admire them.

What a difference it made when I began doing this. Now I see Amy's eyes light up, her spirit lift, and her countenance change when I speak about her potential. It doesn't always happen instantly, but I've noticed her thoughts, words, and feelings shift—just because of words that come from my mouth.

Proverbs 18:21 (NLT) says, "The tongue can bring death or life." It's up to us which one we choose.

Consider this: What would Jesus say about you? Would He focus on your mistakes, your shortcomings, and your limitations? Or would He say, "Here's My son. Here's My daughter. I'm so proud of you. Look how beautifully you're growing. What a remarkable man or woman of God who seeks first the kingdom above all else!"

Giving Up or Gaining

When we're in the dating phase of a relationship, our differences attract us. But once the limerence wears off, those same differences can start to repel us. First, opposites attract—and then opposites attack!

What used to be the most amazing thing about our spouse becomes the thing that frustrates us the most. For example, I thought it was super cool that Todd was in a band, going around playing music to help kids and others know and love the Lord. But after we were married, I got tired of the late-night sessions at our house. I remember having to work the next day, trying to sleep while "the boys" were jamming out and practicing. I would come downstairs, looking like Cruella de Vil, shouting, "Do you have to do this at two in the morning?! I have to work tomorrow—which is now today. *Turn it off!*"

What used to be the most amazing thing about our spouse becomes the thing that frustrates us the most.

We think, *Why can't they be more like this? Why can't they be more like that?* We want to change them—to make them more "compatible" with our own needs, wants, and desires. We try to mold and shape them to be more like us.

But trying to change the other person is manipulation—not to mention playing God. And when we use pressure, threats, or force—that's coercion. There were many times when we both did these things. The hard reality is this: Wherever manipulation or coercion are present, you no longer have a true relationship.

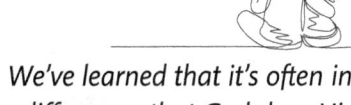

Trying to change the other person is manipulation—not to mention playing God.

If we have to manipulate, convince, or coerce someone to stay with us, it's not a relationship—it's a prison. That's when people say they feel "trapped."

Marriage is a covenant between two people who willingly choose each other. It's a voluntary agreement to love, honor, respect, and support each other. When we try to change our spouse, we're working against the very heart of what a relationship is. The beauty of a real relationship is this: The other person chooses you—just as you are. And you choose them just as they are.

God made us each unique—and He didn't make a mistake when He made your spouse. We need to celebrate our differences and let our spouses be who God created them to be. We've learned that it's often in our differences that God does His deepest work. He helps us become less selfish and to think of others more. He shows us that there's often more than one way of doing things, and "our" way is not always the only

We've learned that it's often in our differences that God does His deepest work.

"right" way. He helps us realize the world doesn't revolve around us!

This is where the hard work comes in. It's easy to look at what your spouse is doing and want to change them. It's much harder to look in the mirror and ask, *What do I need to change?*

Instead of taking the easy way out, looking for greener grass somewhere else, what if we committed to watering our own? Watering is the work, but that's where the transformation happens.

What if God had something beautiful for you to learn and experience *through* those very differences with your spouse—even if those differences sometimes caused pain? Would you say, "No thanks, God?" Would you want to miss out on what He has for you? Or would you say what they say in Todd's men's group: "If it brings me closer to God, bring it on!"

Gratitude

There were many days during our marriage—especially during our separation—when we felt like giving up. We didn't see any hope left. During times like that, it's easy to fall into depression. It's easy to focus on ourselves, on our misery, and just wallow in it. But the Bible reminds us, "So let's not allow ourselves to get fatigued doing good. At the right time we will harvest a good crop if we don't give up, or quit" (Gal. 6:9-10 MSG).

But we learned that one of the quickest ways out of that trap is gratitude.

There's a story about a man who was depressed and went to his pastor for counseling. He shared how his wife was mean, his car broke down, his boss was critical, his house needed a new roof, and his kids were struggling in school.

The pastor said, "It sounds like you have a lot to be thankful for."

"You're crazy—what are you talking about?"

"I just heard you say you're married," the pastor explained. "There are a lot of people out there who wish they were. You said you have a car—many people don't. You said you've got a job—there are folks out there looking for work. You said you have a house—some don't even have shelter. And you've got kids—kids you can hug and talk to. Sounds to me like you have a lot to be thankful for."

It's all in the perspective.

At some point or another, Amy and I were both given the same assignment: Write down three to five things you're thankful for every day. It was hard at first—but we kept at it. Instead of focusing on the bad, we had to be intentional about noticing the good.

The Bible tells us to "Rejoice always, pray continually, give thanks in all circumstances . . . " (1 Thess. 5:16–18 NIV).

Gratitude has the power to shift your focus, your outlook, your mood—even your circumstances—if you're willing to be intentional about expressing it.

We all need to have an attitude of gratitude.

From Catastrophizing to Community

I've always been independent—an introvert and a bit of a loner. When times got tough, I sought solitude. I tried figuring things out on my own. The last thing I wanted was to be around people. Groups drained my energy—like any good introvert.

I also tended to catastrophize anytime something wasn't going well. Okay . . . well, maybe not *just* when things weren't going well. Who am I kidding? I catastrophized all the time. *What if this, what if that . . . ?* All kinds of worst-case scenarios would play out in my head—none of them true—which only made my anxiety worse.

When the world came crashing down after Amy's cancer diagnosis, I tried to go it alone. I didn't think I needed anyone. I sat, night after night, catastrophizing about everything. Finally, God nudged me to reach out and take a chance on joining the separated men's group. It turned out to be the best thing ever.

Being in that community of men was everything. I could reach out and talk to other men daily about what I was facing. They'd talk me down off the catastrophizing cliff. They couldn't change my circumstances—but they could walk through them with me. And I could walk through theirs with them.

God created us for community. We're not made to do life alone.

God created us for community. We're not made to do life alone.

When Amy and I meet with people going through marriage struggles, we often see them trying to tough it out solo—and it breaks our hearts. We watch people spiral into depression and wallow in misery. The old saying "Misery loves company" is real. I can't emphasize enough how important it is to be with other people—and to be vulnerable, especially with those who are walking through those same difficulties.

There's a kind of support you can get only from someone who's also been through it.

It's hard to take that first step. To reach out. To go to that first meeting. I know, because I was there.

When I drove to the courthouse to file the divorce paperwork, I was on the phone with one of the men from my group, and again as I went through the disclosure process. When I didn't know what to do next, when I started spiraling again, I was in meetings with those men. They've been an invaluable resource. I'm so happy that God taught me this principle of community. Now, they're my first go-to. And I've been able to provide that kind of support for countless others. That gives purpose to all the pain. Thank You, Jesus!

When I didn't know what to do next, when I started spiraling again, I was in meetings with those men.

Whose Side of the Street

We all try to exert control at some point or another. Many times, we're doing it even when we think we're not.

It was hard to hear, and even harder to process, just how controlling I'd been—over my wife, my family, my friends, my work . . . honestly, over everyone and everything in my life. I began to see all the ways I had been subtly trying to control things through my words and actions, even when I wasn't consciously aware of it.

During our separation, God was very direct with me. He reminded me that He is in control—and I am not. He is God. I am not.

He made it crystal clear: I've never had control over anything except my own choices. Everything else I thought I could control? That was an *illusion*. There's no such thing as "If it's to be, it is up to me." Psalm 37:23 (NLT) says, "The LORD directs the steps of the godly. He delights in every detail of their lives." Proverbs 16:9 (NLT) says, "We can make our plans, but the LORD determines our steps."

I had to radically shift my thinking—especially when it came to Amy. I had to accept the truth: My wife is an adult. She's her own person. She makes her own choices. And she has to have the freedom to do so. I don't get to control what she's doing, what she's thinking, what she's choosing, or where she's going.

I'd often find myself saying to God, *But look what she's doing . . . What about her? What about what she did?* And God would gently but firmly say, *I don't want to talk about her. She's My daughter—and I've got her. I only want to talk about you and Me!*

God was reminding me to stay on *my* side of the street. We can only control our own actions and responses. We *can't* control what someone else thinks, says, or does. Accepting this truth is essential to living a peaceful and healthy life.

One of the things we see most often is people trying to cross over into their spouse's lane—constantly watching what the other person is doing or not doing. They spend far more time and energy trying to "fix" their spouse than working on themselves.

This is precisely where we're called to let go.

Let go of the control we think we have—but don't.

Let go of our expectations.

Let go of the past hurts.

Let go of resentment and bitterness.

Let go of the fantasies.

Let go of the unrealistic ideals.

Let go of the need to be right.

Let go of comparison.

Let go of assumptions.

Let go of recordkeeping.

Let go of our failures.

Let go of blame.

Let go of worry and anxiety—and give it all to God.

Letting go is the key to holding on to your marriage.

Letting go *is the key to holding on to your marriage.*

Something to Think About

A healthy marriage doesn't grow by accident—it grows through intentional choices. That means choosing to water your own grass instead of waiting for a "greener pasture"—something better—to come along. It means letting go of control, speaking life, and showing up with grace—even when it's hard.

Words matter. What you say to your spouse (and about your spouse) carries weight. As Todd shared, *"When we speak about our spouse as they can be, they begin to rise into that vision."*

You can't control anyone else's journey. But you can tend to your own heart, your own habits, and your own half of the relationship.

Where might God be inviting you to grow—on your side of the street?

Where Am I in This?

1. Where have you seen your marriage drift into "neutral" gear?

   _____

   _____

   _____

_____

_____

2. Do you currently have a weekly date night, check-in,
    or time of shared prayer/study? If not, what can you
    plan with your spouse to devote time to each other?

_____

_____

_____

_____

_____

3. What might "watering your own grass" look like
    in this season of your marriage?

_____

_____

_____

_____

4. How do you talk about your spouse to others? Think of something you have said that, in reflection, would have been better left unsaid.

_____

_____

_____

_____

_____

5. How do you speak *to* your spouse about things you see in them?

_____

_____

_____

_____

_____

6. List ten or more words that describe your spouse's gifts, talents, and unique qualities.

_____

_____

_____

_____

7. Write two or three sentences describing your
   spouse's true "identity" as a son or daughter of
   God. What makes them special? What are their
   callings? What were they created for?

_____

_____

_____

_____

8. What might happen if you make it a habit to
   speak to—and about—your spouse with heaven's
   perspective?

_____

_____

_____

_____

9. What might be some areas where you're still trying to manipulate, fix, or control your spouse?

_____

_____

_____

_____

10. What are you holding on to that God might be asking you to release? (A point to make? A grudge? The need to "teach a lesson"?)

_____

_____

_____

_____

11. In the final words of this chapter, in the section titled "Whose Side of the Street," which of the "let go" lines hit you the hardest?

_____

_____

_____

Hold These Close

There's no coasting in marriage.

A strong marriage requires intentionality. There is no neutral gear. In marriage, you're either moving forward or drifting backward. Without intentional connection, even good marriages can quietly begin to unravel. Every effort becomes an investment in the future you're building together. Even small moments of connection—eye contact, a kind word, a shared laugh—

If someone is staying out of obligation or fear, that's not intimacy—it's captivity.

can keep you growing together instead of drifting apart. Every investment will reap immeasurable rewards to your life and future together.

If we have to manipulate, convince, or coerce someone to stay with us, it's not a relationship—it's a prison.

Love can't thrive where fear or control is in charge. True connection is built on freedom—to choose, to trust, and to stay because you want to, not because you have to. If someone is staying out of obligation or fear, that's not intimacy—it's captivity. God designed love to be powerful, not forceful.

If it brings me closer to God, bring it on!

Not everything that hurts is harmful—sometimes, discomfort is the fire that refines us and the pressure that reveals what we truly need. Pain can feel like the enemy, but when it leads us to deeper dependence on God, it becomes a gift in disguise. The trials we'd never choose often become the turning points we'll never forget. If it makes us more like Christ—more surrendered, more trusting, more whole—it's worth it.

We all need to have an attitude of gratitude.

Gratitude isn't just a nice idea—it's a lifeline. In marriage especially, it shifts our focus from what's lacking to what's lasting. It's a way to *fight* for connection when everything else feels hard. By whatever means necessary—writing it down, saying it out loud, praying it back to God—we choose to focus on what's good because whatever we focus on expands. Our gratitude not only softens our hearts but fuels the other person's growth. It reminds them who they are and invites them to rise. Even on hard days, gratitude helps us remember the good, rekindle connection, and protect the treasures we already have.

Our gratitude not only softens our hearts but fuels the other person's growth.

God created us for community. We're not made to do life alone.

When we isolate, we suffer in silence and carry burdens we were never meant to bear alone. Community brings perspective, comfort, accountability, and strength. The enemy loves to divide and isolate—but healing multiplies in safe, Spirit-led connection. Don't underestimate the power of letting others—whether it's a friend, a small group, or a trusted mentor—walk with you. Connection is one of God's greatest gifts—and it's part of how He heals us.

We can only control our own actions and responses. We can't control what someone else thinks, says, or does. We need to stay on our side of the street.

It's easy to slip into control, blame, or preoccupation with what our spouse is or isn't doing. But growth happens when we take responsibility for our own heart, actions, and choices. Your side of the street is where your power lies. You can't force change in someone else—but you can invite it by living in truth, humility, and integrity. Let God work in you first, and trust Him to handle the rest.

Word for the Journey

You can't force change in someone else—but you can invite it by living in truth, humility, and integrity.

Select the Bible verse below that stands out to you most. Read it slowly. Let it linger in your heart. As you hold onto the words, let them shape your thoughts. Whether you repeat the verse out loud, ponder it in silence, or explore it more deeply through further study, stay open to the Holy Spirit's leading.

> *"We can make our plans,*
> *but the LORD determines our steps."*
> *—Proverbs 16:9 NLT*

"Words kill, words give life; they're
either poison or fruit—you choose."
—Proverbs 18:21 MSG

"Carry each other's burdens, and in this way
you will fulfill the law of Christ."
—Galatians 6:2 NIV

"So let's not allow ourselves to get fatigued doing
good. At the right time we will harvest a good
crop if we don't give up, or quit. Right now,
therefore, every time we get the chance, let us
work for the benefit of all, starting with the people
closest to us in the community of faith."
—Galatians 6:9–10 MSG

"Be always humble, gentle, and patient. Show your
love by being tolerant with one another."
—Ephesians 4:2 GNT

Prayer for the Road

Father,

Thank You for the daily invitation to grow
and for always providing what is needed—
not just in our marriage or household
but in our trust, humility, and love.

When I feel tempted to fix or control, I receive
Your grace to surrender. When I'm tempted to use
pressure or manipulation, help me sit at Your feet
and let it all go. Instead of speaking death, I ask

for Your words of life and power. Give me eyes to see my spouse the way You do—and courage to love them fearlessly. As the Scripture tells us in Galatians 5:22, against these things—such as love, gentleness, and patience—there is no law.

Let our marriage become a garden, a sanctuary, a truly safe space where grace grows and Your presence remains.

In Jesus's name, I pray. Amen.

What's Next

―――――――

TAKE YOUR NEXT STEP WITH US.

Your story doesn't have to end here. Hope, healing, restoration, and freedom are possible—and you don't have to do it alone. Remember, we are made for community.

If this book has stirred something in your heart, we would be honored to walk beside you in your next steps.

Visit MarryMeDaily.com to access the following:

- o Information about upcoming workshops and intensives
- o Videos, reflection guides, and other resources
- o Opportunities to connect with us personally or with our team
- o Our speaking schedule
- o Ways to bring Letting Go principles to your church or community

You can also stay connected by subscribing for updates, event announcements, and new resources.

Start here: MarryMeDaily.com. If you'd like to follow along on social media, find us at:

- o Instagram: @marrymedailyministry
- o Facebook: @marrymedailyministry
- o Email: info@marrymedaily.com

Let's keep growing together—because letting go is only the beginning.

With love and hope,

Todd & Amy Underwood
Authors, *Letting Go: The Key to Holding On to Your Marriage*

> *"Let's not allow ourselves to get fatigued doing good. At the right time we will harvest a good crop if we don't give up, or quit."*
> —*Galatians 6:9 MSG*

Resources

Books and Other Resources We Recommend

Marriage Books

1. *Vertical Marriage: The One Secret That Will Change Your Marriage* by Dave and Ann Wilson

2. *One More Try: What to Do When Your Marriage Is Falling Apart* by Gary Chapman

3. *Sacred Marriage: What If God Designed Marriage to Make Us Holy More Than to Make Us Happy?* by Gary Thomas

4. *Love & Respect: The Love She Most Desires; the Respect He Desperately Needs* by Dr. Emerson Eggerichs

5. *The Meaning of Marriage: Facing the Complexities of Commitment with the Wisdom of God* by Timothy Keller

6.   *Cherish: The One Word That Changes Everything for Your Marriage* by Gary Thomas

7.   *His Needs, Her Needs: Making Romantic Love Last* by Dr. Willard F. Harley Jr.

8.   *How We Love: Discover Your Love Style, Enhance Your Marriage* by Milan Yerkovich and Kay Yerkovich

9.   *The Seven Principles for Making Marriage Work: A Practical Guide from the Country's Foremost Relationship Expert* by John M. Gottman

10. *I Do Again: How We Found a Second Chance at Our Marriage—and You Can Too* by Cheryl and Jeff Scruggs

11. *Torn Asunder: Recovering from Extramarital Affairs* by Dave Carder

12. *Reconnected: Moving from Roommates to Soulmates in Marriage* by Dr. Erin Smalley and Dr. Greg Smalley

13. *Anatomy of an Affair: How Affairs, Attractions, and Addictions Develop, and How to Guard Your Marriage Against Them* by Dave Carder

14. *Fight Right: How Successful Couples Turn Conflict into Connection* by Dr. Julie Schwartz Gottman and Dr. John Gottman

15. *Loving Your Spouse When You Feel Like Walking Away: Real Help for Desperate Hearts in Difficult Marriages* by Gary Chapman

16. *The Love Dare: A 40-Day Challenge for Husbands and Wives to Understand and Practice Unconditional Love* by Stephen and Alex Kendrick

17. *Love Must Be Tough: New Hope for Marriages in Crisis* by Dr. James C. Dobson

Therapy/Recovery Books

1. *No Stones: Women Redeemed from Sexual Addiction* by Marnie C. Ferree

2. *The Body Keeps the Score: Brain, Mind, and Body in the Healing of Trauma* by Bessel van der Kolk

3. *Getting Past Your Past: Take Control of Your Life with Self-Help Techniques from EMDR Therapy* by Francine Shapiro

4. *Untamed* by Glennon Doyle

5. *Waking the Tiger: Healing Trauma* by Peter A. Levine

6. *Your Sexually Addicted Spouse: How Partners Can Cope and Heal* by Barbara Steffens and Marsha Means

7. *Prodependence: Beyond the Myth of Codependency* by Robert Weiss

8. *Codependent No More: How to Stop Controlling Others and Start Caring for Yourself* by Melody Beattie

9. *Facing Love Addiction: Giving Yourself the Power to Change the Way You Love* by Pia Mellody

10. *Hold Me Tight: Seven Conversations for a Lifetime of Love* by Sue Johnson

11. *The Gifts of Imperfection* by Brené Brown

12. *The Betrayal Bond: Breaking Free of Explosive Relationships* by Patrick Carnes

13. *Healing from Trauma: A Survivor's Guide to Understanding Your Symptoms and Reclaiming Your Life* by Jasmin Lee Cori and Robert Scaer

14. *Twelve Steps and Twelve Traditions: The "Twelve and Twelve"—Essential Alcoholics Anonymous Reading* by Alcoholics Anonymous World Services, Inc.

Other Books

1. *The Purpose Driven Life: What on Earth Am I Here For?* by Rick Warren

2. *Love Focused: Living Life to the Fullest* by Bob and Judy Hughes

3. *It's Not Supposed to Be This Way* by Lysa TerKeurst

4. *Forgiving What You Can't Forget: Discover How to Move On, Make Peace with Painful Memories, and Create a Life That's Beautiful Again* by Lysa TerKeurst

5. *The Relationship Principles of Jesus: How to Love like Jesus* by Tom Holladay

6. *Just Enough Light for the Step I'm On: Trusting God in the Tough Times* by Stormie Omartian

7. *Good Boundaries and Goodbyes: Loving Others Without Losing the Best of Who You Are* by Lysa TerKeurst

8. *The Power of a Praying Wife* by Stormie Omartian

9. *The Power of a Praying Husband* by Stormie Omartian

10. *You Are Stronger than You Think: Unleash the Power to Go Bigger, Go Bold, and Go Beyond What Limits You* by Joel Osteen

11. *The Road Back to You: An Enneagram Journey to Self-Discovery* by Ian Morgan Cron and Suzanne Stabile

12. *I Want to Trust You, but I Don't: Moving Forward When You're Skeptical of Others, Afraid of What God Will*

Allow, and Doubtful of Your Own Discernment by Lysa TerKeurst

13. *Putting It Together Again When It's All Fallen Apart: 7 Principles for Rebuilding Your Life* by Tom Holladay

14. *Becoming Us: Using the Enneagram to Create a Thriving Gospel-Centered Marriage* by Beth and Jeff McCord

15. *Redemptive Divorce: A Biblical Process That Offers Guidance for the Suffering Partner, Healing for the Offending Spouse, and the Best Catalyst for Restoration* by Mark W. Gaither

Workshops, Conferences, Intensives, and Movies

1. Weekend to Remember—Family Life, www.familylife.com/weekend-to-remember/

2. Hold Me Tight, www.holdmetightonline.com

3. Relationship Enrichment Center, www.relationshipenrichmentcenter.com

4. Hope Restored—Focus on the Family, hoperestored.focusonthefamily.com/

5. On-site, www.experienceonsite.com

6. Bethesda Workshops, www.bethesdaworkshops.org

7. XO Marriage, www.xomarriage.com

8. *Fireproof* (2008)—a faith-based film about perseverance, forgiveness, and rebuilding marriage

9. *War Room* (2015)—a faith-based film about the power of prayer and spiritual warfare within marriage and family

Acknowledgments

FIRST AND FOREMOST, WE GIVE all glory to God—the true author of this story. Every page, every tear, every moment of surrender belongs to Him. What began in brokenness has become a testimony of His faithfulness, grace, and power to redeem what we thought was lost. Without His healing hand and the gentle work of the Holy Spirit, this book would not exist.

We are profoundly grateful to our senior editor and author coach, Esse Johnson, with HigherLife Publishing, whose guidance, insight, and unwavering dedication made this book possible. Your ability to see through to the heart of the message, and your own heart in delivering that message, is a gift given by none other than God. Thank you for listening deeply, asking the hard questions, and helping us transform our raw experiences and volumes of words into an impactful book that can resonate with and inspire others.

To our families and friends—thank you for walking beside us in seasons of confusion, pain, and hope. Your prayers, your patience, and your belief in what God could still do carried us when we could not carry ourselves. You reminded us that love endures and that grace grows strongest in community.

To my (Amy's) dearest friend, Melodie—thank you for being there for every story, every tear, and every moment for the past twenty-seven of thirty-two years of my marriage. Your unwavering love, laughter, and steadfast support have carried me through the highs and lows. I am endlessly grateful for your friendship and presence in my life.

To my (Amy's) cherished friends who comprise our "five-pack"—Colleen, Lara, Lisa, and Rachel: Thank you for walking alongside me with prayerful support, honest counsel, and encouragement rooted in faith. Your presence has been a reflection of God's love and strength in my life, and I am deeply grateful for each of you. There's nothing better than doing life with girlfriends and God.

To my (Todd's) annoying little sister, Julie—you weren't so annoying after all when I needed to talk night after night after night. Thank you for the long conversations, late nights, wisdom, comfort, and guidance. I guess maybe this makes up for coloring in my *Star Trek* book. Not that I was keeping track. Mom and Dad would be proud.

To our longtime friends, Jenn and Alan—thank you for walking with us, from rebuilding our marriage, to offering support without judgment and love without conditions, to sharing new adventures together. Your love, support, and faithfulness have been a true blessing.

Thank you, Mark, for not giving up on me and for providing an encouraging ear when I needed it. Thank you for continuing to encourage me to do music through the hard times. And no, you were not being like Job's friends.

To our parents, both in heaven and here on earth—thank you for showing us God's love and His sacrifice and setting the foundation from a young age to know that God is who we need to turn to first. He is the same today as He was yesterday and will be tomorrow.

To our mentors, pastors, and counselors—thank you for guiding us with truth and compassion. You created safe spaces for us to wrestle with hard questions and helped us see that letting go is not the end of love but often the beginning of it.

To my separated men's group leader, Randy, for being there day and night and giving so selflessly. Thank you to all the guys in the group—Drew, Randall, Micheal, Daran, Tom, Wes, and so many more. We all learned the hard way what truly surrendering everything really means. Your day-to-day commitment to the group with all the new men coming in is inspiring and life changing. Keep doing the next right thing for the right reason without expectation.

To every reader who finds pieces of your own story in ours—thank you for opening your heart. We pray these words lead you closer to healing, deeper into faith, and nearer to God, who restores all things in His perfect time.

And finally, to each other—thank you for the courage to tell the truth, to forgive, and to keep believing that redemption is possible. Thank you for not just knowing what to do but for staying, showing up, and actually putting in the hard work, day after day. For being a doer of the Word, not just a hearer. This book is our offering of gratitude for what God has done and our hope that it will become a light for others still walking their way home.

About the Authors

TODD AND AMY HAVE BEEN married for more than thirty-two years. They originally raised their three incredible sons in Arizona and now call the beautiful state of Florida home. This new season of life has brought fresh purpose, but their journey has not been without pain. Together, they've **borne** the deep wounds of sexual abuse, abandonment, addiction, and adultery. Yet, by God's grace, they have walked through a powerful process of recovery, reconciliation, restoration, and redemption.

Today, Todd and Amy are wholeheartedly committed to marriage ministry. Their passion is to walk alongside couples in crisis, offering **hope** and guidance on the path to healing. They also strive to equip others with the insight to recognize early warning signs—so they can avoid the heartache Todd and Amy once **endured**. Through openly sharing what God has taught them, they bring encouragement, truth, and renewed hope to marriages in every stage.

In their downtime, Todd and Amy love to travel, be on the water, explore new places, and share their story—testifying and **believing** that even the most broken relationships can be restored through God's transforming power, faith, love, and perseverance.

> *"Love bears all things, believes all things, hopes all things, endures all things" (1 Corinthians 13:7 ESV).*

www.ingramcontent.com/pod-product-compliance
Lightning Source LLC
Chambersburg PA
CBHW061547120626
46550CB00004B/1401